25 years after Beijing
The status of women in Iran

A study by the Women's Committee
of the National Council of Resistance of Iran

February 2020

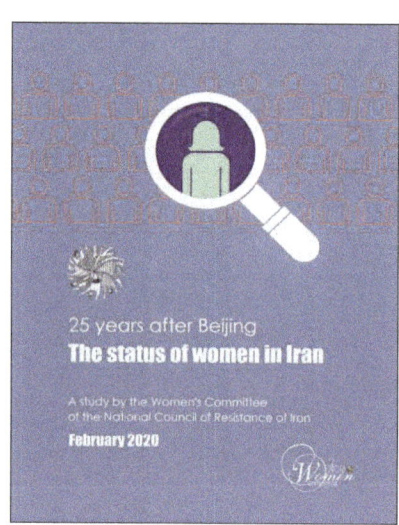

25 Years After Beijing, the Status of Women in Iran

Copyright©2020 by Women's Committee of the National Council of Resistance of Iran (NCRI)
All rights reserved. No part of this publication may be reproduced or transmitted in any form or by any means, electronic or mechanical, including photocopy, recording, or any information storage and retrieval system, without permission in writing from the publisher.

A publication of the Women's Committee of the National Council of Resistance of Iran
February 2020

ISBN: 978-2-35822-019-4

women.ncr-iran.org
@womenncri
@womenncri

TABLE OF CONTENTS

1   PRIORITIES, ACHIEVEMENTS, CHALLENGES AND SETBACKS

41   INCLUSIVE DEVELOPMENT, SHARED PROSPERITY AND DECENT WORK

67   POVERTY ERADICATION, SOCIAL PROTECTION AND SOCIAL SERVICES

109   FREEDOM FROM VIOLENCE, STIGMA AND STEREOTYPES

147   PARTICIPATION, ACCOUNTABILITY AND GENDER-RESPONSIVE INSTITUTIONS

155   PEACEFUL AND INCLUSIVE SOCIETIES

167   ENVIRONMENTAL CONSERVATION, PROTECTION AND REHABILITATION

179   NATIONAL INSTITUTIONS AND PROCESSES

185   DATA AND STATISTICS

TO OUR READERS

Before starting to read this study, it is essential to understand that answering questions on the improvement of the status of women in Iran and the measures adopted by the government in this regard are absolutely irrelevant and not applicable to the so-called Islamic Republic of Iran. The answer to most of the questions should have been a simple NO or NONE. So, the only option left for us was to answer each question by providing an overall picture of the status quo and listing the obstacles to the improvement of women's status and their participation. This was still an extremely difficult task, nearly insurmountable, due to lack of transparency on the part of the dictatorial regime.

So, this study is based on the fact that the clerical regime ruling Iran is inherently a misogynistic regime which lacks the slightest trace of intention to eliminate discrimination against women. The regime opposes the United Nations' Sustainable Development Goals simply because the SDGs seek to promote gender equality.
As a result of this outlook, discrimination against women is entrenched in the law and built within the structure of the government and society.
Iran's fall into the lowest group of the World Economic Forum's gender gap index is due to the laws and structural restrictions imposed on Iranian women.
In an interview with the official IRNA news agency on November 7, 2017, Shahindokht Molaverdi, former presidential deputy for Women and Family Affairs, asserted: "One of the most important reasons for gender gap in the economy is the existence of laws in the economic sphere which expand men's participation and activity. As a result, 'employment and earning of income' have become rights for men, and 'free services at home,' a duty for women."
She further confessed, "Although employment has been recognized in the law as an equal right for all citizens, but in practice men have priority in employment and economic opportunities."
The male-dominated atmosphere in decision-making, law-making and management arenas is also another factor which keeps women away from social, economic and political participation. Women have to earn permission from their husbands, fathers or brothers for making an investment or using shared sources. They also need the signature of a man on their contract to obtain facilities and resources. When they have to travel abroad to sign a contract with non-Iranian parties, they must have their husbands' letter of consent for leaving the country.
In deliberating the status of women in Iran, it is also important to keep in mind that women's rights and freedoms in Iran contradict the regime's general policies. For this reason, advocates of women's rights in Iran become convicted of acting against national security.
An [article](#) published by a state-run website is illuminating in this regard. The state-run didarnews.ir, on March 21, 2019 wrote:
"Women's issues in Iran are political, thus, acting as a fundamental obstacle for the adoption of amendments to the bills involving issues of women. Looking at the process of drafting and examining the bills for women and children, we find that statesmen, and particularly the male MPs, are not only unaware of the bills, but also strongly oppose once they hear about them."
According to didarnews.ir: "There are many reasons why women's political participation and presence as members of parliament or ministerial deputies have little impact on changing the legal procedures in favor of women or on improving their social status. One major reason is that women in the political arena have been picked according to the needs of the power structure

and its selectivity. They do not represent the masses of women. Neither have they emerged from an independent movement of women's associations. Therefore, many women who have a political or managerial position, are not acting as a woman, but as a representative or a manager who is more committed to her party interests than the interests of women in general."

A regime relying on gender discrimination

Due to its misogynistic nature, the mullahs' regime can never be an advocate of women's rights, let alone empower women and promote their political, economic and social participation. They advance their goals by restricting and suppressing women's rights under the banner of Islam. The regime is founded on gender discrimination and male domination over women, and if one day they give up this patriarchy and provide any opportunity for women's participation, they would not be able to maintain their political system.

The first step to promote women's rights and move towards implementing the Beijing Platform for Action in Iran is to sign the Convention for the Elimination of All Forms of Discrimination Against Women (CEDAW), the Council of Europe Convention on preventing and combating violence against women and domestic violence (Istanbul Convention 2011), and other international conventions upholding the rights of women.

The other imperative is to overhaul the Iranian regime's Constitution and recognize the rights of Iranian women to become a leader, a president, and a judge. The Constitution and all other laws of the clerical regime must recognize women as equal human beings with equal worth and rights in all arenas, particularly before the law. Women must enjoy the freedom to choose their own clothing and freely engage in any social activity of their liking. All of which are currently considered existential threats to the rule of the mullahs.

So, this study is an effort to shed light on the conduct of the Iranian regime 25 years after Beijing, and convey the voice of Iranian women suffering under the mullahs' tyrannical regime. Iranian women have never relented their struggle to obtain their legitimate rights, and the time has come for the world to hear their voice and support their cause.

PRIORITIES, ACHIEVEMENTS, CHALLENGES AND SETBACKS

1. What have been the most important achievements, challenges and setbacks in progress towards gender equality and the empowerment of women over the past 5 years?

a. What are general achievements in implementation of the BPfA and CEDAW and SDGs?

BPfA, CEDAW contradict Constitution and laws

The Iranian regime has refused to join the CEDAW because it contradicts the regime's Constitution, Civil Code, Islamic Penal Code, and other laws and legislations.[1]
The articles outlined in the Beijing Platform of Action and the Convention on the Elimination of All Forms of Discrimination against Women starkly contrast the fundamental principles and goals pursued by the Iranian regime.

> **IRAN is not a signatory to CEDAW**
> **Regime accepts EQUITY not EQUALITY**
> **Education 2030 document was scrapped in 2017**
> - BPfA, CEDAW contradict regime's Constitution and laws
> - References to global citizenship and gender equality in SDG4, and promoting peace and non-violence contradict clerical regime's national education system

Discrimination against women has been institutionalized in the Iranian regime's laws and Constitution. All proposals to reform these discriminatory laws have either failed altogether, as was the case with the bill to increase the age of marriage,[2] or were drastically overhauled losing its original purpose as was the case with the bill initially proposed to protect women against violence.[3]

Emphasis on Equity instead of Equality

The regime's officials have always stressed on the word "equity" as opposed to "equality" in all UN conferences and forums, including in the 1995 Fourth World Conference on Women in Beijing. So, it is not reasonable to expect the mullahs' regime of Iran to make the slightest progress towards gender equality and the empowerment of women in the true sense of the word.

---

[1] Why the Iranian regime does not join the CEDAW? A study by the NCRI Women's Committee, March 2016
[2] Marriage age increase rejected by Iran parliament, website of the NCRI Women's Committee, December 25, 2018
[3] Provision of Security for Women bill finalized by Judiciary after 8 years, website of the NCRI Women's Committee, September 19, 2019

Scrapping implementation of Education 2030 document

In a meeting on June 13, 2017, presided by Hassan Rouhani, the regime's President, the Supreme Council for Cultural Revolution decided to stop implementation of the UNESCO Education 2030 document which had been signed just a few months before with reservations. Later, on May 7, 2017, the mullahs' Supreme Leader Ali Khamenei told a meeting of Iranian teachers, "The UNESCO 2030 education agenda and the like are not agendas that the Islamic Republic of Iran should have to surrender and submit to."[4]

Three months later, the semi-official Tasnim news agency wrote, "In the (Education) 2030 Framework for Action, there are references to terms such as global citizenship and gender equality. These issues have been criticized by some experts particularly in the Supreme Council for Cultural Revolution. Some are even convinced that the adoption and implementation of this document would transform national education in many ways. Among them, one can point to the omission of sexual stereotypes, teaching of sex education to children, and omission of some Quranic concepts and values from textbooks to promote peace and non-violence."[5]

Moving in the opposite direction

In fact, the regime has not made any achievements in implementation of the BPfA and CEDAW and SDGs, rather, it has moved in the opposite direction, stripping Iranian women of more of their most basic rights and creating more restrictions for them.

One of the most obvious examples is the security forces' stepped-up use of violence in the past couple of years in dealing with women who oppose the compulsory veil and the mandatory official dress code as recently as in October 2019.[6]

This is the most common form of violence against women in Iran which is "state-sponsored." Vice patrols and police agents who brutally batter women on the streets for not properly observing the veil are encouraged and rewarded by the regime.[7]

b. What have been violations of rights?

Violations of rights take place over a wide spectrum. Discrimination against women is institutionalized in the Iranian regime's laws. Accordingly, a woman's worth, life and testimony are considered half of men.[8] Women also face various restrictions and bans in economic, social and artistic activities as well as in sports. Following is a brief glance over violations of the most basic rights of women in Iran.

---

[4] Khamenei.ir website – May 7, 2017
[5] The state-run Tasnim news agency, May 7, 2017
[6] Security Force beats up young woman walking without the compulsory veil, website of the NCRI Women's Committee, October 30, 2019
[7] Drastic Rise in Violence Against Women in Iran, a report by the NCRI Women's Committee, November 2018
[8] The Iranian regime's Islamic Penal Code, Articles 382 and 550 on blood money for women, Article 716 (f) on blood money on abortion, and Articles 199 and 209 on women's testimony; Misogyny Institutionalized in the laws of the mullahs' regime ruling Iran, website of NCRI Women's Committee, November 8, 2015

The right to life

At least 43 women have been executed in Iran since January 2016. Nine (9) women were executed in 2016; ten (10) women in 2017; six (6) women in 2018; and at least 16 women in 2019. Two (2) women have been executed in January 2020.

Unprecedented were the hanging executions of four (4) women in just eight days from July 16 to 23, 2019, and the hangings of six (6) women in only three weeks in December.[9]

The women executed in Iran are mostly accused of murder. The majority of these women are themselves victims of domestic violence, committing murder of their husbands or other assailants in self-defense.

A good number of these women have committed murder in young age as a minor, so they had already been victims of forced early marriages in addition to domestic violence.

These women are subjected to unfair trials and since they are not aware of their legal rights, they fall victim to the injustices of a misogynous judicial system.

For example, Zeinab Sekaanvand, 24, was hanged in the Central Prison of Urmia, in West Azerbaijan on October 2, 2018. She was accused of killing her husband in 2012 at the age of 17. The UN High Commissioner for Human Rights, Michelle Bachelet issued a statement condemning this execution.[10] She added, "her claims that she was coerced into confessing to the killing, and that she had been a victim of domestic violence, were reportedly not adequately examined during her trial."

---

[9] List of Women Executed Under Rouhani, website of the NCRI Women's Committee
[10] UN High Commissioner for Human Rights, Michelle Bachelet, statement, October 5, 2018

> **WHO ARE THE EXECUTED WOMEN?**
> **IN THE ABSENCE OF ANY LEGAL SUPPORT AND DEPRIVED OF THE RIGHT TO DIVORCE,**
>
> - Most of the convicted women committed murder in self-defense against violence
> - Some were under 18 at the time of crime, and victims of forced early marriages
> - They are convicted in unfair trials without having access to a lawyer

"The sheer injustice in the case of Zeinab Sekaanvand Lokran is deeply distressing… The serious question marks over her conviction appear not to have been adequately addressed before she was executed. The bottom line is that she was a juvenile at the time the offence was committed, and international law clearly prohibits the execution of juvenile offenders."

Forced into marriage at the age of 15, Zeinab Sekaanvand lived two painful years, being battered everyday by her husband. The 24-year-old Iranian Kurdish woman was convicted of killing her abusive husband at the age of 17. She told the judge that her husband's brother, who had raped her several times, had committed the murder.

Also, shocking was the death sentence issued on June 25, 2019, for Soghra Khalili, 36 and mother of two, for defending herself against rape.[11]

She had been in jail for seven years. Her 4-year-old son was staying with her in the Central Prison of Sanandaj. Her other son, 14, lived with his father.

Soghra's husband, Omid Badri, said, "The death verdict was issued in 2015, but the murder my wife committed was in defense of her dignity. There was a man who disturbed my wife and harassed her. The residents of our village know that the victim had harassed several other families in the same way and put pressure on other married women."

Fortunately, in this case, Mr. Badri was able to collect the blood money from charitable persons to pay to the victim's family and win his wife's release.

Many women linger in Qarchak Prison and others on the death row.[12]

In a letter published on July 27, 2019, by former political prisoner Golrokh Ebrahimi Iraee explaining the conditions of female prisoners in Qarchak Prison, she wrote, "In meeting women convicted of murder, I learned that a large percentage of them had murdered their husbands --- instantly or based on a pre-meditated plan—after years of being humiliated, insulted, battered and even tortured by them and because of being deprived of their right to divorce. Although, they consider themselves criminals but are convinced that if any of their repeated appeals for divorce had been granted, they would not have committed such a crime."[13]

---

[11] Soghra Khalili, mother of 4-year-old son, sentenced to death in Sanandaj, website of the NCRI Women's Committee, June 27, 2019

[12] Eleven women imprisoned on death row held in Qarchak Prison, website of the NCRI Women's Committee, October 24, 2018

[13] Mounting repression of women in Iran, in step with growing discontent, Monthly report of the NCRI Women's Committee, July 2019

Heavy prison sentencs for exercising their rights

Defending her clients

Nasrin Sotoudeh — 38 Years / 148 Lashes

Opposing the mandatory Hijab

Yasaman Aryani — 16 Years
Monireh Arabshahi — 16 Years
Mojgan Keshavarz — 23.5 Years
Saba Kord Afshari — 24 Years

Taking part in Labor Day protest

Sanaz Allahyari — 18 Years
Asal Mohammadi — 18 Years
Atefeh Rangriz — 11.5 Years / 148 Lashes
Marzieh Amiri — 10.5 Years / 148 Lashes
Nasrin Javadi — 7 Years / 74 Lashes
Sepideh Qolian — 18 Years

The right to freedom of expression

Any demand for basic freedoms leads to imprisonment and torture.

In 2019, the regime's judiciary has handed down numerous heavy sentences for peaceful activities and demands of rights activists. Many women are presently incarcerated in various prisons for exercising their right to freedom of expression.

Three women's rights activists were sentenced to a total of 55 years and six months in prison.[14] The Revolutionary Court of Tehran informed Yasaman Aryani, Monireh Arabshahi, and Mojgan Keshavarz of their sentences in the absence of their lawyers on July 31, 2019.

Branch 28 of Tehran's Revolutionary Court presided by the notorious judge, Mohammad Moghiseh, sentenced each of these prisoners to 5 years in prison for "association and collusion against national security," one year for "disseminating propaganda against the state," and 10 years for "encouraging and preparing the grounds for corruption and prostitution." In addition to these charges, Mojgan Keshavarz has been sentenced to 7.5 years for "insulting the sanctities."

Saba Kord Afshari, 20, was sentenced to 24 years in prison for "propaganda against the state", "association and collusion against national security", and "promoting corruption and prostitution by removing her veil and walking in the streets without the veil."[15] Her sentence was later commuted to 9 years, which is still a heavy sentence for removing one's veil.

Also, a number of female labor activists were arrested on May 1, 2019 and handed down heavy sentences of up to 11.5 years in prison and lashes of the whip merely for participating in the International Workers' Day demonstration.[16]

Human rights lawyer Nasrin Sotoudeh was arrested at home on June 13, 2018 and taken to Evin prison to serve 5 years in prison.[17] She had been tried in absentia in December 2017, at Branch 28 of the Revolutionary Court in Tehran, presided by judge Mohammad Moghiseh. Again in March 2019, she was sentenced to another 33 years in prison and 148 lashes in a new case against her.[18] Nasrin Sotoudeh is facing nearly four decades in jail and 148 lashes for her peaceful human rights work, including her defense of women protesting the mandatory veil laws.

In a different case on April 24, 2019, a hairdresser was arrested for advertising her beauty shop on a billboard in the city of Babol, northern Iran. She had posted a picture of herself sitting in

---

[14] 55 years for three women's rights activists; website of the NCRI Women's Committee, August 1, 2019

[15] Saba Kord Afshari sentenced to 24 years for refusing video confessions, website of the NCRI Women's Committee, August 27, 2019

[16] On September 7, 2019, Asal Mohammadi, Sanaz Allahyari and Sepideh Qolian were each sentenced to 18 years in prison, a total of 54 years.
Labor activist Atefeh Rangriz was sentenced to 11 years and six months in jail and 74 lashes, on August 31, 2019.
Marzieh Amiri, a journalist and student activist, was sentenced to 10 years and 6 months in prison and 148 lashes, after being tried in Tehran on August 13.
Nasrin Javadi, a female labor activist, was sentenced to 7 years in prison and 74 lashes on August 6, 2019.

[17] Nassrin Sotoudeh, lawyer of human rights defendants, was rearrested, website of the NCRI Women's Committee, June 14, 2018

[18] Human rights lawyer Nasrin Sotoudeh faces 34 years in prison, website of the NCRI Women's Committee, March 6, 2019

front of the billboard on the internet for which she was taken into custody and her beauty shop was sealed.[19]

The right to a decent job and employment

Before the 1979 Revolution, women's participation in the labor force was 12 percent.[20] The World Bank put the average value for Iran from 1990 to 2017 at 14.21 percent with a minimum of 9.83 percent in 1990 and a maximum of 19.41 percent in 2005. While Iran's population, and consequently the population of women, has more than doubled since 1979.[21]

According to the Iranian Law, women are not allowed to hold certain jobs such as presidency and judgeship,[22] while they are discriminated against in having equal opportunity for a decent job. In the meantime, those who have a job are not equally and regularly paid.

As a result of this discrimination against women's access to a decent job, most women including teachers and nurses work on temporary contracts without enjoying job security, any insurance or benefits. Others accept just any job in the unofficial sector where employers are not monitored by the Labor Ministry and have permission to employ workers with salaries way below the minimum wage and without paying their benefits and insurance. Iranian authorities have acknowledged that Iranian women have the largest share in informal jobs.[23]

---

[19] The state-run Tabnak news agency- April 24, 2019
[20] The World Bank, Iran Estekhdam website, April 4, 2016
[21] The population of Iran is currently 83,000,000 with men being 51 percent of the population and women being 49.
[22] Item 115 of the Iranian Constitution, Research Center, official website of the parliament, Constitution of the Islamic Republic of Iran
[23] Massoumeh Ebtekar, director of presidential directorate on Women and Family Affairs, the official IRNA news agency, April 28, 2018

Iran's job market is male dominated.[24] Women's participation rate in the job market in 2017 was only 16.8% which is considered very low compared to the male participation rate of 71.4%.[25] The total labor force in Iran is 21.3 million, with only 3 million being women and 18.3 million men, indicating a wide gender gap.

According to the World Economic Forum, women's wages are 41 percent less than those of men. Taking into account the purchasing power (PPP), this figure drops to 17%. Women's salaries are 17% of men's, underlining the fact that the Iranian regime's conduct in this field has been "one of the worst conducts among the countries of the world."[26]

The United Nations has categorized Iran among the countries which offer the smallest number of job opportunities to women and for this reason have a high rate of unemployment among women.

A report by the International Labor Organization, ILO, which was published on March 8, 2018, on the International Women's Day, indicates that women's unemployment rate in Iran is double that of men.

The Iranian regime has been ranked 148 among 153 countries in the WEF's Global Gender Gap Report 2020. Only five other countries are ranked lower than the Iranian regime: Congo, Syria, Pakistan, Iraq, and Yemen.

Women's participation in the job market in Iran is significantly lower than the average participation in other upper-middle income countries and is lower than the average for all women in the Middle East and North Africa (MENA) region, and one of the lowest worldwide.[27] 85.9% of women under 30 do not have any jobs. In some areas, women's unemployment is nearing 100%.[28] The overall statistics say that unemployed educated females are four times the unemployed educated males.[29]

Iran needs at least 240,000 nurses across the country, whereas right now, there are only 160,000 nurses who provide medical and health services.[30] Nurses are forced to work overtime, but their overtime fees are not paid for between six to ten months.[31]

Sometimes, they are not paid at all for months up to a year.[32] Twenty-eight nurses were brutalized in 2017, and 20 nurses have lost their lives in three years from 2016 to 2018.[33]

Over 50% of teachers in Iran are women, but their living conditions are far below acceptable standards.[34] Going unpaid for months, injustice in the adjustment of their wages with the living costs, and having no medical insurance are amongst the issues that make life difficult for Iranian teachers and consume their energies.

---

[24] The official IRNA news agency, January 17, 2019
[25] The official IRNA news agency, January 17, 2019
[26] World Economic Forum, Gender Gap Report 2018
[27] The state-run Donya-e Eqtesad – September 29, 2015
[28] The state-run Mehr News Agency – January 5, 2016 / the state-run Tabnak website – December 26, 2015
[29] The state-run ISNA news agency – October 5, 2019
[30] Secretary General of Iran's House of Nurses, the state-run ILNA news agency, January 12, 2019
[31] Vice-President of the Nursing Organization, the state-run ILNA news agency, October 31, 2016
[32] Golestan nurses seek one year of wage arears, website of the NCRI Women's Committee, September 24, 2018
[33] Female nurse dies of heart failure on her shift in an Ilam hospital, website of the NCRI Women's Committee, June 23, 2019
[34] Mohammad Javad Abtahi, member of the Education and Research Committee of the mullahs' parliament, the state-run salamatnews.com, September 26, 2018

The right to education

Young women in Iran are also restricted from studying in 77 fields of higher education.[35] Dozens of universities reject female students in various fields. Gender-based quotas strongly favor male students, and the number of gender-based majors exceeds 200.[36]

In December 2015, the Parliament passed Article 5 of the bill on Evaluation and Admission of Students for Complementary Education, emphasizing that the quotas ratified by the Supreme Revolutionary Council and the parliament to limit the number of women and the majors they can study in the higher education system were still valid.[37]

Many children in Iran are deprived of education because contrary to the Iranian Constitution, education is neither free nor mandatory.[38] More and more schools and universities are asking their students to pay tuitions. As a result of prevalent poverty, many students have to leave school because they do not afford to pay tuitions. In the case of girl children, early marriage is an additional factor contributing to school drop outs among them. Poor families give their young daughters to marriage to get rid of their expenses, or receive their dowries as additional revenue.[39]

According to a member of the Education Committee in the mullahs' parliament, the number of illiterates in Iran has reached 11 million making up some 13 per cent of the population of different ages.[40] Approximately two-thirds of this illiterate population are women.[41]

More recent data provided by Wikipedia in September 2019, however, indicates that the number of illiterates in Iran is 13.2 million which amounts to 8.2 million illiterate women.[42]

Some 40 to 50 percent of girls in secondary and high schools in many border provinces, leave school for various reasons including "early marriages", "school being too distant from the village", and "lack of female teachers." [43]

At least a quarter of Iran's students are forced to quit school every year with a large number of them joining the estimated 3 to 7 million child laborers.[44]

The presidential Directorate on Women and Family Affairs published a report in 2015, according to which the illiteracy of women and girl children is in critical conditions in some 40 Iranian cities. Drop-out of girl children, 6 years and older, is widespread particularly in the provinces of Sistan and Baluchestan, Khuzestan, Western Azerbaijan, and Eastern Azerbaijan.

---

[35] The state-run khabaronline website, August 7, 2012
[36] Daneshjoonews.com and the state-run Tabnak website, August 6, 2014
[37] The official website of the Iranian parliament ICANA, February 18, 2016
[38] Ali Bagherzadeh, deputy Minister of Education and head of the Iranian Literacy Movement Organization, the state-run Salamatnews.com, April 25, 2018
[39] Social expert, Sulmaz Sharif, Miyanali.com, September 12, 2011 – Modern Slavery, a publication of the NCRI Women's Committee, August 2018
[40] Seyyed Mohammad Javad Abtahi, member of the parliamentary Education and Research Committee, the state-run salamatnews.com, September 26, 2018
[41] The National Statistics Center, 2011
[42] List of countries by literacy rate, Wikipedia.org
[43] Rezvan Hakimzadeh, deputy Minister of Education in elementary affairs, the state-run Asriran.ir, September 9, 2017; Social Protection, Public Services and Sustainable Infrastructures, a publication of the NCRI Women's Committee, March 2019
[44] Nahid Tajeddin, member of the board of directors of the Social Commission of the Majlis, the state-run Salamat news, September 27, 2017

A total of 4.23 per cent of students dropped out of school in the academic year 2016-2017. Girl students constituted 4.17 per cent of it, meaning that there is a big difference between girls' and boys' dropouts.[45]

The 82% illiteracy rate makes it much more difficult for (female heads of household) to find a job, which has led to their poverty. In such conditions, they are subjected to social harms.[46]

c. What work, roles, or other activities have been prohibited or criminalized for women and girls?
d. What are the obstacles to enjoy rights?

Bans

- While there is no law banning women from entering sports stadiums to watch their favorite teams, the Iranian regime has officially enforced a ban on women. Iranian women opposed this violation of their natural rights, and as an act of protest, kept disguising themselves as men to enter stadiums.
- In September 2019, a young woman –Sahar Khodayari, 29—set herself alight to protest six-month prison sentence for attempting to circumvent the ban on women's entering stadiums and died one week later.
- One month later, on October 10, 2019, after extensive public and international pressure, the Iranian regime allowed a token admission of some 4,000 women into Azadi stadium under tight security control to watch Iran vs. Cambodia game. However, officials said this will not be repeated for national derbies and any woman seen around the stadiums would be arrested and detained.[47]

---

[45] Abbas Soltanian, deputy for mid-level education in the Ministry of Education, the state-run ILNA news agency - June 25, 2018

[46] Shahindokht Molaverdi, former presidential deputy on Women and Family Affairs, the state-run ISNA news agency, TNews.Ir, October 10, 2015

[47] Amir Mehdi Alavi, the spokesman for Iran's Football Federation: "Currently it is not possible for women to be present in league games. Representatives of the World Football Federation (FIFA) who had traveled to Tehran, said that only the national games are in their jurisdiction, and that they respect the laws enforced by countries regarding their premier league." The state-run khabaronline.ir – October 14, 2019

Women are banned from entering sports stadiums contrary to the law

Women who disguise themselves to enter stadiums are sentenced to jail

Sahar Khodayari, 29, set herself alight in September 2019 to protest six-month prison sentence for attempting to enter a stadium

Iran regime was forced to admit a token number of women to watch game of Iran vs. Cambodia on October 10, 2019

But this is not going to be repeated again.

- On numerous occasions, concerts have been cancelled for participation of female players[48] or the concerts were performed after women players left the concert hall altogether.[49]
- Also, women are banned from solo singing. Most recently, a female singer was prosecuted for solo singing during a tour of Abyaneh, a village in Isfahan Province, in May 2019.[50]

---

[48] A member of the Orchestra of Isfahan: "Women always take part in the rehearsals but are not granted permission to participate in the actual performances. Women musicians of Isfahan have not had the permission to go on stage for years." The state-run ILNA news agency, January 15, 2018

[49] Female musicians were banned from playing in a traditional music band supposed to perform in a charity concert at the auditorium of the Azad University of Qazvin. They were not allowed to even sit among the audience. The state-run ILNA news agency – May 23, 2019

[50] On May 21, 2019, the Prosecutor of Isfahan announced that upon the report of "the intelligence police for public security" a case had been filed against Negar Moazzam had travelled to Abyaneh on May 17, 2019, with a sightseeing tour. She sang solo in this village, a video clip of which was circulated on the social media. The state-run Fararu website - May 21, 2019

On July 18, 2019, the charity concert of an all-women musical band called Delyar was cancelled in Urmia, northwest Iran, claiming that they did not written permission from the State Security Force. (The official IRNA news agency – July 17, 2019)

Prohibitions

- As mentioned in the previous section, women are constitutionally deprived of becoming a president or a judge.[51]
- The regime's laws also ban women from travelling without their husband's permission.
- A woman cannot work outside of home without her husband's permission, either.
- Women also cannot open bank accounts for their children, and they cannot have the custody of their children aging over 7 after divorce.
- Women cannot rent rooms in hotels on their own and it should be in the presence of their husband or father.
- Women are also deprived of studying in more than 200 fields of higher education and consequently, 200 fields of work.[52]
- Women can work for only limited hours in places which are sex segregated.[53] Their employment is restricted by government quotas.[54] According to the law, women can be prevented from having a job by their husbands.[55]
- Women are prohibited from riding bicycles in public.[56] The mullahs' supreme leader has on various occasions reiterated the ban on women's bicycling.[57]
70 women cyclists were arrested in Tehran's Vali-Asr Square. Gholam Hossein Ismaeli, spokesman for the Judiciary, confirmed the news when talking to a reporter. He said the 70 women cyclists had been arrested for breaching the rules of "chastity and Hijab." He did not specify the timing of the arrests.[58]

---

[51] Misogyny institutionalized in the laws of the mullahs' regime, website of the NCRI Women's Committee, November 8, 2015

[52] Women's Economic Empowerment in Iran-Moving in the opposite direction, a study by the NCRI Women's Committee, September 2017

[53] Ibid. A legislation adopted in January 2016 stipulates that women's employment in any business must be limited to 7 a.m. to 10 p.m. and they should be confined to a segregated workplace.

[54] In the 2016 Government Employment Exam, 961 job titles had been designated as exclusively for men, and only 16 titles had been considered for recruiting women. The government also ordered in 2014, to allocate only 16 of 2,700 job opportunities to women. The state-run Khabaronline.ir, July 27, 2016

[55] Misogyny institutionalized in the laws of the mullahs' regime, website of the NCRI Women's Committee, November 8, 2015; Article 1117 of the Civil Code

[56] The website of the municipality of Isfahan posted an announcement on May 15, 2019, saying: "We are unable to provide bicycles to the honorable ladies and to youths under 15."
The website published a document according to which the Prosecutor of Isfahan had addressed the police, instructing them to, "stop women bicyclists and confiscate their identification papers. If they do not have ID papers, impound their bicycles and take them to the parking lot."
Women's bicycling banned as illegal by Isfahan's prosecutor, website of the NCRI Women's Committee, May 18, 2019

[57] Khamenei issues fatwa banning women from riding bicycles, website of the NCRI Women's Committee, September 14, 2016

[58] The state-run ISNA news agency – July 30, 2019

Criminalization

- The Iranian regime has criminalized the act of removing the veil. Tehran Police Chief announced that "removing the veil and improper veiling are considered among obvious social crimes."[59]

- According to the regime's law, the punishment for women appearing in public without covering their hair is imprisonment from 10 days to two months and cash fines between 50 to 500 thousand Rials. They could also be punished to 74 lashes for "hurting public chastity."

- However, on February 23, 2019, the State Security Force announced in the state media that "encouraging people to shun the veil applies to paragraph 2 of Article 638 and is punishable by one to ten-year prison sentence which cannot be transformed to alternative forms of punishment."

e. **Does the government have gaps in data? If so, what are these?**

Yes.
- The Iranian regime is not transparent in releasing figures and statistics.
- There is no effective system of collecting statistics.
- Officials usually speak by percentages and not actual numbers.
- When and if they do, they present different figures on the same issue.
- Sometimes, the same official gives contradicting figures.
- There have been a number of occasions where the statistics collected in a particular year were released ten years later. In the case of violence against women, the statistics collected in 2006 has disappeared altogether.

Here are some examples:

Addiction
Officials agree that addiction is spreading rapidly among women:
- Hamidreza Fat'hi, head of the Department for Prevention of Drug Addiction in the Ministry of Health: "Women's share of drug addiction is rapidly on the rise." (The state-run IRNA news agency, February 5, 2017)
- Anoushirvan Mohseni Bandpay, head of the National Welfare Organization: "Addiction is becoming feminine." (The state-run Mehr news agency, February 13, 2018)
- Yasser Rastgar, sociologist and member of the faculty of the University of Hormozgan: "According to the surveys done in 2011, the age of addiction has dropped, and addiction has become feminized." (The official IRNA news agency – August 6, 2019)

---

[59] Tehran Police Chief Hossein Rahimi, the state-run ROKNA news agency, June 1, 2019

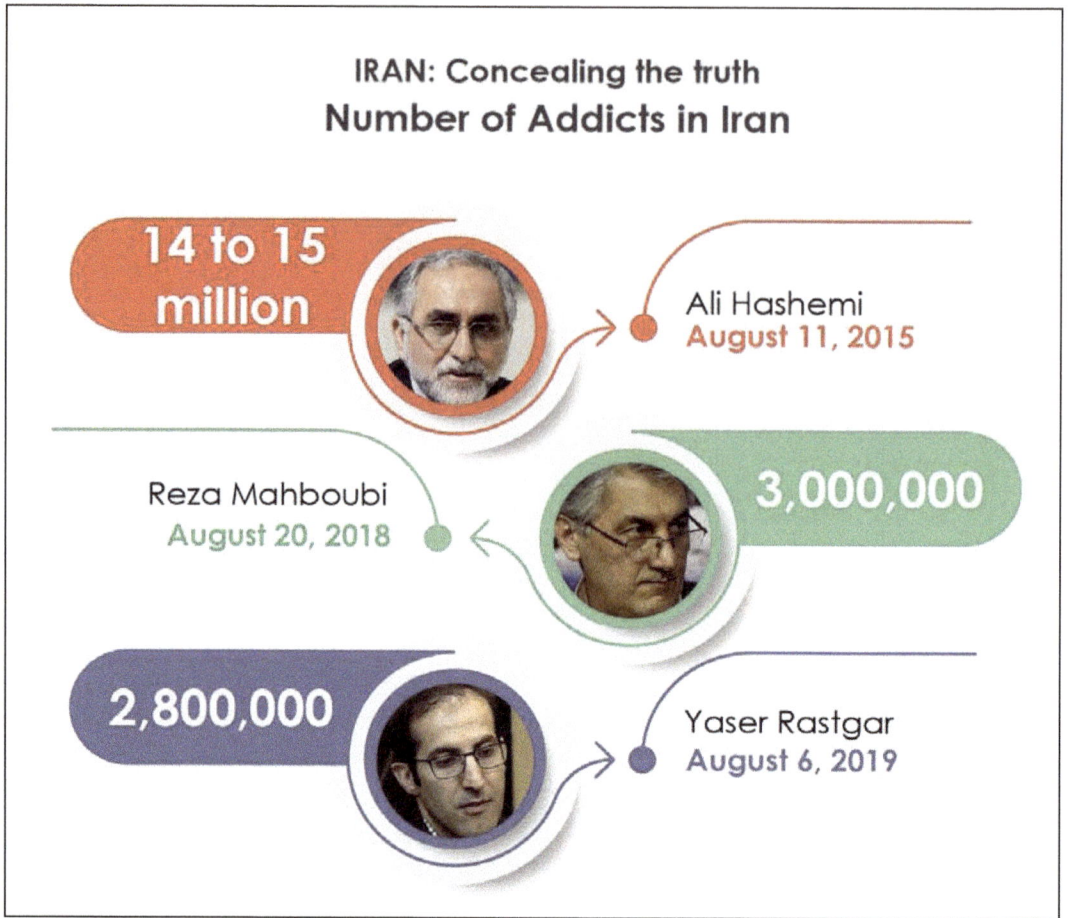

However, they present different figures on different dates on the number of addicted women and the total number of addicts in Iran. The number of addicts varies from 2.8 million to 3 million to an implied 7.5 million people. While according to the same officials, the number of addicts has not grown in 1.5 years from February 2018 until August 2019.

- Farid Barati, Welfare Organization's deputy for preventing addiction: "There are 165,000 addicted women in the country." (The state-run Salamtnews.ir – July 31, 2019)
- Yasser Rastgar, sociologist and member of the faculty of the University of Hormozgan: "According to official figures, there are some 2,800,000 persons involved in addiction and women's share is 10 percent (which amounts to 280,000)." (The official IRNA news agency – August 6, 2019)
- Reza Mahboubi, deputy for social affairs in the Center for Social and Cultural Affairs in the Interior Ministry: "There are 3 million addicts in the country." (The official IRNA news agency – August 20, 2018)
- Afrashteh, executive deputy for the mullahs' parliament: "Presently, there are 2 million and 800,000 persons addicted to narcotic drugs." (The state-run Tasnim news agency – February 28, 2018)

- Seyed Mohammad Mousavi, the State Security Force Commander of Gachsaran, in Kohgiluyeh and Boyer-Ahmad Province: "We have to accept that there are more than 750,000 drug addicted women in the country." (The state-run ILNA news agency, August 17, 2018)
- Ali Hashemi, head of the Independent Committee Fighting Narcotic Drugs in the State Expediency Council: "This phenomenon is in front of people's eyes and at least 14 to 15 million people in the families are addicted." (The state-run ISNA news agency, August 11, 2015)

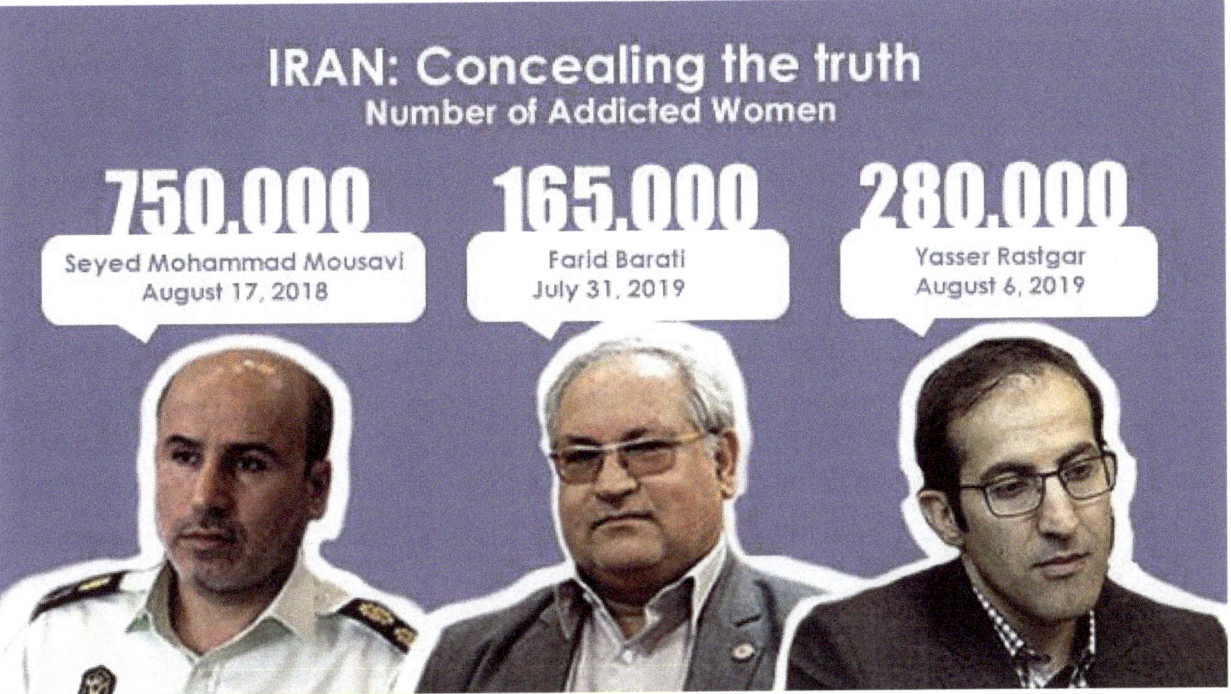

Officials agree that the average age of addiction has dropped conspicuously, however, the figure goes from 13 years of age in 2015 to 12 in 2018, and suddenly rises to 15 in October 2018 without explaining the reason. And then in 2019, the official does not give an age at all:

- Shahindokht Molaverdi, presidential deputy on Women and Family Affairs: "The average addiction age has dropped to 13 years for girls." (The state-run ISNA news agency, September 4, 2015)
- Seyed Mohammad Mousavi, the State Security Force Commander of Gachsaran, in Kohgiluyeh and Boyer-Ahmad Province: "The age of drug addiction in Gachsaran has dropped to 12, and today the government cannot fight addiction to narcotic drugs on its own." (The state-run ILNA news agency, August 17, 2018)
- Akram Mosavvari Manesh, executive director of women's studies and research: "Addiction age has dropped to the 15-18 range and even under 15." (The official IRNA news agency, October 15, 2018)
- Yasser Rastgar, sociologist and member of the faculty of the University of Hormozgan: "According to the surveys done in 2011, the age of addiction has

dropped, and addiction has become feminized." (The official IRNA news agency – August 6, 2019)

Different officials offer different percentages for addicted women while the same figures do not correspond with their acknowledged rapid spreading of addiction among women.
While one official puts the percentage of addicted women at 5 percent in 2001 and 10 percent in 2011, other officials claimed the percentage remained at 10 in 2017 and 2019 despite passage of six to eight years and the growing poverty of the population. These figures also contradict official acknowledgements in 2015 and 2018 of 2 to 30 percent growth in the number of addicted women.

- Parviz Afshar, spokesman for the Staff Fighting Narcotic Drugs: "10 percent of addicts are women... There are concerns that addiction is increasingly spreading among women of lower age group. This is seriously alarming... In 2001, some 5 percent of addicts were women, but this figure doubled in 2011."
(The official IRNA news agency – February 13, 2018)
- Ahmad Kaheh, general director of public education at the Social Directorate of the State Security Force: "The percentage of women used to be three per cent in the past, but unofficial figures indicate that it has risen to 12 per cent of the population of addicts." (The official IRNA news agency, May 12, 2018)
- Anoushirvan Mohseni Bandpay, head of the National Welfare Organization, citing statistics compiled in the Persian year 1394 (March 2015-March 2016): "There is one addicted woman for every 6.6 addicted men in the age range of 15 to 25 (i.e. 15 percent)." (The state-run salamatnews.com, July 11, 2018)
- Hamidreza Fat'hi, head of the Department for Prevention of Drug Addiction in the Ministry of Health: "The latest official statistics show that one woman is addicted in Iran for every 9 male addicts. (i.e. 10 percent)." (The state-run IRNA news agency, February 5, 2017)
- Firouzeh Jaafari, deputy for women's affairs in the Staff of Fighting Narcotic Drugs: "Seven (7) per cent of the population of addicts in the country were women in (the Persian year) 1396 (which spans from March 2017 to March 2018) where as in 1398 (March 2019 to March 2020), this has increased to at least 10 per cent." (The official IRNA news agency – August 6, 2019)

Employment, unemployment, economic participation
- In Iran, the participation rate for the female work force has dropped from 17 per cent in 2005 to 12 per cent in 2014. (Website of the Statistics Center)
- In 2015, the National Statistics Center had announced that women's economic participation was 13.3 per cent.[60]
- In 2016, the National Statistics Center announced a 1.6-percent drop in women's economic participation but instead of 11.7 announced the figure of 14.3 percent.[61]

---

[60] https://www.amar.org.ir/Portals/0/Files/abstract/1394/ch_ntank_94.pdf
[61] https://www.amar.org.ir/Portals/0/Files/fulltext/1395/n_nank_95_3_v2.pdf

- Economic participation among Iranian women older than 10 years, is 13.8 per cent. (The state-run Fars news agency, January 4, 2016)
- Sussan Bastani, deputy for strategic studies at the directorate for Women and Family Affairs: "Two million girls have graduated from universities in the past 20 years. However, unemployment rate among women has increased. Women's economic participation has also dropped from 39.5 to 27 per cent." (The state-run ISNA news agency, February 13, 2016)
- World Bank put the average value for Iran from 1990 to 2017 at 14.21 percent with a minimum of 9.83 percent in 1990 and a maximum of 19.41 percent in 2005.

The average rate for participation of the female work force is 50 per cent in the world, and 20 per cent in the Middle East and North Africa.

Illiteracy

The statistics on literacy or illiteracy in Iran are scarce, inaccurate and conflicting.

- Seyyed Mohammad Javad Abtahi, member of the parliamentary Education and Research Committee: The number of illiterates in Iran has reached 11 million making up some 13 per cent of the population of different ages. (The state-run salamatnews.com, September 26, 2018)
- National Statistics Center, 2011 statistics: The population of illiterates is 9,483,028. Approximately two-thirds of this population, i.e. 6,250,965, are women.
- Ali Bagherzadeh, deputy Minister of Education and head of the Literacy Movement Organization: Based on the census done in 2016 in Iran, the number of illiterates in the 10-49 age group was 2.3 million, 60 per cent of whom are women (i.e. 1.38 million women). (The state-run Salamatnews.com, April 25, 2018)
- Ali Bagherzadeh, deputy Minister of Education and head of the Literacy Movement Organization: "There are some 2.7 million illiterates between 10 and 49 years of age in Iran, nearly 1.8 million of whom are women." (The state-run ILNA news agency, March 31, 2018)
- The statistics collected in 2006 and published ten years later in the state press in 2016, indicate that there are over 3.2 million children deprived of education in Iran. (The state-run Mehrkhaneh website, December 5, 2016)
- The parliamentary Research Center published a report in 2015 indicating the number of students deprived of education as 4 million.
- There are more than 15 million school-age Iranians, but the student population is only 13 million. This means that at least 2 million Iranian students have not been able to go to school. (The state-run salamatnews.com, September 26, 2018)

g. What laws need to be changed?

The Iranian regime's entire Constitution, Civil Code, Penal Code and all other rules and regulations contradict CEDAW, the SDGs, the planet 50-50 goals, and therefore need to be overhauled.

- As it was stated earlier, just Article 1 of the CEDAW, contradicts the regime' laws in 90 instances, according to the regime's religious scholars and experts. Here is a vivid example:
- Rouhani government's acceptance with reservations of UNESCO Education 2030 document in 2016, wreaked havoc within the Iranian regime.[62] Officials viewed the Education 2030 document as a "disgraceful" document "bearing a colonialist content" which manifests "one of the most bitter examples of infiltration" and promotes "educational transformation", "elimination of sexual stereotypes", "gender equality", and "global citizenship", causing grave "security" concerns.
- Opposition to the UNESCO document built up and the supreme leader weighed in. Finally, in June 2017, the regime's president, Hassan Rouhani, presided a meeting of the Supreme Council of Cultural Revolution (SCCR) which decided to stop implementation of the Education 2030 document and consider the Fundamental Reform Document of Education (FRDE) adopted under Mahmoud Ahmadinejad in December 2011, as the benchmark for all educational affairs in the country.
- The reason why this "non-binding" document with the genuine goal of equitable education and learning opportunities for all sends such tremors through the ruling clique in Iran, can be clearly seen in the following paragraph from the state-run Tasnim news agency:
- "In the (Education) 2030 Framework for Action, there are references to terms such as global citizenship and gender equality... The adoption and implementation of this document would transform national education in many ways. Among them, one can point to the omission of sexual stereotypes, teaching of sex education to children, and omission of some Quranic concepts and values from text books to promote peace and non-violence."[63]

h. Are there public awareness programs about women's legal rights?

The government does not sponsor any public awareness programs on women's legal rights. Contrarily, the regime arrests and imprisons members of independent NGOs that try to provide such education for women.

---

[62] Education 2030 Framework for Action (SDG4) and Iranian officials' hysteric reactions to it, NCRI Women's Committee, June 2017
[63] The state-run Tasnim news agency, May 7, 2017

Case of the Voice of Iranian Women Association (April – September 2019):
- Members of the Voice of Iranian Women Association (*Anjoman-e Neday-e Zanan-e Irani*) were arrested and charged with "promoting corruption and prostitution", "formation of the Iranian Women Association", "association and collusion against national security", and "propaganda against state."
- Akram Nasirian was arrested on April 29, 2019 and detained in solitary confinement at Ward 209 of Evin Prison for a month. Ms. Nasirian is an activist in the literacy movement and had been actively engaged in sending aid to flood victims. She was charged with disrupting the public opinion and encouraging women to shun their veils.
- Nahid Shaqaqi, a women's rights activist, was brutalized and arrested on May 15, 2019, and detained at ward 209 of Evin Prison. She had made a speech on the International Women's Day on the roots of violence against women.
- Maryam Mohammadi was arrested on July 8, 2019, in the city of Garmsar and taken to solitary confinement in the Intelligence Ministry Ward 209 in Evin Prison. She was confined for a month in solitary and subsequently transferred to the Women's Ward.
- Esrin Derkaleh, 36, was arrested on July 28, 2019, in Garmsar and taken to Ward 209 of Evin Prison. She was in prison for more than 40 days. Maryam Mohammadi and Esrin Derkaleh had been active in the field of women's empowerment and women's literacy.
- Parvin Nokhostin, whose activities focus on the rights of children lacking identity papers, was summoned to the Department of Intelligence on July 24, 2019.
- Mahboubeh Farahzadi, retired teacher and a member of the Voice of Iranian Women Association, was interrogated at the Prosecutor's Office of Evin for several hours on September 8, 2019.

Case of lawyers and human rights activists (September 2018):
- Women's rights activists, Hoda Amid, a lawyer, and Najmeh Vahedi, a sociology graduate, were arrested at their homes in Tehran on September 1, 2018. The two women used to hold workshops for women to educate them about their rights.
- Another women's rights activist and student of gender studies, Rezvaneh Mohammadi, was arrested by security forces on September 3, 2018. Ms. Mohammadi was detained in the Women's Ward of Evin Prison after undergoing interrogations for nearly one month.

Amnesty International issued a statement on September 3, 2018, warning that the human rights situation in Iran had reached "crisis point" and that the arrests of lawyers and women's rights activists in Iran signal intensifying crackdown on civil society.[64]

---

[64] Iran: Arrests of lawyers and women's rights activists signal intensifying crackdown on civil society, **Amnesty International, September 3, 2018**

2. Which of the following have been important for accelerating progress for women and girls in your country?

The laws, policies and practices of the Iranian regime generally and fundamentally seek to restrict, marginalize and hinder the progress of women. As explained in the case of Education 2030 document, the regime cannot tolerate gender equality, and it even refuses using the word equality, replacing it with the word, "equity."
So, one cannot expect this regime to take steps which would accelerate women's progress.

○ Equality and non-discrimination under the law and access to justice

Under the Iranian law, women are considered half-humans. This is why the regime refuses to use the terms "equality" and "gender equality," rather, they use the word "equity."
Women's testimony,[65] blood-money,[66] and inheritance[67] are always half of men's. Women are discriminated against in holding leadership position as a president[68] or a decision-making position as a judge.[69] Accordingly, women are discriminated against in every realm of law and justice.

- Article 1133 of the Civil Code states, "A man can divorce his wife any time he so chooses." But a woman cannot get divorce unless she proves that her husband is either impotent, a drug addict, unable to provide for a family or living away from home for more than six months."
- As a result, the law does not provide protection for victims of domestic violence and make it difficult for them to escape violence through divorce. Under the Civil Code, women seeking to obtain a divorce as a result of domestic violence must first prove that the abuse was intolerable (*osr va-haraj*).

---

[65] According to Articles 199 and 209 of the regime's Islamic Penal Code, testimonies of two women are equal to the testimony of one man and are not considered at all if not accompanied by a male witness.
[66] According to Article 382 of the Islamic Penal Code, if a Muslim man deliberately murders a woman, he will not be punished in kind (as called for by the principle of Retribution) unless the victim's parents pay half of the man's blood-money to his parents. While if a woman murders a man, she may be executed upon request of the victim's parents.
Article 550 of the Islamic Penal Code – The blood money for murder of a Muslim woman (whether deliberate or undeliberate) is half of the blood money for a Muslim man.
[67] Based on articles 861 – 949 of the Civil Code on heritage, the wife and daughter's share of heritage is half that of the husband and son.
[68] Article 115 of the Iranian constitution views the right to hold the office of presidency as limited to only "religious and political statesmen."
[69] Article 163 of that constitution has made qualifications for a judge contingent upon the "principles of religious jurisprudence," stating: "The conditions and qualifications to be fulfilled by a judge will be determined by law, in accordance with principles of religious jurisprudence."
The "Law on Conditions for Appointing Judiciary Judges" (ratified in April 1982), states, "Judges will be appointed from among men with the following qualifications: 1. Practical faith, justice, and commitment to Islamic principles and loyalty to the system of Islamic Republic of Iran…"
In 1985, amendments were made to the above law allowing women to hold advisory positions or become investigative magistrates in judicial bodies. But they still cannot draft judgments.

- One of the most abusive articles of the Iranian Constitution is on marriage of girls. According to the law, the legal age of marriage is 13 for girls and 15 for boys, but if a father decides that he wants to wed his daughter in younger age, the law permits him to do so. This has paved the way for a growing number of early marriages in Iran.
- Early marriages violate the rights of girl children and young women and are considered a form of violence against women.
- A judiciary official, Ali Kazemi, announced in March 2019, that around 600,000 girl children officially get married in Iran every year, but there are more marriages that are not officially registered.[70]
- The Iranian census organization has released new statistics indicating that 234,000 marriages of girl children under 15 years of age were officially registered by this organization from March 2017 to March 2018 (Persian year 1396). 194 of these were marriages of girl children under 10 years old.[71]
- The parliamentary judicial and legal committee rejected the plan to increase the minimum age of marriage for girls in December 2018.[72]
- Also, a bill called the Law to Support Disadvantaged, Defenseless and Abandoned Children was passed by the Iranian regime's Parliament on September 22, 2013, which sanctions marriage between the girl child and her guardian, with the approval of a court.
- According to the regime's law, fathers and grandfathers are considered owners of blood and they are not punished if they kill their children, hence sanctioning honor killings of young women by their fathers and grandfathers.[73]

⭕ Quality education, training and life-long learning for women and girls

According to Principle 30 of the Iranian Constitution, "The government is obliged to provide free elementary and high school education for all members of the nation and facilitate free higher education for all until the country is self-sufficient." In practice, however, education is neither free nor mandatory.[74]

- The latest figure on the number of illiterates announced by a parliamentary deputy was 11 million,[75] two-thirds of which are women and girls. This shows 1.5-million increase in 7 years considering the figure of 9,483,028, announced by the National Statistics Center (NSC) in 2011.
- According to the figures announced in 2018, at least 2 million out of a total of 15 million school-age children in Iran are deprived of education. Again, two-thirds of these children

---

[70] The state-run daily Entekhab, March 4, 2019
[71] The state-run Iran daily newspaper, October 30, 2019
[72] The state-run Fars news agency, December 23, 2018
[73] Misogyny institutionalized in the laws of the mullahs' regime, website of the NCRI Women's Committee, November 8, 2015; Article 717 of the Islamic Penal Code
[74] Ali Bagherzadeh, deputy Minister of Education and head of the Literacy Movement Organization, the state-run Salamatnews.com, April 25, 2018
[75] Seyyed Mohammad Javad Abtahi, member of the parliamentary Education and Research Committee, the state-run salamatnews.com, September 26, 2018

are girls who are forced to drop out of school due to poverty, early marriages, lack of high schools in their villages, lack of transportation, etc.
- Hundreds of young women and girls become victims of bad roads,[76] old transportation vehicles,[77] worn-out schools,[78] dysfunctional heating,[79] in schools and universities, every year.
- Baha'i students are systematically deprived of continuing their college education and every year dozens of Baha'i students are dismissed from their universities or not admitted due to their faith.
- Student activists are also imprisoned and deprived of continuing their education for a higher degree. Most recently, student activist Soha Mortezaii has been deprived of continuing her education for a Ph.D. She has been sentenced to six years in prison for participating in anti-government protests in January 2018.

O Poverty eradication, agricultural productivity and food security

Poverty is the most common problem the people of Iran face contrasting the country's immense national wealth and oil. The middle class has all but diminished and at least 80 per cent of Iranians live below the poverty line.[80]
- A socio-economist was cited as saying that one third of low-income Iranians, i.e. around 5 million people, who earn only 1 million tomans a month ($74) are living in extreme poverty and hunger, while 67% of people live below the relative poverty line.[81]
- Poverty has become feminized. Social ills, suicide, runaway girls, addiction, and a rising number of female prisoners are some of the issues in Iran.[82]
- The face of poverty in Iran has become feminine. This was acknowledged by Rouhani's deputy in women and family affairs.[83] Other officials have also echoed the same theme.
- "Poverty has become feminine… Today, more than 64 per cent of impoverished families covered by our Relief Committee are female heads of household."[84]

---

[76] Eleven high school girls from Kermanshah got wounded with broken arms and legs when their minibus overturned on Kangavar-Sahneh road. The state-run ISNA news agency, April 22, 2019

[77] On December 25, 2018, a bus crash on the campus of the Sciences and Research Branch of Azad University in Tehran, led to the deaths of eight including 3 female students. 28 students were injured.

[78] A 7-year-old Kurdish girl, Donya Veisi, died when the wall crumbled on her at school in Sanandaj. The state-run Tasnim news agency – October 8, 2018

[79] Four pre-school and elementary girl students lost their lives in a fire at a non-governmental girls' school in Osveh Hassaneh in Zahedan, capital of Sistan and Baluchestan Province. The state-run Tasnim news agency, December 18, 2018

Twenty-five girls were poisoned after being exposed to carbon monoxide leak from the heating system in their elementary school in Bam, Kerman Province. The state-run ISNA News Agency, January 29, 2019

[80] The official website of the Iranian regime's parliament, ICANA, March 13, 2018

[81] Fa.shafaqna.com, February 28, 2018

[82] Zahra Shojaii, secretary general of the so-called reformist women's assembly, the state-run dustaan.com, June 20, 2018

[83] In a gathering on women and employment, Shahindakht Molaverdi said the most important challenge to Iran's economy is the unemployment predicament. She said: "The growing trend of female heads of households and feminization of poverty leaves no room for questioning the need to give priority to these women." The state-run ILNA news agency, September 6, 2014.

- "50 per cent of beggars and panhandlers are women."[85]
- "The most significant problem in the city of Tehran is the feminization of social ills."[86]
- Poverty of women and its consequent social ailments are mainly and basically due to the regime's official policies and laws which discriminate against women.
- According to the head of Welfare Organization, "We are lagging with respect to economic indices, such as providing jobs and employment for women. Of course, this is mainly due to country's policies where we have 22 women employed compared to every 100 men with employment. Women's employment rate in Iran is 12 percent, at best."[87]
- A parliamentary deputy explained, "Having no guardians, this stratum of women (heads of households) is responsible for the custody of their children, and due to financial poverty, unemployment and their consequences, they are subjected to harms. This is while, because of budget constraints, the Welfare Organization cannot take appropriate measures to empower and create jobs for women heads of household."[88]
- Working age women comprise a population of 32,252,090, but only 4,289,528 of them are economically active and the other 27,962,562 women [87 per cent] have no role in the country's economy.[89]

Rural women

Despite the fact that rural women are actively engaged in work, but their occupation has not been considered in any program.[90] Usually, the statistics is based on owners of the production units, and since women do not own production units, they have not been mentioned in the official statistics and their employment has not been considered, either.[91]

- Rural women must do various difficult jobs like working in farms and agricultural fields at all stages and shepherding, as well as housework and handicraft. These women have a large economic and social share in all the works and production in every village.[92] But they are deprived of social or economic security. There is no secure future for them and

---

[84] Mer'at Rassouli, director of the state-run Relief Committee (charity) in Shiraz, the state-run ISNA news agency, August 26, 2015.
[85] Kamran Gardan, spokesman for the City Council of Hamadan, the state-run ISNA news agency, July 24, 2018.
[86] Farzad Hooshyar Parsian, General Director of Tehran's Welfare, Social Services and Cooperation Organization, the state-run IRNA news agency, August 16, 2015.
[87] Anoushirvan Mohseni Bandpay, head of the National Welfare Organization, the state-run Tabnak website, February 13, 2018
[88] Hassan Lotfi, a member of the social commission of the mullahs' parliament, May 2018
[89] The state-run Ettelaat newspaper, August 15, 2015
[90] Zahra Faraji, general director for Women and Family Affairs in the Central Province's Governorate, the state-run ISNA news agency, January 25, 2015
[91] Forough-os Sadat Bani-Hashem, general director of the Development Office of Agricultural Activities of Rural and Nomad Women in the Ministry of Agricultural Crusade, the website of the presidential directorate of Women and Family Affairs, October 22, 2017 - http://women.gov.ir/fa/news/7803
[92] The state-run ISCANEWS website, October 17, 2016

when they are disabled, widowed, or divorced, and when they become sick or elderly, there is no social security system to give them support.[93]
- Women who plant rice do more than 60 percent of the planting and harvesting of rice, but their wage is 10,000 tomans less than the wage of their male counterparts. A seasonal female worker participates in all stages of plantation and harvest of rice. In other seasons, they work in other farms.[94]
- Harvest of potatoes is also part of the agricultural work women engage in, but women workers harvest between 50 to 70 sacks of potatoes every day for only 350,000 tomans ($30). In other agricultural sectors, despite doing the same work for the same number of hours, women end up with half of the pay allocated to their male counterparts.[95]
- Iranian women make 75 percent of the handicraft industries' products, 40 percent of agricultural products, and 80 percent of the carpet industry productions.[96] Most of these women are women heads of household.[97]

Food security

As for food security, in many Iranian villages, people are living below the minimum humane conditions.
- The inhabitants of Hosseinabad village, in the middle of a desert, eat hay as their main food. They do not have drinking water. They use the little water they have for farming to sow several hundred square meters of hay near their sheds. Some of the hay sown is used for the livestock and some is kept for human consumption.[98]
- Not all the villagers can easily procure food from cities. This is why their food security is jeopardized, leading to the displacement of rural inhabitants who finally have to change their territory.[99]
- Poor urban women resort to the trash bins to find food leftovers, a scene which has become all too common these days in Tehran and other major capitals. [100]

---

[93] The state-run ISCANEWS website, October 17, 2016
[94] Iranwire.com, October 16, 2017
[95] The official IRNA news agency, November 22, 2018
[96] Massoumeh Ebtekar, head of the presidential directorate for women and family affairs, the official IRNA news agency, May 4, 2019
[97] The official IRNA news agency – May 16, 2018
[98] The state-run Asr-e Iran website, January 21, 2018
[99] The state-run ISNA news agency October 16, 2017
[100] Mousavi Chelek, deputy of Welfare Organization, the state-run ILNA news agency, October 8, 2016

○ Eliminating violence against women and girls

Not only the clerical regime's Constitution and laws institutionalize violence against women and sanction the death penalty and cruel punishments of flogging, stoning and blinding, but the regime systematically and formally undertakes violent measures against Iranian women day and night, throughout the country.

VAW in Iran is state sponsored
- Violence against women is not a cultural issue in Iran, but a state-sponsored phenomenon.
- The most common form of violence against women in Iran are the measures to force Iranian women to observe the compulsory veil. Hossein Ashtari, the Commander of the State Security Force (SSF), announced in September 2016 that, "Some 2000 women who wear improper clothing are arrested every day in Tehran and some other provinces."[101] This amounts to 730,000 arrests in a year, a minimized figure both due to lack of transparency on the part of the regime, and the increase in suppression of women as manifested in the video clips this year.
- At least 105 women have been executed since August 2013 when Rouhani became the clerical regime's president.

---

[101] The state-run Tasnim news agency, September 29, 2016

Official violence against women has sanctioned and promoted domestic violence against women, as well, so much that the regime's experts have been talking about the drastic rise in domestic violence against women in Iran.

- Iran has one of the highest statistics on violence against women.[102]
- Violence (against women) has become institutionalized.[103]
- Currently, domestic violence against women is pervasive in society.[104]
- Violence against women occur in various forms in society.[105]
- According to Tehran's forensics officials, after road accidents and street fights, the main reason for women referring to the Coroner's Office in Tehran is being battered by their husbands. In 2017, they reported an average of 52 women refer to the Coroner's Office every day.[106]
- 66 per cent of Iranian women experience domestic violence in their lifetime. [107] Although the figure is double the world average of one-in-every-three women (or 33%), it must be considered a blatant mitigation of the reality.
- Violence against wives ranks second only after violence against children in Iran.[108]
- Domestic violence against women in Iran saw a 20% rise from March 2017 to March 2018.[109]

Ill-fated VAW bill

- A VAW bill was finalized by the Iranian regime's Judiciary and sent to the government on September 17, 2019.[110] The bill called "Provision of Security for Women (PSW)" had been stalled for eight years in the labyrinths of decision making in the parliament, the Guardian Council and the Judiciary Branch.[111]
- After the bill was rejected in August 2017 by the parliamentary legal and judicial committee, the Judiciary changed the bill's name to "Protection, Dignity and Provision of Security for Women Against Violence."
- They removed at least 41 articles of the original bill ostensibly because they overlapped with the Islamic Punishment Code and the Criminal Procedures Regulations, or because

---

[102] VAW expert Parastoo Sarmadi, the state-run ILNA news agency, September 18, 2018
[103] Parvaneh Salahshouri, member of the mullahs' parliament, the state-run ILNA news agency, September 18, 2018
[104] Parvaneh Salahshouri, head of women's faction in the mullahs' parliament, the state-run IRNA news agency, November 25, 2017
[105] Parvaneh Salahshouri, head of women's faction in the mullahs' parliament, the state-run IRNA news agency, November 25, 2017
[106] Tehran's forensic officials, January 2017
[107] Fatemeh Ghassempour, head of the Research Center on Women and Family in Tehran, the state-run ISNA news agency, November 16, 2018
[108] Kamel Delpasand, sociologist and a researcher in social sciences, interview with the official IRNA news agency, July 18, 2018
[109] Reza Jafari, head of the Social Emergencies, interview with the official IRNA news agency, July 18, 2018
[110] Provision of Security for Women bill finalized by the Judiciary after 8 years, website of the NCRI Women's Committee, September 19, 2019
[111] Annual Report 2019 of the NCRI Women's Committee, March 7, 2019

they contradicted the regime's so-called policy of de-imprisonment. The present bill has been re-written in five chapters and 77 articles.[112]
- Some experts say a major deficiency in the new bill is replacing the word "women" with "ladies" which refers only to married women. Therefore, girls under 18, single women, victims of social ills and those subjected to such harms, are not covered by this bill.
- Neither does the bill criminalize sexual harassment, rape, and sexual exploitation of women and it does not contain any punishment for the assailants.
- Another serious problem is the lack of effective and sufficient guarantees in the bill to prevent violence against women or counter it. The bill has totally turned a blind eye on the state-sponsored violence against women to enforce the compulsory veil, as the main systematic form of VAW.

○ Access to health care, including sexual and reproductive health and reproductive rights

- According to Article 717 of the Islamic Penal Code, abortion is considered a crime and if a woman has an abortion, she must pay the blood money for the aborted fetus.

○ Political participation and representation

Iranian women are excluded from any real power. Iranian women's participation and representation in the formal political structure is among the lowest in the world.
The most senior women in government are only three so-called vice-presidents who do not have any executive powers or influence on key economic, foreign policy, political, cultural, or social matters.

- In August 2017, when Hassan Rouhani was elected for a second term as the mullahs' president, he failed to appoint even one woman as cabinet minister.
- Despite being strongly criticized for excluding women again from his second-term cabinet, Hassan Rouhani did not include any women among the new governors he appointed on September 13, 2017.[113]
- The mullahs' parliament voted down a proposal to allocate a one-sixth quota of parliamentary seats to women on April 16, 2019. Women's participation in the Iranian parliament is 5.9 percent in 2019 compared to the world's average of 24.3 percent.[114]
- As far as the number of parliamentary seats allocated to women is concerned, Iran ranks 180 among 191 countries in the world. Only Nigeria, Thailand, Sri Lanka, Lebanon, Maldives, Kuwait, Haiti, Oman, Yemen and Guinea rank lower.[115]
- A report published by the Iranian regime's parliament on the city councils' elections accounts only for the main cities and claims that women constitute some 12% of the city councils.

---

[112] The official IRNA news agency, September 17, 2019
[113] The state-run ISNA news agency, September 14, 2017
[114] Parvaneh Mafi, MP, the state-run Iran daily - April 17, 2019
[115] Parvaneh Mafi, MP, the state-run Iran daily - April 17, 2019

- Another state-run news outlet studied the decrease in women's participation only in provincial centers, setting the current number of women at 42.[116]
- However, a study done by the Women's Committee of the National Council of Resistance of Iran found out that in a total of 500 big and small cities, only 64 women were elected as members of City Councils compared to 3,724 male members. That amounts to a meager 1.7% participation for women in the City Councils.[117]
- In the administration of Iranian cities and provinces, women hold only 13 out of 2,653 positions as provincial governors, governors, district governors, and mayor, which is a mere 0.5 percent participation.[118]
- Massoumeh Ebtekar, Rouhani's deputy in Women and Family Affairs, once admitted that "women almost disappear in senior management positons."[119]

○ Right to work and rights at work (e.g. gender pay gap, occupational segregation, career progression)

Right to work

As explained in answer to questions 1-c in this section, Iranian women confront an array of restrictions and are denied equal access to employment.

- First of all, they are restricted from entering certain professions and 77 fields of education, while denied equal benefits at work, basic legal protections.
- Secondly, employers give priority to men and the social and economic infrastructure is built to exclude women from the job market. Often, employers are reluctant to hire women because their ability to travel depends on their husband's permission.
- From the 27 million women over the age of 10 in Iran, only three million are employed and the remaining 24 million are not in the workforce.[120]
- The number of unemployed women in Iran has increased by 200,000 from 830,996 in 2011 to more than 1,037,000 women in 2017. That is a 25% increase in just seven years.[121]
- Unemployment rates among young people, women and educated women, are alarmingly high particularly in western provinces. In some of these provinces, youth unemployment rates range from 50% to 63% and educated women's unemployment rates in the same provinces fluctuate between 63% and 78%.[122]
- Unemployment rate among young women under 30 was 85.9%.[123]

---

[116] The state-run Iran newspaper, May 29, 2017
[117] A study on women's participation as governors, mayors and members of city councils, June 2017, website of the NCRI Women's Committee
[118] A study on women's participation as governors, mayors and members of city councils, June 2017, website of the NCRI Women's Committee
[119] The state-run ISNA news agency, October 31, 2017
[120] The state-run Mehr news agency - June 8, 2016
[121] Report by the Centre of Strategic Statistics and Information of the Iranian Labor Ministry, October 2018
[122] The state-run ISNA news agency - November 21, 2018
[123] The state-run Mehr News Agency – January 5, 2016 / the state-run Tabnak website – December 26, 2015

- A survey done in 2016 and 2017 indicated that out of 3.2 million jobless people in Iran, more than 1.3 million or 42% of the unemployed population held university degrees. This comes as only 24% of jobholders in the same year were university graduates.
- Women with higher education are regarded as a new sector who are either unemployed or have been forced to engage in menial jobs with low wages. Many women with college education have to resort to peddling in the streets, working in restaurants or as secretaries in offices and accept salaries as low as one-third of the minimum wage. Women with bachelor's degrees are working in welding workshops, and a graphics major is now a simple worker.
- In its annual survey of Iran's labor force, the National Statistics Center (NSC) also confirmed gender inequality in the job market of Iran in the 10-year period spanning from 2008 to 2017.
- The NSC findings indicate that the 63% average participation rate of men in the job market was four times greater than women's participation rate of only 14% in the said period.
- The survey also indicated that out of every 100 persons holding jobs in Iran, 84 were men and only 16 were women, a clear indication that the job market is male dominated.
- A survey by the Labor Ministry's Center for Statistics and Strategic Information found unequal access to wage-earning jobs for men and women. According to this study done for the period spanning from March 2016 to March 2017, men's share of wage-earning jobs was 82.7 per cent compared to women's 17.3 per cent share, indicating a fivefold access for men to wage-earning opportunities compared to women.[124]
- According to the figures compiled by the NSC, the rate of unemployment among young women between 20 and 30 years of age is double that of men in the same age range.[125]

Working rights
- Working women receive 77% of men's wage for equal work, and as such they lag 10 years behind their male colleagues.[126]
- Half of Iranian women workers receive only one third of their real wage.[127]
- Women workers work in step with men in production units, but do not receive equal wages. They are not aware of their legal rights. Therefore, they do not even find out if their insurance has been considered in their payrolls. But they do not file any complaints in this regard since they fear being fired by their employers.[128]
- Temporary three-month contracts have deprived female workers of job security. Sometimes, employers mistreat women workers for the smallest flaw in their work. They face long working hours but are deprived of many rights and benefits.[129]

---

[124] The state-run Mehr news agency – January 23, 2018
[125] The state-run Asr-e Iran website – December 20, 2017
[126] Hassan Ta'ii, job market advisor to the Minister of Labor, the state-run ISNA news agency, September 2, 2017
[127] A Rouhani advisor, the official IRNA news agency, April 21, 2015
[128] Fatemeh Pourno, Secretary of the Union of Women Workers in Qazvin (a state institution), The official IRNA news agency - May 3, 2018
[129] Fatemeh Pourno, Secretary of the Union of Women Workers in Qazvin (a state institution), The official IRNA news agency, May 3, 2018

- There is a wide gap in the salaries of nurses and doctors. In most countries this difference is three folds at most, but in Iran it is 100 folds. Sometimes, the doctors' payrolls are 500 times greater than those of nurses.[130]
- The number of women working in the rice fields is less than the market demand, but many farm owners prefer to employ women because their wages are always lower than men's.[131]
- In some agricultural sectors, despite doing the same work for the same number of hours, women end up with half of the pay allocated to their male counterparts.[132]
- Some women are working more than the legal working hours and the wages they receive are rather small... Women are kept at their workplace for long hours and they are paid wages less than men…. (They) go to work at these production centers since early morning and work up to 12 hours with a meager (monthly) wage of 400,000 tomans ($35).[133]

○ Women's entrepreneurship and women's enterprises

- Despite the regime's propaganda, many women who wish to start and are capable to run a business, have great difficulties in receiving loans for the initial investment, because bank managers think that women would not be able to pay back.[134]
- The Directorate for Women and Family Affairs' proposal to distribute 18 million tomans of investment in villages to invest on women's entrepreneurship and employment networking, has gotten nowhere due to limits in the fiscal budget.[135]

---

[130] Female nurses in Iran entangled in a web of damaging problems, website of the NCRI Women's Committee, February 27, 2019
[131] The state-run ILNA news agency, March 4, 2018
[132] The official IRNA news agency, November 22, 2018
[133] Ahmad Amirabadi Farahani, a member of the presiding board of the mullahs' parliament from Qom, the state-run ISNA news agency, May 1, 2018
[134] Fatemeh Zolqadr, member of the Labor Committee of the parliament, said, "Many women who wish to start a business, do not have the initial capital despite their capability to run one. When we speak of supporting employment and occupation for women, the first thing is to provide the initial capital, and accordingly, women who wish to start a business must be able to be granted loans… Getting loans is more difficult for women compared to men. Thinking that women would have more problems in paying back their loans compared to men, banks refuse to grant them loans." The state-run ILNA news agency, October 9, 2019
[135] The state-run ILNA news agency, October 9, 2019

Working rights of Iranian women

- The majority of them are hired in informal sectors
- Most of them are hired on temporary three-month contracts
- They are laid off for the slightest flaw
- They face longer working hours, unsafe conditions and smaller wages

They receive 77% of men's wage for equal work — **77%**

They make up 80% of uninsured job holders — **80%**

Half of them receive one third of their real wage — **50%**

- Iran ranks 54 among 58 nations according to a MasterCard ranking of countries with regards to women's entrepreneurship. The countries that lag Iran are Saudi Arabia, Algeria, Bangladesh and Egypt.[136]
- Women's economic participation in Iran has grown only less than 7 percent from 9.2 percent in 1956 to 16 percent in 2019 in a span of 63 years despite doubling of the country's population and women's higher education.[137]
- It can be concluded that despite Iranian women's efforts to increase their economic participation, they face numerous structural obstacles that go beyond employers' mentalities. These obstacles include lack of support for women's entrepreneurship where women are not trusted by banks and have difficulty in receiving loans and are required to place deposits.[138]

---

[136] The state-run ILNA news agency, November 24, 2019
[137] Ibid.
[138] Ibid.

Q 1-4 PRIORITIES, ACHIEVEMENTS, CHALLENGES AND SETBACKS

O Unpaid care and domestic work / work-family conciliation (e.g. paid maternity or parental leave, care services)

- The regime's general approach is for women to stay home and do not engage in any outside work. As a result, they are not prone to work-family conciliation. The limited steps they have taken in this regard either remain on the paper or are not implemented due to lack of funds.
- It was reported that the government began deducing child benefits from the payrolls of women heads of household in Autumn 2017.[139] The decision was implemented abruptly and the amounts previously paid to them were withdrawn from their accounts, at once.
- A number of government officials have also admitted that despite legislations which allow working women enjoy maternity leave, at least 74,000 women are dismissed every year when they return to work after delivering their babies.[140]

O Gender-responsive social protection (e.g. universal health coverage, cash transfers, pensions)

Only 19 percent of the total number of insured individuals in Iran are women.[141]

- Women have the largest share in informal jobs, which means they are hired by small workshops and production units which are not officially registered and, therefore, not monitored by the government.[142]
- Women working in the informal sector work longer hours under unsafe conditions, are paid less, and are denied benefits and insurance, including medical and retirement insurance.[143]
- The General Board of Directors of the Administrative Court of Justice rescinded a directive by the general director of the Labor Ministry which had banned laying off working mothers for two years while they nurse their children.[144]

---

[139] Zahra Sa'ii, spokeswoman for the parliamentary Social Commission, the state-run salamatnews.com, March 28, 2018

[140] Fatemeh Sadeqi, Professor and member of faculty of Teachers' Training University, the state-run Fars news agency, June 16, 2015
The state-run ISNA news agency, June 30, 2015; the state-run entekhab.ir website, August 1, 2015

[141] Vahideh Negin, Labor Minister's advisor, the state-run Tejarat-e Emrouz website, April 24, 2015
http://tejaratemrouz.ir/fa/news/2988

[142] Massoumeh Ebtekar, presidential deputy for Women and Family Affairs, Labor Ministry gathering in Tehran, April 28, 2018

[143] The official IRNA news agency, April 28, 2018

[144] The state-run Tasnim news agency, September 15, 2017

○ **Basic services and infrastructure (water, sanitation, energy, transport etc.)**

- Lack of access to clean and adequate water is one of the greatest infrastructural problems of rural women in Iran.
- Reports on the situation of 100 villages in Golestan Province,[145] 44 villages in Sistan and Baluchestan Province,[146] and dozens of villages in the four corners of the country[147] reveal that most villages do not have water pipelines. The inhabitants receive water by tankers, and only 15 liters per person and only 2 or 3 times per week. As a result, they do not have enough water for bathing and they use the water for basic needs such as drinking and farming. Often people can take a bath every three months.[148]
- The roads leading to many villages are unpaved and difficult to pass. They are blocked with any slight rain or snow and there is no public transportation.[149]
- Sixteen (16) women including a pregnant woman died in four bus accidents in various parts of Iran from January 9 to 20, 2020.
- According to the state-run media in Iran, every half an hour, one Iranian woman loses her husband or father due to road accidents.[150]
- In investigating the causes of increase in road accidents in Iran, many domestic and international experts believe that the lack of standard roads and traffic infrastructures, worn-out and sometimes out-of-date vehicles, lack of traffic signs on the roads, population growth and rising number of cars, poverty and economic pressure on drivers are among the causes of road accidents in Iran. This is in addition to mismanagement by a kleptocratic regime.
- Iran ranks the world's number one with the highest death toll, in 800,000 road accidents per year (1.5 times the world average).
- In terms of casualties caused by road accidents, Iran ranks 189th among 190 countries.

○ **Strengthening women's participation in ensuring environmental sustainability**

The Iranian regime does not allow citizen's participation to ensure environmental sustainability and keeps arresting conservationists under various pretexts. Most recently, on November 20, 2019, six environmental experts including two women were sentenced to 4 to 10 years in prison after 20 months of pre-trial detention.[151]

---

[145] Alireza Ebrahimi, secretary of the assembly of representatives of Golestan Province, the state-run Tasnim news agency, December 28, 2017
[146] The state-run salamatnews.com, October 22, 2017
[147] The state-run Raja News website, July 10, 2017; Bartarinha website, August 29, 2017; The state-run Tasnim news agency, December 20, 2017; The state-run Kashmari website, January 27, 2018; ...
[148] The state-run Raja News website, July 10, 2017
[149] The official IRNA news agency, October 30, 2017
[150] The state-run salamatnews.com, January 25, 2020
[151] Montrealgazette.com, November 22, 2019, Iran sentences McGill-trained scientist to 10 years in prison: reports

The clerical regime does not give priority to environmental protection. The Environmental Protection Organization is a small department with limited budget which is only one-tenth of a percent of the country's total budget.[152]

Tremendous damages have been done to the environment during the 40 years of the clerical rule in Iran. Deforestation, drying up of major lakes, water shortages, soil erosion, and heavy air pollution in Tehran, Khuzestan and other provinces are just some of the major environmental issues in Iran which have not been addressed by the organization.

- The extent of damages done to Iran's nature and environment became evident during the flashfloods in spring 2019 which afflicted at least 25 out of the 31 provinces in Iran.
- The main reason behind Iran's devastating, lethal flash floods was 40 years of environmental mismanagement and government led deforestation.[153]
- Rain has decreased by 20% in the past 50 years while Iran's floods have increased by 50%.[154]
- Every year, around 600 hectares of northern forests are destroyed. Some 200,000 hectares of northern forests have been destroyed in forest fires in the past 40 years.[155]
- Iran ranks the world's first in terms of soil erosion. The average depth of Iran's soil is just three centimeters compared to the world average of around three meters. It takes more than 300 years for one centimeter of soil to form. The main cause of soil erosion in Iran is the destruction of vegetation as a result of deforestation and the unrestrained building of villas in northern Iran.[156]

○ **Gender-responsive budgeting**

Budgeting for the Presidential Directorate on Women and Family Affairs which is the only agency following up on the issues of women is very small compared to other government departments and ministries. That small budget has been cut off year by year.

- In the fiscal year 1397 (March 2018 – March 2019), the credit for empowering women heads of household was lowered from 20 billion tomans ($1.74 million) in the previous year to 15 billion ($1.3 million) in the Sixth Development Program.[157]
- Also the budget for insurance of housewives with more than three children was cut down by more than 30%.[158]

---

[152] Gholam-Ali Jafarzadeh Imenabadi, member of parliament from Rasht, Mojnews.com, January 26, 2019: Share of environment from 1398 budget is one-tenth of a percent.
[153] The state-run Shafaqna.com news agency, March 24, 2019
[154] The state-run Shafaqna.com news agency, March 24, 2019
[155] The state-run Shafaqna.com news agency, March 24, 2019
[156] Esa Kalantari, director of the Environmental Protection Organization, the state-run Shafaqna.com news agency, March 24, 2019
[157] Parvaneh Salahshouri, a member of the Cultural Committee of the mullahs' parliament, the state-run ISNA news agency – December 18, 2017

- While the budget considered for the Directorate of Women and Family Affairs was only 21 billion tomans ($1.8 million), the budget allocated to the Policy Making Council for Women's Seminaries, which is part of the regime's religious propaganda machine, was 270 billion tomans ($23.5 million).[159] Ironically, the Iranian regime considers this allocating funds to the cause of gender equity!
- There was a 39% cut in the budget allocated to women heads of household in the Iranian fiscal year 1397 budget, while the budget of some other cultural agencies remained the same or doubled.[160]
- The parliamentary Research Center evaluated the budget for 1398 fiscal year for women, family and children. Persian year 1398 started on March 21, 2019 and will end on March 20, 2020.
- The Research Center studied the credit predicted for the two policy-making institutions, i.e. the Presidential Directorate for Women and Family Affairs and the Social and Cultural Council of Women and Family, and concluded that the total credit allocated to these two institutions dealing with women had been reduced by 30% from 22.5 billion tomans to 15.7 billion tomans. It said the reduction was due to the cut in the total credit for the Directorate for Women and Family Affairs from 21 billion tomans ($1.83 million) in 2018 to 14.2 billion tomans ($1.2 million) in 2019, which is a 32 percent budget cut tantamount to 7 billion tomans.[161]
- Due to insufficient funds in the 1398 fiscal year, 88% of women heads of household eligible for Poverty Preventing Plan were excluded from the program. Only 5,000 of the 40,000 women heads of household nominated by the Ministry of Health and Medical Education to be covered by the Poverty Prevention Plan for Pregnant and Lactating Women, were included in the plan.[162]
- The number of women heads of household who were taught skills to find jobs was only 12,000.[163] There are 3.6 million women heads of household in Iran. 82% of these women do not have any jobs, and only 180,000 of them receive a meager monthly support from the Welfare Organization.[164]

---

[158] Parvaneh Salahshouri, a member of the Cultural Committee of the mullahs' parliament, the state-run ISNA news agency – December 18, 2017
[159] The state-run donya-e-eqtesad.com, December 20, 2017
[160] Zohreh Ashtiani, secretary of the Family Faction of the mullahs' parliament (Majlis), the state-run Shahrvand daily, July 10, 2018
[161] The state-run Etemad online, December 26, 2018
[162] Ahmad Maidari, Deputy Minister of Cooperatives, Labour and Social Welfare, the state-run IRNA News Agency – February 12, 2019
[163] Zahra Javaherian, deputy for planning and coordination in the Presidential Directorate on Women and Family Affairs, the state-run ISNA news agency, December 11, 2019: "12,000 women heads of household were covered by plans in 1398 to teach them skills to find jobs."
[164] Massoumeh Ebtekar, head of the Presidential Directorate on Women and Family Affairs, the official IRNA news agency, October 7, 2018.

- Contradicting the Research Center of the mullahs' parliament, officials of the women's directorate announced this year (2020), that they received 20.3 billion of the allocated 21 billion toman budget of the Persian fiscal year 1398.[165]
- Officials of the Presidential Directorate on Women and Family Affairs are boasting that they are going to receive 19% more budget in the new Persian 1399 fiscal year (March 2020-March 2021), amounting to 25 billion tomans ($2.17 million).[166] In the meantime, they acknowledge that this is a very small budget compared to other agencies and institutions.
- One of the main criticisms to the 1399 budget bill is omission of the credits for insurance of women heads of households and women with bad guardians. The articles 19 and 22 of the 14th amendment to the 1398 bill which concerned credits for insurance of women heads of households and women with bad guardians have been omitted altogether.[167]
- Neither were any funds allocated to paragraph d of Article 80 of the Sixth Development Program for the empowerment of women.[168] This is while the Welfare Organization has a one trillion toman deficit for implementation of paragraph d of Article 80 of the Sixth Development Program.[169]
- Also, the budget for Women's Cultural and Social Council has been cut by 18% because of omission of the plan for strategic researches without any clear reason.[170]
- In the discussions about the new year's budget, it was revealed that from the meager 300 billion tomans allocated in the 1398 fiscal year to the insurance of housewives, only 12 percent of it had been granted by July, and by January, it was still not clear if they had received the actual credit for it.[171]
- Welfare Organization officials have also revealed that implementation of the Comprehensive Plan for Empowerment of Women requires 322 billion tomans, which is 13 times the entire budget of the women's presidential directorate.[172] They also acknowledged that they have no credits for providing support to 245,000

---

[165] Zahra Javaherian, deputy for planning and coordination in the Presidential Directorate on Women and Family Affairs, the state-run ISNA news agency, December 11, 2019: "21 billion tomans had been adopted for the directorate's budget in 1398 but only 20.3 billion tomans was granted to the directorate."
[166] Zahra Javaherian, deputy for planning and coordination in the Presidential Directorate on Women and Family Affairs, the state-run ISNA news agency, December 11, 2019: "The budget allocated this year to the presidential directorate on Women and Family Affairs is 25 billion tomans which shows a 19% growth compared to last year, which is of course very small in comparison to many other agencies and institutions."
[167] Zahra Javaherian, deputy for planning and coordination in the Presidential Directorate on Women and Family Affairs, the state-run ISNA news agency, December 11, 2019; Tayyebeh Saivoshi, member of the mullahs' parliament, the state-run javanonline.ir, January 2, 2020
[168] Farideh Olad Ghobad, member of the mullahs' parliament, the state-run ICANA.ir, December 17, 2019
[169] Derakhshani, member of the Social Directorate of the Welfare Organization, the state-run ICANA.ir, December 17, 2019
[170] Tayyebeh Saivoshi, member of the mullahs' parliament, the state-run javanonline.ir, January 2, 2020
[171] Farideh Olad Ghobad, member of the mullahs' parliament, the state-run ICANA.ir, December 17, 2019
[172] Derakhshani, member of the Social Directorate of the Welfare Organization, the state-run ICANA.ir, December 17, 2019

women heads of household, 60,000 families and 77,000 students who are on the Welfare Organization's waiting list.[173]
- The 1399 budget bill has allocated only 3 billion tomans for screening and health while the budget needed for screening is 17.5 billion tomans and 50 billion tomans for health care. The Welfare Organization officials also said they needed 600 billion tomans of credit to provide housing to the families who need to receive support from this organization.[174]
- In the Persian fiscal year 1399, in the absence of oil revenues, the Iranian regime has based its budget on revenues from taxes on property and water to be exacted from the Iranian public. With the majority of the populace living under the poverty line, there is no guarantee for them to secure this revenue.

○ Gender-responsive disaster risk reduction and resilience building

---

[173] Ibid.
[174] Ibid.

Disaster risk reduction and resilience building is non-existent in Iran. Every time, there is an incidence of flood or earthquake, it becomes evident that the buildings had been constructed with bad material, not resistant or resilient to earthquakes and floods.
The relief efforts have always been poor. Women and children are the most vulnerable in these situations. Following are some examples:

Flashfloods in Spring 2019

- During the floods in Spring 2019, many buildings and bridges were destroyed or extensively damaged by the flashfloods. At least 20 women and several girl children died in the devastating floods throughout Iran. No exact figures have been announced by the regime officials. But real evidence, including the number of submerged villages and the cities destroyed by floods indicates that the actual figures must be much greater.[175]
- A middle-aged woman by the name of Ana Sultan, in Golestan Province, described their situation after the devastating floods. "We were stuck for one-and-a-half days on the upper storey of the house, without any food or toilets. People came with trucks. We jumped from up there and were saved."
- A flood-hit girl in Lorestan Province said, "We have not received any assistance, so far. We sleep in cars at night. We have no place to go. We have no tents and did not receive one from the government."

Earthquake in Kermanshah

- In the earthquake in Kermanshah, apartment complexes built by government contractors were destroyed and their residents rendered homeless.[176]
- The teams assigned to help the people, left them alone. The contractors employed to rebuild the stricken areas, abandoned their projects and banks did not grant loans to the victims of earthquake.[177]
- More than 750 families in the earthquake-stricken areas are still living in trailers, two years after the earthquake.[178]
- The freezing cold weather in Kermanshah Province led to the deaths of a number people, including children and infants.[179]
- One of the residents said, "The situation is particularly bad for women. Many have suffered miscarriages and pregnant women are living in difficult conditions in tents."[180]

---

[175] NCRI Women's Committee monthly report, February-March 2019 and April 2019
[176] Parviz Fattah, head of the Relief Committee, the state-run Tasnim news agency, January 14, 2018
[177] The state-run ICANA news agency, November 7, 2018; Farhad Tajarri, MP from Qasr-e Shirin, Sarpol-e Zahab and Gilan-e Gharb, the state-run BORNA news agency, November 8, 2018
[178] The state-run Young Journalists Club, January 19, 2020
[179] Deaths of 11 pregnant women, 39 children under 5 in Kermanshah, website of NCRI Women's Committee, December 6, 2017
[180] Women's condition deplorable four months after the quake, website of NCRI Women's Committee, March 17, 2018

He said, "Pregnant women had been promised to get a trailer. Our neighboring woman went to get hers; she was told that she could get a trailer only if she was eight or nine months pregnant."
- Some women had to deliver their babies in the tents, and they have nowhere else to go. Then they contract infections and face thousands of other problems.[181]

Despite so many problems for women in the disaster-hit areas, the measures undertaken by the regime are limited to a few educational workshops.

◯ Changing negative social norms and gender stereotypes

- The culture promoted by the ruling regime has led to further male domination and violence against women. The legal, judicial and disciplinary structures are such that men allow themselves to imply force and commit violence against women.[182]
- Male domination and its related prejudices have grown in the younger generation, and based on the culture promoted, men consider domestic violence against women as a right they are entitled to.[183]

---

[181] The state-run salamatnews.com, March 15, 2018)
[182] Ahmad Bokharaii, director of social damages group affiliated with the Sociology Association, interview with the official IRNA news agency, July 18, 2018
[183] Interview with a sociology expert, the official IRNA news agency, July 18, 2018

○ Other

Gender gap due to laws in economic sphere
In an interview with the official IRNA news agency on November 7, 2017, Shahindokht Molaverdi, who presently serves as Rouhani's deputy for citizen's rights, gave a good picture of the plight of women in Iran's male-dominated job market, their rights to work and their working rights. Excerpts of her interview are illuminating:

One of the most important reasons for gender gap in the economy is the existence of laws in the economic sphere which expand men's participation and activity and have made employment and making income rights for men, and free services at home a duty for women.

Although employment has been recognized in the law as an equal right for all citizens, but in practice men have priority in employment and economic opportunities.

This is a problem that has remained unsolved despite passage of four decades since the Islamic Revolution and despite women's endeavors to prove their capabilities.

Men are authorized to prevent their wives from having a job. This is another restriction women face in economic participation which has made women's unemployment twice as much as the unemployment of men.

The male-dominated atmosphere in decision-making, law-making and management arenas is also another factor which keeps women away from the excitements of presence and participation. This means that women have to earn the permission of their husbands, fathers or brothers for making an investment or using shared sources. They also need the signature of a man on their contract to obtain facilities and resources. When they have to travel abroad to sign a contract with non-Iranian parties, they must have their husbands' letter of consent for leaving the country. These factors have frustrated and disappointed women and over time, they have left the scene in favor of their male rivals.

Having job experience in senior positions of management is another obstacle and condition for the presence of women in political and economic fields.

Women's participation in the parliament, governorates, municipalities and other political arenas is an indication of the reality.

3. Over the past five years, has the state acted to prevent discrimination and promote the rights of women and girls who experience multiple and intersecting forms of discrimination?
None, whatsoever. The regime justifies discrimination against women and does not endeavor to prevent them or promote the rights of women and girls.

4. Have conflicts, climate-induced or other disasters or other events affected the implementation of the BPfA/CEDAW in your country?
The Iranian regime does not intend to implement the BPfA or the CEDAW and is not a signatory to the international convention. As a result, the recurrent disasters could not make the situation worse for the regime in implementing the BPfA/CEDAW. Whereas they caused tremendous difficulties and problems for women and children whose rights are not protected by any government or private entity.

INCLUSIVE DEVELOPMENT, SHARED PROSPERITY AND DECENT WORK

5. What actions has your country taken to advance gender equality in relation to women's role in paid work and employment?

- Ensured the same employment opportunities for women as men, including the application of the same criteria for selection in matters of employment

Discrimination against women's employment

Women in Iran are systematically discriminated against in the law, in employment and the job market.

- In July 2013, the mullahs' parliament adopted a bill[184] according to which employment priority in all public and private sectors is given to married men who have children. Next in line are married men who do not have children. Women who have children are the third in line while women who do not have any children do not even exist on the list.[185]
- The Iranian parliament put further restrictions on women's employment by passing the bill of "protecting hijab and chastity" on January 3, 2016. According to item 5 of this bill, women's employment is limited to businesses that have segregated workspace, and only from 7 a.m. to 10 p.m.
- In addition, "the bill to reduce the working hours of women who have special conditions," was passed on February 1, 2016. Rouhani's deputy for Women and Family Affairs, Shahindokht Molaverdi, admitted that the bill would effectively result in gradual elimination of women from the workforce.[186]
- The recruitment of women in government jobs has confronted more obstacles every year.
- According to government orders in 2014, only 16 of 2,700 job opportunities were allocated to women.[187]
- The Ministry of Education employs one woman per every five men. From the 3,703 individuals selected by the Ministry of Education through the employment exam, 3,073 were men and 630 were women.[188]
- In 2017 government employment test, 961 job opportunities were allocated to men and only 16 were allocated to women.[189]
- The United Nations has categorized Iran among the countries which offer the smallest number of job opportunities to women and for this reason have a high rate of unemployment among women.

---

[184] Population growth, mullahs' hoax to exploit women, the NCRI Women's Committee website, July 6, 2015
[185] The state-run Hamshahri Online website, April 9, 2014
[186] The state-run Mehr news agency (February 1, 2016) and donya-e-eqtesad.com, February 3, 2016
[187] The state-run donya-e-eqtesad.com website, September 29, 2015
[188] The state-run Arman newspaper, August 9, 2015
[189] The state-run Khabaronline.ir, July 27, 2016

- A report by the International Labor Organization, ILO, which was published on March 8, 2018, on the International Women's Day, indicates that women's unemployment rate in Iran is double that of men.

Male-dominated job market
Iran's job market is male-dominated and there is wide gender gap.
- According to a survey by the National Statistics Center on the Iranian work force for the Iranian year 1395 (March 21, 2016 – March 20, 2017), from 20,654,750 people who held jobs in Iran, only 16.2 per cent were women and 83.8 per cent were men. 48.1 per cent of women with employment had higher education compared to 26.1 per cent of employed men. In addition to the gender gap, this data shows a discriminatory approach to the employment of women despite their better education.
- According to another official report, women's participation rate in the job market in 2017 was only 16.8% which is considered very low compared to the male participation rate of 71.4%.[190]
- Iran's total labor force is 21.3 million, which includes only 3 million women out of 27 million working age women.[191]
- A survey by the Labor Ministry's Center for Statistics and Strategic Information found unequal access to wage-earning jobs for men and women. According to this study done for the period spanning from March 2016 to March 2017, men's share of wage-earning jobs was 82.7 per cent compared to women's 17.3 per cent share, indicating a fivefold access for men compared to women.[192]
- Before the 1979 Revolution, women's participation in the labor force was 12 percent. The World Bank put the average value for Iran from 1990 to 2017 at 14.21 percent.[193]
- Iranian women's participation in the job market is significantly lower than the average participation in other upper-middle income countries and is lower than the average for all women in the Middle East and North Africa (MENA) region, and one of the lowest worldwide.[194]
- According to the World Economic Forum's 2020 report, Iran ranks 149th in terms of women's earnings which is less than one-fifth of the earnings of men.[195]

---

[190] The official IRNA news agency, January 17, 2019
[191] The state-run Mehr news agency, June 8, 2016
[192] The state-run Mehr news agency, January 23, 2018
[193] The GlobalEconomy.com, the World Bank
[194] The state-run Donya-e Eqtesad, September 29, 2015
[195] The state-run khabaronline.ir, December 29, 2019

Economic Participation of Women in Iran

Rouhani:
860,000 women were fired in 4 years

Participation in job market

16.8% 71.4%

Share of wage-earning jobs

17.3% 82.7%

Unemployment rate

educated women: 63% to 78%

women under 30: 85.9%

80% of uninsured job holders are women

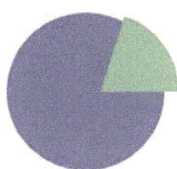

An average of 100,000 women get fired every year.

25% increase in unemployment in just 7 years

- The number of unemployed women in Iran has increased by 200,000 from 830,996 in 2011 to more than 1,037,000 women in 2017. That is a 25% increase in just seven years.[196]
- An average of 100,000 women get fired every year.[197]
- Addressing his rivals in the election campaign, the mullahs' president Hassan Rouhani said 860,000 women had been expelled from their jobs in four years.[198]
- 85.9% of women under 30 do not have any jobs.[199]
- One study indicates that 52 per cent of female university and college graduates are "economically inactive," meaning that they have given up looking for jobs.[200]
- The number of women with bachelor's degrees working as simple workers is on the rise. These women rather not mention their degrees to be able to get hired.[201]
- Unemployment rates among young people, women and educated women, are alarmingly high particularly in western provinces. In some provinces, educated women's unemployment rates fluctuate between 63% and 78%.[202]
- The National Statistics Center of Iran declared in summer 2016 that the average unemployment rate for young women in Iran reached 47.3% in summer 2015.
- The unemployment rate of young women in 2015 had reached the highest level in 20 years.[203]
- "Women have the highest rate of unemployment" and "women's economic participation is not noteworthy" in Iran.[204]

---

[196] Report by the Iranian Labor Ministry's Centre for Strategic Statistics and Information, October 2018, the state-run ISNA news agency, November 21, 2018
[197] Abol Hassan Firouzabadi, deputy Minister of Labor and Social Welfare, the official IRNA news agency, September 6, 2015
[198] The state-run Tasnim news agency, May 9, 2017
[199] The state-run Mehr news agency, January 1, 2016; the state-run Tabnak website, January 5, 2016
[200] The state-run Kayhan daily newspaper, June 20, 2017 http://kayhan.ir/fa/news/106849
[201] Hossein Akbari, a member of the Workers Services Association, the state-run Asr-e Iran daily, September 23, 2015
[202] The state-run Dana news agency, July 2, 2016
[203] Shahindokht Molaverdi, former presidential deputy for women and family affairs, the state-run psychnews.ir, January 22, 2017
[204] Alireza Mahboub, General Secretary of the House of Workers (a government foundation) and member of the Social Committee of the mullahs' parliament, the official IRNA news agency, April 28, 2018

- **Strengthened / enforced laws and workplace policies and practices that prohibit discrimination, including on the grounds of marriage, pregnancy or maternity in the recruitment, retention and promotion of women in the public and private sectors, and equal pay legislation**

    - Women's unemployment index has gone up, partly because of the wave of expulsions of women. An average of 100,000 women get fired every year for taking a maternity leave.[205]
    - The General Board of Directors of the Administrative Court of Justice rescinded a directive which had previously banned laying off working mothers for two years while they nurse their children.[206]
    - The rescinded directive No. 49517, dated June 9, 2014, issued by the general director for labor relations and service compensation at the Ministry of Labor and Social Welfare, had stated that "laying off working women during their maternal leave and the period while they nurse their children (up to two years) is forbidden under whatever pretext."
    - Employers in the private and informal sectors have set conditions on the marital status of women, making them sign papers and agree to be fired if they get pregnant.[207]
    - Starting in Autumn 2017, child benefits were no longer paid to women heads of household. The decision was implemented abruptly and the amount which had been previously paid to them were withdrawn at once from their accounts.[208]

- **Provided social security for women, particularly in cases of retirement, unemployment, sickness, invalidity and old age and other incapacity to work, as well as the right to paid leave Retirement**

    - Women in Iran basically do not enjoy social security or any form of social protection.
    - The majority of working women, work in the informal sector which is greenlighted by the government to make their workers work longer hours, pay them less, and deny them benefits and insurance.[209]
    - Again, the majority of women working in the informal sector are women heads of household.[210]
    - Lack of social security is one of the three main problems women heads of household face in Iran. The three main problems are discrimination and inequality, unemployment, and lack of social security.[211]

---

[205] The state-run ISNA news agency, June 30, 2015; the state-run entekhab.ir website, August 1, 2015
[206] The state-run Tasnim news agency, September 15, 2017
[207] The state-run Shaffaf website, August 2, 2015 http://www.shafaf.ir/fa/news/335310
[208] Zahra Sa'ii, spokeswoman for the parliamentary Social Commission, the state-run Salamatnews.com, March 28, 2018
[209] The official IRNA news agency, April 28, 2018
[210] Fatemeh Pourno, Secretary of the Union of Women Workers in Qazvin, the official IRNA news agency, May 3, 2018

- There are at least 3.6 million women heads of household in Iran and every year 60,300 more women are added to this population.[212] Anoushirvan Mohseni Bandpay, head of the Welfare Organization, acknowledged that only 180,000 women heads of household consistently receive aid from the organization and 100,000 receive social insurances. Bandpay said, "With regards to job loans to women without guardians or with bad guardians, however, the organization faces major challenges."[213]
- The amount of Welfare Organization's aid is a monthly pension of around 70,000 tomans ($5) which is nothing compared to the poverty line of 8 million tomans ($700).
- Women have the largest share in informal jobs.[214]
- Only 1.5 million, i.e. 50 per cent, of working women have insurances and the other half work in the informal sector, without any social or legal support.[215]
- An official of the Interior Ministry's Social Security Organization Research Institute said 80 percent of uninsured job holders in Iran are women.[216]
- The number of insured women is only 19 per cent of the total number of employed individuals in Iran, because women are mainly recruited by the unofficial sector.[217]
- The minimum wage and food basket is not paid to the workers… Recently, I was in a meeting in Tehransar, where 200 needy female workers were in attendance. None of these women had received subsidies to support their livelihood. This was asserted by Soheila Jelodarzadeh, former member of parliament.[218]

---

[211] Susan Bastani, strategic studies deputy at the directorate for women and family affairs, the official IRNA news agency, May 4, 2019
[212] Moussavi Chalak, chair of the Social Aid Association in Iran, the state-run salamatnews.com, May 19, 2018
[213] The state-run Tabnak website, February 13, 2018
[214] Massoumeh Ebtekar, presidential deputy for Women and Family Affairs, Labor Ministry gathering in Tehran, April 28, 2018
[215] Minister of Labor and Social Welfare, the state-run Mehr news agency, June 8, 2016
[216] The state-run khabaronline.ir, November 24, 2016
[217] Vahideh Negin, Labor Minister's advisor, the state-run Tejarat-e Emrouz website, April 24, 2015 http://tejaratemrouz.ir/fa/news/2988
[218] The state-run ILNA news agency, February 1, 2020

- **Improved financial inclusion and access to credit, including for self-employed women**

One of the main groups of self-employed women are carpet weavers, and the majority of them do not have access to credit or any form of insurance.

- 70% of Iran's one million carpet weavers are women and a large percentage of them are heads of household. By this account the number of women weaving carpets amounts to at least 700,000. Only 320,000 of carpet weavers (both men and women) have insurance.[219]
- Women lack support for entrepreneurship since they are not trusted by banks and have difficulty in receiving loans. They are required to place deposits.[220]
- Women who wish to start and are capable to run a business, have great difficulties in receiving loans for the initial investment, because bank managers think that women would not be able to pay back.[221]
- At the same time, women are not permitted to open short-term or long-term bank accounts for their children. The opening of an account must be at the presence of the father. This is a legal issue and comes from Articles 1180 and 1181 of the Civil Code. All banks, especially state-run banks, must abide by it.[222]
- Article 1180 of the Civil Code states: A minor is under the compulsory guardianship of his/her father and the father's father. The same is the case for immature and insane children who are considered minors.
- Article 1181 of the Civil Code states: The father or the father's father are guardians of their children.

---

[219] Abdollah Bahrami, the CEO of National Union of Hand-woven Carpet Producers, cited by the state-run ILNA news agency, May 16, 2018
[220] The state-run ILNA news agency, November 24, 2019
[221] Fatemeh Zolqadr, member of the Labor Committee of the parliament, said, "Many women who wish to start a business, do not have the initial capital despite their capability to run one. When we speak of supporting employment and occupation for women, the first thing is to provide the initial capital, and accordingly, women who wish to start a business must be able to be granted loans... Getting loans is more difficult for women compared to men. Thinking that women would have more problems in paying back their loans compared to men, banks refuse to grant them loans." The state-run ILNA news agency, October 9, 2019
[222] Mehdi Bagheri, a banking expert, the state-run ILNA news agency, August 11, 2014

- **Supported the transition from informal to formal work, including legal and policy measures that benefit women in informal employment**

"Employment not an issue for women"

The overall attitude and vision dominating the Iranian regime and its policies is against women's economic participation and their formal employment. So, the government could not be expected to support the transition from informal to formal work, or adopt legal and policy measures that would benefit women in informal employment.

- Ali Khamenei, the supreme leader of the clerical regime, explicitly says, "God has created women for a particular area of life … Employment is not a major issue for women."[223]
- His representative in Mashhad, mullah Ahmad Alam-ol Hoda, says, "One of the problems our society has to deal with today, is women's excessive involvement in economic matters and in their husbands' economic activities which is not appreciated in Islam because external (outside the house) and economic issues must not be relayed to women whatsoever."[224]
- Economically, the government is unable to create jobs. The presidential directorate on women and family affairs has been promoting women's employment in the private and informal sectors, as well as their self-employment at home.
- In the private and informal sectors, there are no compliance mechanisms to hold employers accountable for advancing gender equality and women's economic empowerment, and women end up with inadequate earnings, without any job security or safe working conditions. The employers also have a free hand in easily laying off women.
- A study done in June 2017 revealed that educated women with BA and BS degrees were hired without legal contracts and without insurance, for a monthly salary of 150-300 thousand tomans ($13-26). The employers sometimes get blank checks from these women so that they would not be able to file complaints against their employers.[225]
- Most of the women in the workers' community are heads of household, but they face long working hours and are deprived of many rights and benefits.[226]

- **Ensured the right to organize collective action and freedom of movement**

According to the Iranian Constitution, women are not allowed to leave home without their husband's permission. This is also true for travel and for getting employed for a job.

Article 1105 of the Civil Code: Heading the household is the inherent duty of the man and the woman cannot even leave home without his permission.

---

[223] The official website of Ali Khamenei, April 19, 2014
[224] The state-run Alef website, July 12, 2017
[225] The state-run shahrvand-newspaper.ir, June 28, 2017
[226] The official IRNA news agency, May 3, 2018

- Niloufar Ardalan, 30 and captain of women's national football team, could not travel with the team to the Asian Championship competitions, because her husband disagreed with her participation in the Asian games. He did not hand in her passport.[227]
- The Hiking Board of Razavi Khorasan Province issued a directive on November 4, 2018, to all hiking clubs in the province, instructing them that "married women must have their husbands' permission, and single women as well as young women under 20 years must have their fathers' permission before they can participate in any hiking or nature tours."[228]

- **Devised mechanisms for women's equal participation in economic decision-making bodies (e.g. in ministries of trade and finance, central banks, national economic commissions)**

The government in Iran has not devised any mechanisms for women's equal participation in economic decision-making bodies. Data and information in this regard are also scarce.
- According to a report published in July 2014, the latest statistics announced by the National Statistics Center of Iran shows a wide gap in economic participation of men and women. The situation is worse in management and decision-making. The same is true for the banking system in Iran.[229]
- Women's presence in the parliament is about 3 per cent and only one per cent in the decision-making and power structures, a situation that is embarrassing for the government.[230]

A table on women's management positions in the banking system, showed that in the 22 main Iranian banks surveyed in this study, there was only one woman in the board of directors of these banks, who was retired in 2008.[231]
Only one woman sits as the deputy for human resources.[232]
Fourteen women held positions of manager in 22 banks, and 13 women headed various departments.[233]
As evident from this table, one can conclude that women have not occupied top management or decision-making positions in the banking system.

---

[227] The state-run Tasnim news agency, September 14, 2015
[228] The official IRNA news agency, November 13, 2018
[229] The state-run Asr-e Bank website, July 24, 2014
[230] Former presidential deputy on Women and Family Affairs, Shahindokht Molaverdi, the state-run Mizan website, September 8, 2015
[231] Farideh Geraminejad worked as head of the Treasury Department from 1978 to 2008 in Bank-e Tejarat (Bank of Commerce). She is presently retired.
[232] Maryam Eslami, head of the Department of Human Resources in the Bank of Industries and Mines.
[233] The state-run Asr-e Bank website, July 24, 2014

Banking system's management positions at the disposal of women[234]

R	Bank	Board of Directors	Deputy	manager	head of department
1	Melli	0	0	0	0
2	Maskan	0	0	0	4
3	Tose'eh Ta'avon	0	0	0	0
4	San'at va Ma'dan	0	1	0	0
5	Tejarat	0	0	0	0
6	Pasargad	0	0	0	0
7	Eqtesad-e Novin	0	1	0	1
8	Refah	0	0	0	0
9	Saman	1	0	4	0
10	Gardeshgari	0	0	1	5
11	Saderat	0	0	0	1
12	Khavar Mianeh	0	0	0	0
13	Parsian	0	0	0	0
14	Karafarin	0	0	4	0
15	Iran Zamin	0	0	0	0
17	Shahr	0	0	2	0
18	Hekmat Iranian	0	0	0	1
19	Sina	0	0	1	0
20	Ghavamin	0	0	0	0
21	Ayandeh	0	0	2	0
22	Sepah	0	0	0	1

6. What actions has your country taken in the last five years to recognize, reduce and/or redistribute unpaid care and domestic work and promote work-family conciliation?

• Included unpaid care and domestic work in national statistics and accounting (e.g. time-use surveys, valuation exercises, satellite accounts)

There are no accurate statistics available in the case of working rural and nomad women. At the same time, the employment of rural women and girls has not been defined. Even though these women are actively engaged in work, but their occupation has not been considered in any program.[235]

---

[234] Ibid.
[235] Zahra Faraji, general director for Women and Family Affairs in the Central Province's Governorate, the state-run ISNA news agency, January 25, 2015

- Five million women between 18 and 62 years of age in Iran are estimated to be potentially ready for work.[236]
- Usually, the statistics are based on owners of the production units, and since women do not own production units, they have not been mentioned in the official statistics and their employment has not been considered, either.[237]

- **Expanded childcare services or made existing services more affordable**

The statistics on childcare services are very scarce. The limited information available indicates that there have not been any attempts on the part of the government to expand childcare services or make the existing services more affordable.

- A report by the Research Center of the Parliament studying the 1398 fiscal year budget, noted a reduction of credits for supporting female workers.[238]
- The Ministry of Labor and Social Welfare had a 35 percent reduction in its activities to guide and support the daycare centers for women working in economic institutions, also for the plans to provide physical and psychological self-care for female workers at the work environment.[239]
- The report also noted that in the 1397 fiscal year budget, the government had been obliged to cover 7,000 female workers by allocating 300,000 tomans ($26) to each. This amount was reduced to 200,000 tomans ($17) for every woman in the 1398 budget.[240]
- With regards to daycare services, the Labor Ministry had been obliged to support 40 daycare centers by granting 25 million tomans ($2,174) to each. This is 14 million tomans less than the 39 million tomans ($3,391) specified for each daycare in the previous year.[241]

Such credit cuts for plans which affect direct support for female workers aggravates their vulnerability considering high inflation rates which have shrunk the food basket for workers' families.

---

[236] Forough-os Sadat Bani-Hashem, general director of the office for the development of agricultural activities of rural and nomad women in the Ministry of Agricultural Crusade (Jihad-e Sazandegi), the state-run ISNA news agency, January 25, 2015 - https://www.isna.ir/news/93110502224
[237] Forough-os Sadat Bani-Hashem, general director of the Development Office of Agricultural Activities of Rural and Nomad Women in the Ministry of Agricultural Crusade, the website of the presidential directorate of Women and Family Affairs, October 22, 2017 - http://women.gov.ir/fa/news/7803
[238] Research Center of the Iranian Parliament, January 14, 2019
[239] Ibid.
[240] Ibid.
[241] Ibid.

- **Expanded support for frail elderly persons and others needing intense forms of care**

    - A study of the characteristics of the elderly population in Iran shows that there are 97 elderly men for every 100 elderly women in Iran. Officials say this correlation will become 88 elderly men for every 100 women by 2021, a phenomenon which they describe as feminization of the elderly population. While the total population of Iran's elderly is said to have exceeded 8 million.[242]
    - About 95% of nursing homes for the elderly are private and managed at the expense of charities and the families of the elderly.
    - There are only 150 government-run centers in Iran which provide care for 20,000 elderlies whose identities are mostly unknown. The maximum fund allocated by the government for each elderly in these centers is 200,000 tomans a month ($17).[243]
    - According to the Director General of the Office of Well Being of the Elderly, the monthly cost of care for every elderly person is not more than 550,000 tomans ($48).[244]
    - Private centers, however, receive between 1.2 to 6 million tomans ($104 - $522) per month for every elderly, depending on the geographical area and type of services they provide, which does not include physiotherapy and health care.[245]
    - A Welfare Organization official while criticizing the government for not allocating sufficient funds to the care centers for the elderly, announced that the organization intends to raise the fees. In his remarks, one can see how the government has cut down on the budget needed for persons who need intense forms of care. He said, "The welfare organization estimates that implementing the law on protection of the rights of persons with disabilities would require 12 trillion tomans ($1.05 billion), but the parliament's specialized commissions have allocated only 1.1 trillion tomans ($95.65 million), less than one tenth of the estimated fund to implement the law."[246]

---

[242] The state-run salamatnews.com, April 27, 2019
[243] Homayoun Hashemi, head of the parliamentary faction supporting people with disabilities, the state-run Mashreqnews.com, August 24, 2014
[244] Ibid.
[245] Ibid.
[246] Vahid Ghobadi Dana, head of the Welfare Organization, the official IRNA news agency, January 13, 2019

- **Introduced or strengthened maternity/paternity/parental leave or other types of family leave**

On the paper and according to the legislated acts, Iranian women who have a job are entitled to six to nine months of maternity leave. In practice, however, many women find out after returning to work after six or nine months that they have been dismissed.

In fact, there are no provisions to oblige employers to safeguard a woman's right to maternity leave. In addition, the government's adoption of a plan to extend women's maternal leave has caused added restrictions on employment of women.

- Some employers have set conditions on the marital status of women they plan to employ and make them sign papers and agree to be fired if they get pregnant.[247]
- Many private sector employers terminate employment of female workers as soon as they find out that they are pregnant. In some workshops the employer limits the benefits for the number of dependents to two children; if a woman has a third child, they terminate her contract.[248]
- According to official figures, over a period of ten years, 74,000 women have been expelled from their jobs each year after returning from maternity leave.[249]
- In 2014-2015, 74,000 out of 145,000 women who had taken a six-month maternity leave of absence were fired.[250]
- The General Board of Directors of the Administrative Court of Justice rescinded a directive which had banned laying off working mothers for two years while they nurse their children.[251]
- The rescinded directive No. 49517, dated June 9, 2014, issued by the general director for labor relations and service compensation at the Ministry of Labor and Social Welfare, had stated that "laying off working women during their maternal leave and the period while they nurse their children (up to two years) is forbidden under whatever pretext."

---

[247] The state-run Shaffaf website, August 2, 2015 http://www.shafaf.ir/fa/news/335310
[248] Working mothers, hiding their children and signing to be fired voluntarily, the official IRNA plus news agency, November 3, 2019; semi-official Tabnak website, August 15, 2017
[249] Fatemeh Sadeqi, Professor and member of faculty of Teachers' Training University, the state-run Fars news agency, June 16, 2015
[250] The state-run ISNA news agency, June 30, 2015; the state-run entekhab.ir website, August 1, 2015
[251] The state-run Tasnim news agency, September 15, 2017

- **Ensured that women engaged in unpaid work or in the informal sector have access to non-contributory social protection**

Due to economic recession, institutionalized restrictions on employment of women, and widespread corruption of the ruling clique, more and more women are driven into informal, substandard and unpaid jobs which do not grant them any social protection.
In the meantime, the policy of Iran's labor market has been based on temporary labor force in recent decades, removing legal protections for workers and employees versus the employer and the government.[252]

Informal sector

- Another official confessed that despite their high productivity and diligence, women are taken advantage of because they are desperate to have just any job with any amount of difficulty.[253]
- Women work with heavy machinery in uninspected closed environments and are given only 5 days of insurance for the whole month.[254]
- Many women work between 10 to 12 hours at home applying glue on envelopes or sewing spangles on fabric, but their daily wage is around 5,000 tomans which is less than 50 cents. These women do not even have a specific employer and their products are sold through intermediaries who pocket most of their revenues.[255]

Unpaid work

- In Iranian villages, rural women often work continuously for up to 20 hours a day, farming, breeding livestock, or weaving carpets. This is coupled with all the tedious and hard work related to the daily routine of rural life. So, their employment is limited to family-based and unpaid work, which do not bear any direct material benefits for them.[256]
- Although female carpet weavers carry the economic burden of the family, but they do not even own their house. Their husbands own everything. The majority of carpet weaving women are deprived of insurance.[257]
- Rural women also face numerous obstacles in entrepreneurship due to lack of adequate financial and legal support.[258]

---

[252] The state-run meidaan.com, May 30, 2018
[253] Pour Moussa, the Secretary General of the Supreme Assembly of Labor Councils, the state-run ISNA news agency, February 27, 2015
[254] Fatemeh Pourno, Secretary of the Union of Women Workers in Qazvin, the official IRNA news agency, May 3, 2018
[255] Ahmad Amirabadi, a member of the presiding board of the mullahs' parliament, the state-run ISNA news agency, May 1, 2018
[256] Iranwire website, October 16, 2017 - https://iranwire.com/fa/features/23608
[257] The state-run ILNA news agency, May 16, 2018
[258] Fatemeh Zolqadr, member of the Labor Committee of the parliament, said, "Many women who wish to start a business, do not have the initial capital despite their capability to run one. When we speak of supporting employment and occupation for women, the first thing is to provide the initial capital, and accordingly, women

- Most of the women living in Hengam Island do fishing since their childhood until they die. The Labor Law does not recognize them although they do fishing for 50 years.[259]

Unpaid formal workers and employees

One of the forms of unpaid work in Iran is workers and employees working for many months without receiving their wages.

- Studies on the employment of women in Iran's labor market show that most employed women are working in the services sector, and that the share of women's employment in the agricultural and services sectors is more than men.[260] But according to the National Statistics Center of Iran (NSC),[261] 60% of the employees of the commercial and services sector did not receive any salary in 2015.[262]
- The fees and salaries of nurses working for the hospitals affiliated with the Medical Sciences University of Golestan Province (northern Iran), were not paid for one year.[263]
- The Literacy Movement's educators systematically do not receive their wages for several months while being deprived of job security.[264]
- Casual teachers must also be considered as unpaid workers. These well-qualified teachers work on an hourly basis. They do the same work as teachers who are formally and permanently employed by the Education Ministry but they receive less than half the salary of an officially hired teacher and are deprived of all privileges of their hired peers. They enjoy no job security and have no privilege in the subsequent hiring season. They are not paid for summer and not granted New Year bonuses.[265] The principle of same work, same pay is not applied to casual teachers.
- Some 250 physicians, nurses and medical personnel of the largest hospital in Karaj, including a large number of women, held at least 35 rounds of protests, marches, strikes and sit-ins from May till end of December 2018 to demand payment of their salaries not paid for over a year.
- According to a social researcher, "What happens in the Iranian economy is that due to recession and lack of production, the non-wage and wage-earning sector is expanding, reaching 45 to 46 percent of the total workforce. The first characteristic of this kind of employment is that <u>they are not covered by the labor law</u>, their probability of being

---

who wish to start a business must be able to be granted loans… Getting loans is more difficult for women compared to men. Thinking that women would have more problems in paying back their loans compared to men, banks refuse to grant them loans." The state-run ILNA news agency, October 9, 2019

[259] The state-run ROKNA news agency, February 10, 2020
[260] The state-run agronic.ir, June 23, 2017
[261] The official website of the National Statistics Center of Iran, June 12, 2018
[262] The state-run ISNA news agency, June 25, 2018
[263] The state-run ILNA news agency, September 18, 2018
[264] Mohammad Javad Abtahi, member of the Education and Research Committee of the mullahs' parliament, the state-run salamatnews.com, September 26, 2018
[265] The state-run Fars news agency - August 9, 2019; the state-run ILNA news agency, February 6, 2020

insured is low, the minimum wage laws are not respected, the education level of workers is lower, and the probability of being laid off is higher...

"The number of insured workers in Iran is about 15 million and 6.5 million workers have no insurance at all. These people are not wage-earners and at least 80% of them are women."[266]

- **Invested in time- and labor-saving infrastructure, such as public transport, electricity, water and sanitation, to reduce the burden of unpaid care and domestic work on women**

Lack of access to clean and adequate water is one of the greatest infrastructural problems of rural women in Iran.

- The situation of 44 villages near Chabahar, in Sistan and Baluchestan Province, southeast Iran, and their lack of access to water is tragic. These villages do not have pipelines. Their water is provided by worn out tankers that bring them unsanitary and unclean water with long delays and in small amounts.
- Due to severe shortage of water, people have dug out ditches, called *Hootag*, to collect rainwater. The ditches attract flies and mosquitoes. This water is used for bathing, laundry and doing the dishes at the same time. Sometimes, when the *Hootag* water is fresh or the water tanker has delays, people also drink the same water as animals do. For every person living in these villages, only 15 liters of water has been considered which is not sufficient at all.[267]
- More than 100 villages in Golestan Province lying by the Caspian Sea receive their water by tankers and villagers are deprived of minimum basic services.[268]
- Water condition is the same in villages across the country. People reportedly do not have access to drinking water in Jelaran villages[269] near the border of Afghanistan, Calshour village[270] in North Khorasan Province, Kaftar village[271] in Eghlid (southern Iran) and Gandombar village[272] in Kashmar (in the northeast).

---

[266] Hessam Nikoupour, a research associate at the Institute for Social Security Research, the state-run khabaronline.ir, June 28, 2017
[267] The state-run Salamat news, October 22, 2017
[268] Alireza Ebrahimi, secretary of the assembly of representatives of Golestan Province, the state-run Tasnim news agency, December 28, 2017
[269] The state-run Raja News website, July 10, 2017
[270] Bartarinha website, August 29, 2017
[271] The state-run Tasnim news agency, December 20, 2017
[272] The state-run Kashmari website, January 27, 2018

Hygiene is a real problem in Iranian villages.
- For example, there are no public baths or toilets in Jilaran village.[273] Families have put clods together and made an outdoor toilet. Bathing depends on water tankers and whenever they arrive. If the weather is good and water arrives in the village, and if there is more water than for basic needs such as drinking, some of the inhabitants can bathe. Often people can take a bath every three months.
- More than 80% of the children in South Khorasan's villages suffer from skin problems due to water shortage. Due to water shortage the people don't have enough hygiene and cannot have a bath correctly. About 480 villages in South Khorasan Province suffer from water shortage and they receive water by tankers. Many of the watercourses there have dried up.[274]

The roads leading to many of these villages are unpaved and difficult to pass. They are blocked with any slight rain or snow and there is no public transportation. At the same time, bad roads and worn-out vehicles lead to the deaths of thousands of women every year.
- Moor-e Zard-e Zilaii village in Boyer Ahmad (southwestern Iran) with a population of 773 people has no proper roads. In one instance, a woman who had suffered

---

[273] The state-run Raja News website, July 10, 2017
[274] Mohammad Bagher Ebadi, MP from Birjand, the state-run ILNA News Agency, May 24, 2018

high blood pressure died because she could not be taken quickly to any medical center because the village's road had been blocked after rainfall.[275]
- A bus accident on Tehran- Shiraz Road led to the deaths of nine passengers including five women. Another 18 passengers were injured in this bus accident including four women.[276]
- Sixteen (16) women including a pregnant woman died in four bus accidents in various parts of Iran from January 9 to 20, 2020.
- According to the state-run media in Iran, every half an hour, one Iranian woman loses her husband or father due to road accidents.
- Experts say addiction, prostitution, divorce, street children and child labor are some of the consequences of road accidents affecting women and children. (The state-run salamatnews.com -January 25, 2020)
- In investigating the causes of increase in road accidents in Iran, many domestic and international experts believe that the lack of standard roads and traffic infrastructures, worn-out and sometimes out-of-date vehicles, lack of traffic signs on the roads, population growth and rising number of cars, poverty and economic pressure on drivers are among the causes of road accidents in Iran. This is in addition to mismanagement by a kleptocratic regime.
- Iran ranks the world's number one with the highest death toll, in 800,000 road accidents per year (1.5 times the world average).
- In terms of casualties caused by road accidents, Iran ranks 189th among 190 countries.

- **Promoted decent work for paid care workers, including migrant workers and domestic workers**

    - 78.5% of Iranian nurses are women. By September 22, 2017, the total number of nursing personnel employed by the medical sciences universities, including the personnel for operation rooms, anesthesia, and medical emergencies, amounted to 117,639 persons which included 92,442 female nurses.[277]
    - Despite the sensitivity of their job, and its inherent pressure and harms, the majority of female nurses in Iran are not permanently employed, and the majority of them work on temporary contracts. As a result, they are offered a small salary which is not regularly paid.
    - Due to shortage of nurses and medical personnel in Iran, work conditions for nurses are appalling, worse than the nurses' situation in Kenya and Iraq.[278]
    - Nurses are forced to do mandatory shifts and overtime work but their overtime fees are not paid for between six to twelve months. Nurses working for the

---

[275] The official IRNA news agency, October 30, 2017
[276] The state-run Rokna news agency, January 28, 2020
[277] Female nurses in Iran entangled in a web of damaging problems, NCRI Women's Committee, February 27, 2019
[278] Ali Asghar Dalvandi, president of the National Nursing Organization, the state-run Mehr news agency, January 12, 2019

hospitals affiliated with the Medical Sciences University of Golestan Province (northern Iran), were not paid their overtime fees and salaries for one year.[279]
- According to an official in the Nursing Organization, discrimination and injustice against the nursing community in Iran has aggravated in the past five years.[280]
- "We need at least another 150,000 nurses. The world standard of the ratio of nurses to hospital beds is 1 to 8 (12.5%), while in our country this ratio is 0.7% (i.e. 7 for every 1000 beds). This shows we are way below the standards."[281]
- "To provide adequate nursing services, we must have four nurses for (every 1000 persons in) the population. Of course, the world's average is six nurses for every 1000 persons in the population. So, if we want to have the minimum number of nurses for the 80 million population (of Iran), we must have at least 240,000 nurses working across the country, whereas right now, there are only 160,000 nurses who provide medical and health services."[282]
- The government, however, does not allocate sufficient funds and budget for recruitment of additional nurses. Due to financial restrictions and the policy of not granting new licenses, there are 30,000 unemployed nurses in Iran.[283]
- The budget for recruitment of new nurses in the Persian year 1398 (from March 21, 2019- March 20, 2020), was rejected. While half of the nursing graduates remain without jobs, the responsibility of recruiting new nurses is passed from one government agency to the other.
- Due to this situation, some 1,000 nurses leave Iran and migrate to other countries every year.[284]
- Shortages of nurses create additional pressure at work, causing professional distress, increasing the possibility of nurses making mistakes, and consequently increasing the possibility of deaths in hospitals.[285]
- Female nurses in Iran are not only missing their monthly salaries but are enduring great pressure at work. Since they cannot respond to everyone's needs, they become directly face to face with the patients and their companies and are often insulted and even brutalized.
- Twenty-eight nurses were brutalized in 2017, and 20 nurses have lost their lives due to work stress from 2016 to 2018.[286]

---

[279] The state-run ILNA news agency, September 18, 2018
[280] Ali Asghar Dalvandi, president of the National Nursing Organization, the state-run Mehr news agency, January 12, 2019
[281] Ibid.
[282] Mohammad Sharifi Moghaddam, secretary general of Iran's House of Nurses, the state-run ILNA news agency, January 12, 2019; the state-run Young Journalists Club website, October 29, 2018
[283] Mohammad Sharifi Moghaddam, secretary general of Iran's House of Nurses, the state-run ILNA news agency, January 12, 2019
[284] Ibid.
[285] Abbas Eskandari, chair of the board of directors of the Nursing Organization of Isfahan, the state-run ILNA news agency – January 12, 2019
[286] [Female nurses in Iran entangled in a web of damaging problems](#), NCRI Women's Committee, February 27, 2019

- As a result of the above factors, nurses and care workers in Iran could not be considered to have a decent job.

- **Introduced/ strengthened programs that address the particular problems faced by rural women including their work in the non-monetized sectors of the economy**

No, there has not been any effective programs to address problems faced by rural women working in the non-monetized sectors.

- Rural women do not own their production tools. Most rural women do not receive any wages.[287]
- A group of women work on other people's farms, i.e. their activities are outside their family businesses, but the amount of wage they receive is far less than what men get (for equal work).
- A woman with four children, from Kalat Abi village in Mazandaran Province, says, "Normally, I wake up at 4 a.m. I do the housework, feed the birds and the livestock, prepare the lunch and then accompany my husband to the land. I return home around noon, feed the children, and go back to the land… In the afternoon, I go to the fruit garden along with other women to harvest the fruit. Amid all this work, I have to remember to milk the cow, oversee my children's homework, and take care of my disabled mother-in-law. Every day, I have to bake the bread and twice a week, I bake breads for sale. I must bake at least 500 breads on my own. At nights, I come back home around 7 p.m. I prepare the dinner, prepare tea for my husband, tidy the house and do the sewing after dinner."
  She does not receive any wage from anybody for the work she does. Even the wage for her work on the farm and in the fruit garden is directly paid to her husband.[288]
- Women who plant rice do more than 60 percent of the planting and harvesting of rice but their wage is 10,000 tomans less than the wage of their male counterparts. A seasonal female worker participates in all stages of plantation and harvest of rice. In other seasons, they work in other farms.
  Most of these women suffer from rheumatism and arthritis. They tie their knees with cloth and go to work again. Often, the farm owner does not allow them to wear boots or use gloves. Many of these women start training at the age of seven without receiving any wage. Then, they have to do the work for lifetime, even in the final months of their pregnancy. Their hands get blistered and bruised. They contract fungal diseases and fever. They do not have insurance and they do not own any land. But their work is not limited to the land they work on.
- In the hours they do not work on the farm, they have to do all the housework. From early in the morning until they go to the farm, they have to tend the poultry, do the housework, wash the clothes, cook the food, etc. After returning from the farm,

---

[287] General director of the office in charge of rural and nomad women's affairs, the state-run salamatnews.com, October 17, 2016
[288] The state-run salamatnews.com, October 17, 2016

they have to bake bread, tend the livestock, and do other chores around the house.[289]
- Harvest of potatoes is also part of the agricultural work women engage in but women workers harvest between 50 to 70 sacks of potatoes every day for only 350,000 tomans ($30).[290] In other agricultural sectors, despite doing the same work for the same amount of hours, women end up with half of the pay allocated to their male counterparts.[291]
- Most of the women living in Hengam Island do fishing since their childhood until they die. The Labor Law does not recognize them although they do fishing for 50 years.[292]

- **Adopted gender-responsive social protection floors to ensure that all women have access to essential health care, childcare facilities and income security**

There have been no reports of the adoption of specific gender-responsive social protection floors to ensure women's access to essential health care, child facilities and income security. On the contrary, there have been many reports indicating deaths of women and children due to lack of access to essential health care.
- There is one medical center for every 3 to 4 villages in Iran and most villagers have problems receiving medical care.[293]
- Rural and nomad women have little access to specialist doctors and dentists. Many rural and nomad women die before reaching a medical center when they get sick.[294]
- The inhabitants of Hassanabad village have to ride camels to get to normal roads where cars travel. One of the inhabitants who had suffered a heart stroke, died before getting to a city hospital.[295]
- A sick woman lost her life in Hashin village near Ardabil due to the absence of a medical center and bad roads.[296]
- The villages in Damavand and Firouzkouh face medical and health problems.[297]
- Chahak village with a population of 8,000 does not have even one permanent medical center. The only physician available to this village is a conscript soldier that visits patients from morning until noon. In this time period, he can visit only 15 out

---

[289] Iranwire website, October 16, 2017
[290] The state-run IRNA news agency, November 14, 2017
[291] The official IRNA news agency, November 22, 2018
[292] The state-run ROKNA news agency, February 10, 2020
[293] Moussa Reza Servati, member of the Social Committee of the Parliament, the state-run Mehr news agency, December 31, 2016
[294] Parichehr Soltani, secretary of the working group on rural and nomad women living in underprivileged areas, the state-run ISNA news agency, October 5, 2016
[295] The state-run Asr-e Iran website, January 21, 2018
[296] Balal Eskandari, head of Firouz Governorate in Ardabil, the official IRNA news agency, December 25, 2016
[297] Qassem Mirzaii Nikou, deputy from Damavand and Firouzkouh, the state-run Fars news agency, February 1, 2018

of some 60 patients who need to be visited. In other times, people have no access to any doctor or medics and emergency patients usually do not survive on the way to hospital in a distant location. The distance between the last village in this district to the nearest city is 60 kilometers.[298]

- People living in Ermian village of Shahroud, northeastern Iran, face serious medical problems. A doctor visits this village occasionally, only once a month. Sometimes, no doctor visits this village for 4 to 5 months. Inhabitants of this village have to pay at least 100,000 tomans for transportation to go to the nearest medical center.[299]
- More recently, during the 5.9 magnitude earthquake in East Azerbaijan, on November 8, 2019, two little girls and two women got killed. According to press reports, Zahra Abedi, 10, was killed because there was no hospital in Varnakesh village and the nearby village had a power outage, not able to help save the girl's life.[300]
- Fatality of newborn infants in Iran is five times greater than in developed countries.[301]
- Every year, 15,000 infants[302] and some 300 mothers die during delivery.[303]
- A considerable part of infant mortality occurs in underprivileged areas and villages, because there rarely are any medical centers in these areas.[304]
- In poor, uneducated rural communities, girl children are given to marriage and become pregnant. Mothers under 19 years of age have a very risky pregnancy. While they need more medical care and attention, there are no such services in their villages.[305]
- 170 citizens in Dinaran village of Ardel, in Charmahal and Bakhtiari Province, became sick for drinking polluted water, 10 of whom were in critical conditions.[306]
- At least 300 women, children and even infants were infected with HIV virus in Chenar Mahmoudi village, in Lordegan county of Charmahal Bakhtiari Province, due to repeated use of disposable syringes for diabetes test by the clinic in this village.[307] One of the residents said 500 people had taken HIV tests and all had positive results.

People who do not afford hospital expenses are treated in two ways, either they are not admitted to begin with, or they are held hostage after treatment.

---

[298] The state-run Ostani Hamshahri website, October 22, 2017
[299] The state-run Dana website, February 8, 2015
[300] The state-run ISNA news agency, November 8, 2019
[301] Ali Akbar Sayyari, deputy Minister of Health, the state-run Asr-e Iran website, January 21, 2018
[302] The state-run Tabnak website, February 2, 2017
[303] The state-run Asr-e Iran website, January 21, 2018
[304] Iraj Khosronia, head of the GI Specialists' Association, the state-run Tabnak website, February 2, 2017
[305] Fereshteh Sarbazi, member of the Association of Women and Midwives, the state-run ILNA news agency, August 29, 2017
[306] Hassan Nouri, deputy for Emergency Operations, the state-run Jam-e Jam Online, August 29, 2017
[307] The state-run ROKNA news agency, October 2, 2019

- In February 2018, a 35-year-old mother from Mashhad who had normal delivery, was taken hostage for 5 days and not allowed to leave the hospital due to lack of financial resources to pay her hospital bill. Hospital officials had insisted that she would be able to leave the hospital only if she made full payment of 1.2 million tomans ($89). It should be noted that with the passing of everyday 380,000 tomans ($28) were added to her bill. This despite the fact that the state's health rules specifically point out that natural births are free of charge.[308]
- Officials of a hospital in Tehran's poor neighborhood of Yaftabad took one of the newborn twin hostage for 27 days until their mother paid the expenses for the delivery of a second infant. The young mother, Jamileh, had sold all her belongings to pay for the expenses of a delivery in hospital. However, hospital officials told her that because she had given birth to twins, she would have to pay expenses in addition to the 1.7 million tomans that she had already paid for the delivery. They released the mother and her newborn daughter, but kept the newborn son until his mother provided the money they asked for. Jamileh said her infant was not taken care of in the hospital and he had become very weak after 27 days. She had to pay 7 million tomans ($2,300) to get her son.[309]
- In August 2014, a young pregnant woman gave birth to her baby in the hospital's toilet because the hospital refused to admit her. Parvaneh who was in severe pain when she went to the hospital in Kohdasht, but was told that she had to go to the hospital in Khorramabad. Having no choice, she went to the hospital's dark toilet with the help of her sister to give birth to her child.[310]
- Kowthar Obstetrics and Gynecology Hospital in Urmia, which is the only specialized maternity hospital, has only 62 beds for the city with 73,000 inhabitants. Most women who go to this hospital, give birth to their children in the corridor, spend their recovery in the corridors of the hospital and are discharged from there.[311]
- In September 2018, Zahra Barghi, 3, died due to blood infection after the state hospital refused her admittance despite the treating physician's order, saying there were no empty beds for non-emergency patients. Despite her father's insistence that he would hold his daughter in his arms and stay in the hallway, he was thrown out of hospital using foul language and insults. On the way to another hospital, little Zahra suffered seizures and nausea and died less than 24 hours later.[312]
- An 18-year-old orphan girl was kept as a hostage for at least seven days in March 2016 in the city of Yazd for not being able to pay for her treatment cost. She went to the hospital's emergency room where she underwent surgery. The cost of treatment for her seven-day stay was 4 million tomans ($296) but she could only

---

[308] The state-run Asriran.ir, January 26, 2018; the state-run ROKNA news agency, January 24, 2018
[309] The state-run Tabnak and Jam-e Jam websites, January 20, 2016
[310] The state-run khabaronline.ir, August 19, 2014
[311] The state-run Tasnim news agency, July 7, 2018
[312] The state-run Young Journalists Club, September 9, 2018

afford to pay one million of the amount, and the hospital prevented her discharge.[313]

- **Conducted campaigns or awareness raising activities to encourage the participation of men and boys in unpaid care and domestic work**

Not only the Iranian regime has not campaigned for or encouraged participation of men and boys in unpaid care and domestic work, but the culture promoted by the ruling regime has led to further male domination and violence against women.

- Regardless of the existing cultural backgrounds promoting male domination, the legal, judicial and disciplinary structures are such that men allow themselves to imply force and commit violence against women.[314]
- Male domination and its related prejudices have grown in the younger generation, and based on the culture promoted, men consider domestic violence against women as a right they are entitled to.[315]

- **Introduced legal changes regarding the division of marital assets or pension entitlements after divorce that acknowledge women's unpaid contribution to the family during marriage**

Under the Iranian regime's laws, man is the only party who can divorce his wife at any time and for any reason. Outside the law and at the time of marriage, however, women can register a precondition in their marriage document indicating that she can get divorced, should the circumstances arise.

The only thing a woman can receive after divorce is her own dowry, but she is not entitled to any pension or division of marital assets for her unpaid contribution during marriage.[316]

---

[313] Destitute girl, 18, held hostage after treatment, website of NCRI Women's Committee, April 7, 2016

[314] Ahmad Bokharaii, director of social damages group affiliated with the Sociology Association, interview with the official IRNA news agency, July 18, 2018

[315] Interview with a sociology expert, the official IRNA news agency, July 18, 2018

[316] The state-run Young Journalists Club website, January 10, 2020

7. Has your country introduced austerity/fiscal consolidation measures, such as cuts in public expenditure or public-sector downsizing, over the past five years?

In the fiscal year 1397 (March 2018 – March 2019), the credit for empowering women heads of household was lowered from 20 billion tomans ($1.74 million) in the previous year to 15 billion ($1.3 million) in the Sixth Development Program.[317]
Also the budget for insurance of housewives with more than three children was cut down by more than 30%.[318]
While the budget considered for the Directorate of Women and Family Affairs was only 21 billion tomans ($1.8 million), the budget allocated to the Policy Making Council for Women's Seminaries, which is part of the regime's religious propaganda machine, was 270 billion tomans ($23.5 million).[319] Ironically, the Iranian regime considers this allocating funds to the cause of gender equity!
There was a 39% cut in the budget allocated to women heads of household in the Iranian fiscal year 1397 budget, while the budget of some other cultural agencies remained the same or doubled.[320]

The parliamentary Research Center evaluated the budget for 1398 fiscal year for women, family and children. Persian year 1398 started on March 21, 2019 and will end on March 20, 2020.

The Research Center studied the credit predicted for the two policy-making institutions, i.e. the Presidential Directorate for Women and Family Affairs and the Social and Cultural Council of Women and Family, and concluded that the total credit allocated to these two institutions dealing with women had been reduced by 30% from 22.5 billion tomans to 15.7 billion tomans. It said the reduction was due to the cut in the total credit for the Directorate for Women and Family Affairs from 21 billion tomans ($1.83 million) in 2018 to 14.2 billion tomans ($1.2 million) in 2019, which is a 32 percent budget cut tantamount to 7 billion tomans.[321]

Due to insufficient funds in the 1398 fiscal year, 88% of women heads of household eligible for Poverty Preventing Plan were excluded from the program. Only 5,000 of the 40,000 women heads of household nominated by the Ministry of Health and Medical Education to be covered by the Poverty Prevention Plan for Pregnant and Lactating Women, were included in the plan.[322]

---

[317] Parvaneh Salahshouri, a member of the Cultural Committee of the mullahs' parliament, the state-run ISNA news agency – December 18, 2017
[318] Parvaneh Salahshouri, a member of the Cultural Committee of the mullahs' parliament, the state-run ISNA news agency – December 18, 2017
[319] The state-run donya-e-eqtesad.com, December 20, 2017
[320] Zohreh Ashtiani, secretary of the Family Faction of the mullahs' parliament (Majlis), the state-run Shahrvand daily, July 10, 2018
[321] The state-run Etemad online, December 26, 2018
[322] Ahmad Maidari, Deputy Minister of Cooperatives, Labour and Social Welfare, the state-run IRNA News Agency – February 12, 2019

The number of women heads of household who were taught skills to find jobs was only 12,000.[323] There are at least 3.6 million women heads of household in Iran. 82% of these women do not have any jobs, and only 180,000 of them receive a meager monthly support from the Welfare Organization.[324]

Contradicting the Research Center of the mullahs' parliament, officials of the women's directorate announced this year (2020), that they received 20.3 billion of the allocated 21 billion toman budget of the Persian fiscal year 1398.[325]

Officials of the Presidential Directorate on Women and Family Affairs are boasting that they are going to receive 19% more budget in the new fiscal Persian year 1399 (March 2020-March 2021), amounting to 25 billion tomans ($2.17 million).[326] In the meantime, they acknowledge that this is a very small budget compared to other agencies and institutions.

One of the main criticisms to the 1399 budget bill is omission of the credits for insurance of women heads of households and women with bad guardians. The articles 19 and 22 of the 14th amendment to the 1398 bill which concerned credits for insurance of women heads of households and women with bad guardians have been omitted altogether.[327]

The government's budget bill to the parliament pointed out that support for women heads of household is unnecessary and the budget for their insurance was removed altogether.[328]

---

[323] Zahra Javaherian, deputy for planning and coordination in the Presidential Directorate on Women and Family Affairs, the state-run ISNA news agency, December 11, 2019: "12,000 women heads of household were covered by plans in 1398 to teach them skills to find jobs."
[324] Massoumeh Ebtekar, head of the Presidential Directorate on Women and Family Affairs, the official IRNA news agency, October 7, 2018.
[325] Zahra Javaherian, deputy for planning and coordination in the Presidential Directorate on Women and Family Affairs, the state-run ISNA news agency, December 11, 2019: "21 billion tomans had been adopted for the directorate's budget in 1398 but only 20.3 billion tomans was granted to the directorate."
[326] Zahra Javaherian, deputy for planning and coordination in the Presidential Directorate on Women and Family Affairs, the state-run ISNA news agency, December 11, 2019: "The budget allocated this year to the presidential directorate on Women and Family Affairs is 25 billion tomans which shows a 19% growth compared to last year, which is of course very small in comparison to many other agencies and institutions."
[327] Zahra Javaherian, deputy for planning and coordination in the Presidential Directorate on Women and Family Affairs, the state-run ISNA news agency, December 11, 2019; Tayyebeh Saivoshi, member of the mullahs' parliament, the state-run javanonline.ir, January 2, 2020
[328] Simin Kazemi, a sociologist, the state-run asriran.ir, January 2, 2020

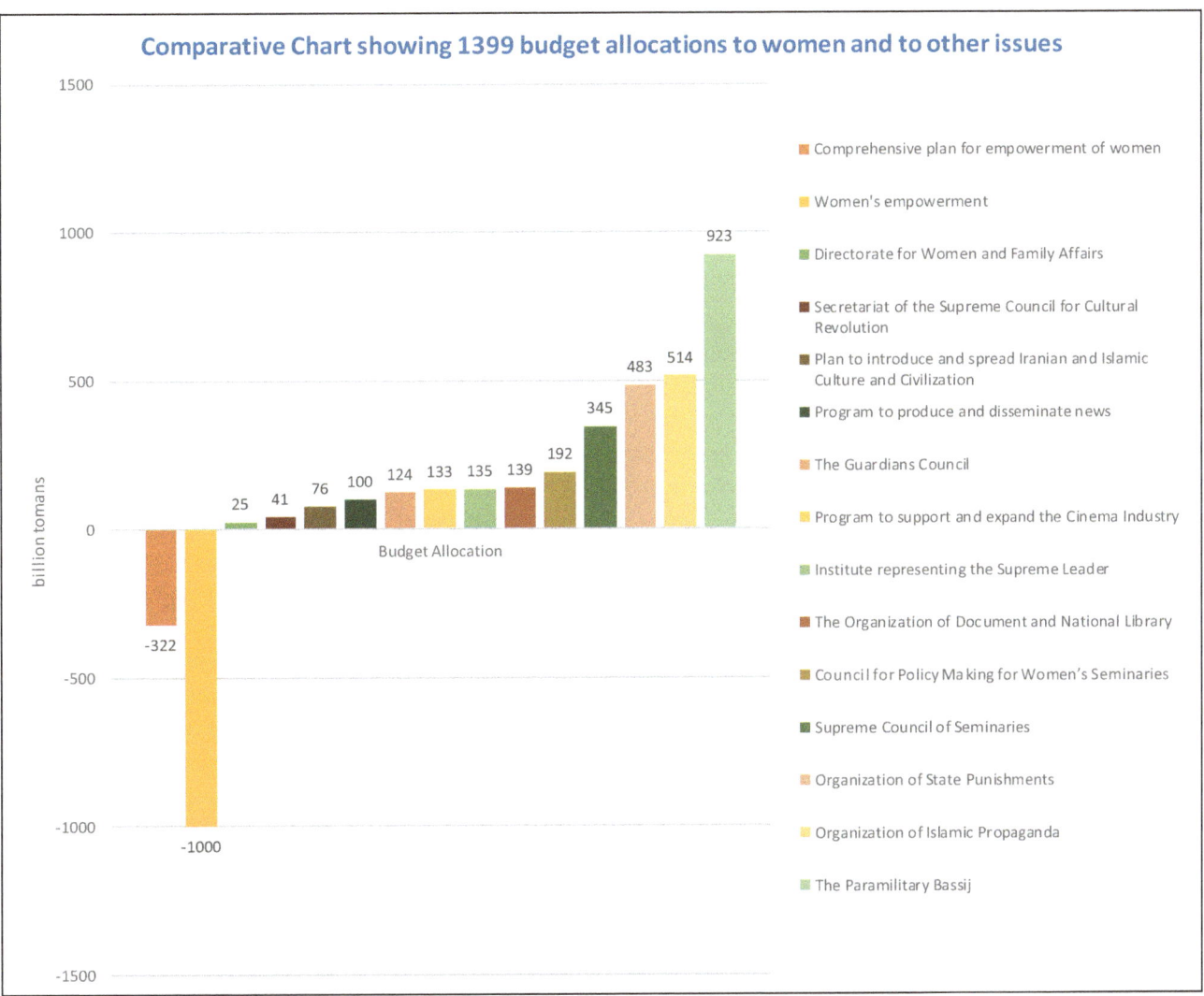

The above chart for Persian fiscal year 1399 (March 2020-March 2021) compares the budget allocated to the Directorate on Women and Family Affairs compared to the budget granted to other plans and departments. While the women's directorate has been granted only 25 billion tomans, the women's empowerment plan in Article 80 of the Sixth Development Program has not received any budget while it lacks 1 trillion tomans for being implemented. This is while the seminaries and the agencies in charge of Islamic propaganda and even cinema (133 billion) and production of news (100 billion) have been granted higher budgets. The Council for Policy Making for Women's Seminaries has been granted 192 billion tomans.

Neither were any funds allocated to paragraph d of Article 80 of the Sixth Development Program for the empowerment of women.[329] This is while the Welfare Organization has a one trillion toman deficit for implementation of paragraph d of Article 80 of the Sixth Development Program.[330]

Also, the budget for Women's Social and Cultural Council has been cut by 18% because of omission of the plan for strategic researches without providing any clear reason.[331]
In the discussions about the new year's budget, it was revealed that from the meager 300 billion tomans allocated in the 1398 fiscal year to the insurance of housewives, only 12 percent of it had been granted by July, and by January, it was still not clear if they had received the actual credit for it.[332]

Welfare Organization officials have also revealed that implementation of the Comprehensive Plan for Empowerment of Women requires 322 billion tomans.[333] They also acknowledged that they have no credits for providing support to 245,000 women heads of household who are on the Welfare Organization's waiting list. The 1399 budget bill has allocated only 3 billion tomans for screening and health while the budget needed for screening is 17.5 billion tomans and 50 billion tomans for health care.

In the Persian fiscal year 1399, in the absence of oil revenues, the Iranian regime has based its budget on revenues from taxes on property and water to be exacted from the Iranian public. With the majority of the populace living under the poverty line, there is no guarantee for them to secure this revenue.

---

[329] Farideh Olad Ghobad, member of the mullahs' parliament, the state-run ICANA.ir, December 17, 2019
[330] Derakhshani, member of the Social Directorate of the Welfare Organization, the state-run ICANA.ir, December 17, 2019
[331] Tayyebeh Saivoshi, member of the mullahs' parliament, the state-run javanonline.ir, January 2, 2020
[332] Farideh Olad Ghobad, member of the mullahs' parliament, the state-run ICANA.ir, December 17, 2019
[333] Derakhshani, member of the Social Directorate of the Welfare Organization, the state-run ICANA.ir, December 17, 2019

POVERTY ERADICATION, SOCIAL PROTECTION AND SOCIAL SERVICES

8. What actions has your country taken in the last five years to reduce/ eradicate poverty among women and girls?

Over the past five years, the people of Iran have become much poorer. The middle class has all but diminished and more than 80 percent of the Iranian people live under the poverty line.[334] So, the Iranian regime has not taken any steps towards reducing or eradicating poverty, especially among women and girls. In fact, various regime officials have admitted that the face of poverty in Iran has become feminine.

- One of the officials of the state-run Relief Committee acknowledged, "Poverty has become feminine... Today, more than 64 per cent of impoverished families covered by our Relief Committee are female heads of household."[335]
- An official of Tehran's Welfare, Social Services and Cooperation Organization acknowledged: "The most significant problem in the city of Tehran is the feminization of social ills."[336]
- Another official involved with women's issues said, "Poverty has become feminized. Social ills, suicide, runaway girls, addiction, and a rising number of female prisoners are some of the issues we face."[337]
- 33 percent of Iran's population, i.e. nearly 26 million people, are suffering from absolute poverty, and six percent, or five million people, are starving. They are not even able to buy enough food, while they also have other expenses like housing, transportation, and clothing.[338]
- According to this economist, a family of four living in an urban area with a monthly income below 40 million Rials (roughly $347) is living in poverty. Families in rural parts with an income of less than 20 million Rials per month live in poverty.

Where are the oil revenues going?
Before the comprehensive sanctions and oil embargo imposed on Iran, the Iranian regime used to have around 1,500 trillion Rials of oil revenues, notwithstanding the taxes and the government's other sources of income. The women's share of these revenues, however, amounts to a meager 200 billion Rials.

---

[334] Shahab Naderi, member of the parliamentary Economic Committee, the official website of the Iranian regime's parliament, ICANA, March 13, 2018
[335] Mer'at Rassouli, director of the state-run Relief Committee (charity) in Shiraz, the state-run ISNA news agency, August 26, 2015.
[336] Farzad Hooshyar Parsian, General Director of Tehran's Welfare, Social Services and Cooperation Organization, the state-run IRNA news agency, August 16, 2015.
[337] Zahra Shojaii, secretary general of the so-called reformist women's assembly, the state-run dustaan.com, June 20, 2018
[338] Hossein Raghfar, Iranian economist, the state-run ISNA news agency, April 7, 2018

The total credit for the directorate for Women and Family Affairs slipped from 210 billion Rials ($1.83 million) in 2018 to 142 billion Rials ($1.2 million) in 2019, which is a 32 percent budget cut of 70 billion Rials.[339]

Compare the 142-billion-rial budget of Women and Family Affairs' Directorate with the 250 billion Rials allocated to the *Rahian-e Nour* Central Staff whose mandate is disseminating the official accounts of the Iran-Iraq war and arrange trips for high school students to the former warfront zones.[340]

The budget allocated to women heads of household in 1397 budget was cut by 39% due to insufficient funds, and 88% of women heads of household eligible for Poverty Preventing Plan were excluded from the program,[341] while the budget of some other so-called cultural agencies doubled or remained the same.[342]

The budget allocated to defense and security affairs was 620 trillion Rials in 1398 (2019), the budget allocated to the state radio and television and other propaganda organs was 5.3 trillion Rials. The Policy-making council for Friday prayer leaders received 3.350 trillion Rials and the giant financial conglomerate of Astan-e Qods-e Razavi was exonerated from paying taxes worth 300 billion Rials.[343]

- Promoted poor women's access to decent work through active labor market policies (e.g. job training, skills, employment subsidies, etc.) and targeted measures

- Supported women's entrepreneurship and business development activities

The official policy in Iran is tuned to eliminate women from the job market, not providing them equal opportunities for a decent job. So, there is no evidence on promoting poor women's access to decent work.

Iran's job market is male-dominated and women have been pushed to the informal sector. The official Iranian news agency reported a wide gender gap in the job market: "Women's participation rate in Iran's job market in 2017 was only 16.8% which is very low compared to the male participation rate which was 71.4% in the same year."[344]

Women's employment in Iran is insignificant compared to developing countries. Women are constantly denied the right to work and are generally employed in informal, low-paid sectors.[345] The unofficial or informal sector of the job market has become feminine because women are cheap labor force and because they need to earn their living, they accept such jobs.[346]

---

[339] The state-run Etemad online, December 26, 2018
[340] Budget Bill of 1398, BBC Persian website, December 26, 2018
[341] Ahmad Maidari, Deputy Minister of Cooperatives, Labour and Social Welfare, the state-run IRNA News Agency, February 12, 2019
[342] Zohreh Ashtiani, secretary of the Family Faction of the mullahs' parliament, interview with the state-run Shahrvand newspaper, July 10, 2018.
[343] Budget Bill of 1398, BBC Persian website, December 26, 2018
[344] The official IRNA news agency, January 17, 2019
[345] The official Iran Estekhdam website, April 4, 2016
[346] Shahindokht Molaverdi, Rouhani's deputy on Women and Family Affairs in the weekly meeting with the state media and press, the state-run ISNA news agency, August 24, 2015.

Not much access to decent work

NO training programs for poor women and women heads of household

Little employment opportunities for women with higher education

Educated women forced to accept:
- part time jobs
- in the informal sector
- with low salaries
- no insurance or benefits

Unemployed   = Unemployed

78%  = **economically inactive**

Astara, Gilan Province
Educated women earn 400,000 tomans ($34) a month

KURDISTAN
38% of educated women are unemployed

 **30,000 nurses are unemployed**
The budget for recruitment of new nurses was rejected by the parliament

Not only there are no training programs for poor women and women heads of household, but there are not sufficient employment opportunities for women with higher education.

A large number of educated women do not find jobs for their level and field of education; thus they are forced to accept part time jobs in the informal sector with low salaries and no insurance or benefits.

In one of her latest remarks, Massoumeh Ebtekar, Rouhani's deputy for Women and Family Affairs, said, "The number of unemployed educated females are four times greater than unemployed educated males."[347]

One study indicates that 52 per cent of female university and college graduates are "economically inactive", which is a euphemism used to refer to the unemployed.[348]

A government official admitted that 38% of women with higher education in Kurdistan Province are unemployed.[349] Another report indicated that highly educated women in the city of Astara, Gilan Province, are working with low monthly salaries of 400,000 tomans ($34) to avoid being isolated at home.[350]

The Special Commission for the Protection of National Production and Monitoring of the Implementation of Article 44 of the Constitution, dated November 21, 2018, reported "the unemployment rate of young educated women reaches 78 percent."

Sometimes, unemployment is due to lack of funds to pay for new recruitments.

The secretary general of the House of Nurses revealed that there are at least 30,000 unemployed nurses in Iran due to financial restrictions and the policy of not granting new licenses.[351]

The budget for recruitment of new nurses in the Persian year 1398 (from March 21, 2019- March 20, 2020), was rejected by the parliament. While half of the nursing graduates remain without jobs, the responsibility of recruiting new nurses is passed from one government agency to the other.[352]

---

[347] The state-run ISNA news agency, October 5, 2019
[348] The state-run Kayhan daily newspaper, June 20, 2017 http://kayhan.ir/fa/news/106849
[349] Leila Ajhir, Director General of Women and Family Affairs in Kurdistan, the state-run Fars news agency, November 9, 2019
[350] The state-run salamatnews.com August 17, 2019
[351] Mohammad Sharifi Moghaddam, secretary general of Iran's House of Nurses, the state-run ILNA news agency, January 12, 2019
[352] Mohammad Sharifi Moghaddam, the General Secretary of the House of Nurses, the state-run ILNA news agency, December 31, 2018

- **Broadened access to land, housing, finance, technology and/or agricultural extension services**

The regime's MPs have time and again admitted that what they adopt in the parliament has no financial backing to be carried out.[353] It also frequently happens that despite the availability of funds for a project, the contractor just pockets the money and gets away.[354]

In the absence of an accountable census system, there is no way of finding out whether any of the plans the regime talks about, is actually implemented in practice.[355] This is very much true for the Directorate for Women and Family Affairs which has the smallest budget and funding and the least executive powers. What remains is the evidence from which we can draw conclusions.

- It is a fact that except for a small 4% of super rich families, the whole Iranian population has become extremely poor and the middle class has diminished altogether.
- It is a fact that shantytowns and slums have expanded to many provinces in Iran, and most of their residents come from villages.
- A presidential deputy said seven percent of the rural population has been displaced. One of the reasons for such migration is that the income every village man can earn in the village is 40 per cent less than what he can earn in a city.[356]
- A sociologist says class difference is so deep that the food and things a poor man can find in a city trash bin is more than what he can earn in his own village.[357]
- It is estimated that more than 11 million Iranians live in slums.[358] Others put the actual figure at 16 million[359] and even 19 million.[360] It is also estimated that 34,000 villages have been abandoned and annihilated.[361]
- Since the male-female ratio in the Iranian population is 51-49, it can be deduced that between 5.5-9 million Iranian women live in the slums.

---

[353] In remarks made on April 14, 2019, Pezeshkian, deputy speaker of the mullahs' parliament, revealed that the Iranian regime is neither capable nor it wants to compensate for the damages the people of Iran suffered as a result of the devastating floods. He said, "It is impossible for the government to respond to these problems just by-passing legislations... When it gets to action, the government has no money to do it. It cannot dredge or repair the dams."

[354] The state-run BORNA news agency, November 3, 2018

[355] People sarcastically call this "hope-therapy," which refers to the regime's prominent feature of lots of talking and doing nothing.

[356] The official IRNA news agency, January 18, 2018 http://www.irna.ir/fa/News/82799767

[357] The state-run Mehrkhane website, November 9, 2016 http://mehrkhane.com/fa/news/29640/

[358] The official IRNA news agency, January 18, 2018 http://www.irna.ir/fa/News/82799767

[359] Saeed Reza Jandaghian, a municipal deputy in Tehran, ISNA news agency, July 9, 2019. "There are about 11.4 million people living in slums, according to official figures, but the actual numbers are much higher, and today, 16 million Iranians, one-fifth of the population, live in slums."

[360] Salman Khodadadi, member of the parliamentary Social Committee, the state-run Ensaf news agency, April 6, 2018 "Official statistics say that we have 11 million people, and if we also count worn-out places and settlements, 19 million marginalized people are living in slums."

[361] The official IRNA news agency, January 16, 2018 http://www.irna.ir/fa/News/82797957

- A member of the City Council has admitted that wrong policies and lack of proper planning in attending to the problems of villages has led to migration of their inhabitants to major capitals such as Tehran.[362] He says, "Many of those living in the slums and shanty towns, those sleeping on cardboard boxes in the streets and those who panhandle in various parts of Tehran, are people who originally owned lands in their cities and villages, but migrated to the capital and its outskirts because they did not have any jobs or assets."

From these facts, one can conclude that not much is being effectively done as far as extension services are concerned for women who live in the deprived villages across the country.

- **Introduced or strengthened social protection programs for women and girls (e.g. cash transfers for women with children, public works/employment guarantee schemes for women of working-age, pensions for older women)**

Iranian women do not enjoy any social protection and no job security. They are the first to be dismissed from their jobs in any economic ups and downs.

- The head of the Presidential Directorate on Women and Family Affairs has confirmed that "rural women are deprived of social or economic security. There is no secure future for rural women and when they are disabled, widowed, or divorced, and when they become sick or elderly, there is no support for them. There are no social security systems to give them support."[363]
- As for women who live in the cities, they are the last to be employed and the first to be dismissed from offices and factories. They have no job security. Sometimes, employers mistreat female workers for the smallest flaw in their work.[364] Since the job market policy is to hire women on temporary three-month contracts, female workers are basically deprived of job security.[365]
- Women have the largest share of jobs in the unofficial or informal sector.[366] As it was mentioned earlier, the workshops and businesses in the informal

---

[362] The state-run Shafaf website, October 9, 2017 http://www.shafaf.ir/fa/news/443373
[363] Shahindokht Molaverdi, head of the directorate for women and family affairs, the state-run ISCANEWS website, October 17, 2016 - http://www.iscanews.ir/news/686728
[364] Fatemeh Pourno, Secretary of the Union of Women Workers in Qazvin, interview with the official IRNA news agency, May 3, 2018.
[365] Fatemeh Pourno, Secretary of the Union of Women Workers in Qazvin (a state institution), The official IRNA news agency, May 3, 2018
[366] Massoumeh Ebtekar, director of Women and Family Affairs Directorate, the official IRNA news agency, April 28, 2018

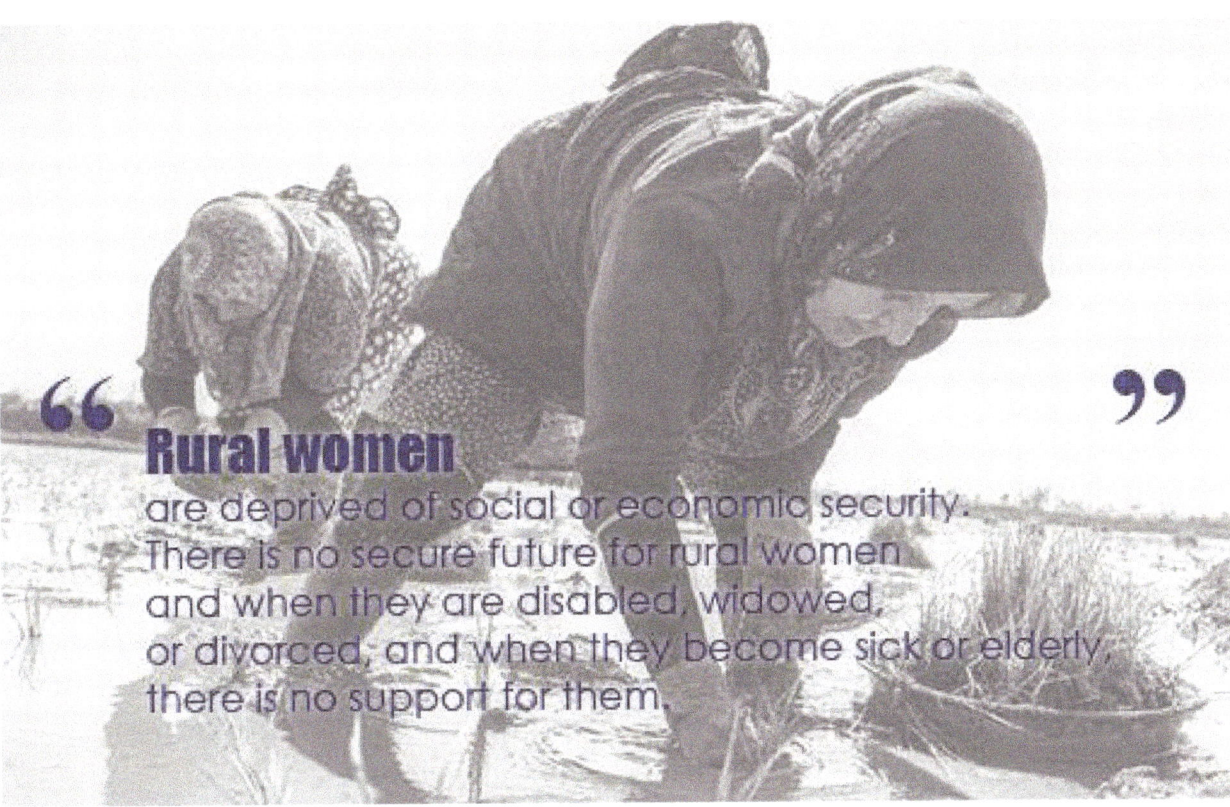

> **Rural women** are deprived of social or economic security. There is no secure future for rural women and when they are disabled, widowed, or divorced, and when they become sick or elderly, there is no support for them.

sector are not monitored by the government. So, women who work in this sector accept to work with low pay under unsafe conditions without receiving any benefits, insurance or social security. Or they are forced to do hazardous jobs such as peddling in the metro stations to stay away from social harms.[367]

- The majority of women working in the informal sector are women heads of household who work long hours but are deprived of their rights and benefits.[368]
- Not only they are deprived of social protection, but the few benefits some of them enjoy are taken away from them.
- In 2018 statistics, the number of insured women was one-sixteenth of insured men.[369]
- It was reported that the government began deducing child benefits from the payrolls of women heads of household in Autumn 2017.[370] The decision was implemented abruptly and the amounts previously paid to them were withdrawn from their accounts, at once.

---

[367] The state-run ILNA news agency, April 20, 2019
[368] The official IRNA news agency, May 3, 2018
[369] The state-run faratab.com, March 8, 2018
[370] Zahra Sa'ii, spokeswoman for the parliamentary Social Commission, the state-run salamatnews.com, March 28, 2018

- The head of the Welfare Organization once asserted that, "the organization faces major challenges" in granting job loans to women without guardians or with bad guardians. [371]
- A government official reported that women heads of household even sell their organs in order to support their families.[372]
- In a video clip posted on the internet,[373] a young woman who is going through the administrative stages for selling her kidney, says, "I work from 6 a.m. until 8 p.m. but my salary is not sufficient. I have to pay for the expenses of my two sisters. I have referred to different places to get loans or any form of assistance, but their answers were negative. Those who responded positively, intended to take (sexual) advantage (of me). People in some government places told me that I do not need help. I can pay all my debts in one month with my looks. If I don't pay my debts in two weeks, I will be taken to jail."
- In the fiscal Persian year 1398 budget, only 4 trillion tomans ($347.8 million) was allocated to the National Welfare Organization which is supposed to provide the basic needs and support services for low-income and needy sectors. This is less than 50,000 tomans ($4) per person.[374]
- Welfare Organization officials have also revealed that implementation of the Comprehensive Plan for Empowerment of Women requires 322 billion tomans, which has not been granted to them.[375] They also acknowledged that they have no credits for providing support to 245,000 women heads of household, 60,000 families and 77,000 students who are on the Welfare Organization's waiting list.[376]
- No funds have been allocated to paragraph d of Article 80 of the Sixth Development Program for the empowerment of women.[377]
- The Welfare Organization has a one trillion toman deficit for implementation of paragraph d of Article 80 of the Sixth Development Program.[378]
- Also, the budget for Women's Social and Cultural Council has been cut by 18% because of omission of the plan for strategic researches without providing any clear reason.[379]

---

[371] Anoushirvan Mohseni Bandpay, head of the National Welfare Organization, the state-run Tabnak website, February 13, 2018.
[372] The state-run Mehr news agency, October 8, 2015 - An official in Kermanshah admitted: "Often we witness women heads of household taking desperate measures and resorting to unconventional methods to provide the needs of their families including selling their kidneys!"
[373] Aparat.com, December 20, 2016 http://www.aparat.com/v/nSvxE
[374] The state-run ISNA news agency, December 29, 2018
[375] Derakhshani, member of the Social Directorate of the Welfare Organization, the state-run ICANA.ir, December 17, 2019
[376] Ibid.
[377] Farideh Olad Ghobad, member of the mullahs' parliament, the state-run ICANA.ir, December 17, 2019
[378] Derakhshani, member of the Social Directorate of the Welfare Organization, the state-run ICANA.ir, December 17, 2019
[379] Tayyebeh Saivoshi, member of the mullahs' parliament, the state-run javanonline.ir, January 2, 2020

- **Introduced/strengthened free or low-cost legal services for women and girls living in poverty**

Despite hollow publicity stunts about plans to provide affordable legal or educational services to women, there is no sign or statistics of any practical measures or steps taken in support of Iranian women.

- The minimum cost of legal services in 2018 were listed as the following:[380]
- Basic charge to hire a lawyer = 1 million tomans and up
- Writing a defense bill = 250,000 tomans and up
- Writing indictments = 100,000 tomans and up
- Writing legal appeals = 100,000 tomans and up
- Notary and registration jobs = 150,000 tomans and up
- Writing an affidavit = 50,000 tomans and up
- Writing contracts = 250,000 tomans and up

Obviously, Iranian women the majority of whom are unemployed or earn very low income, would hardly be able to use such services.
To receive free services, a woman needs to prove that she does not afford to pay for legal services, something that is nearly impossible in the mullahs' corrupt bureaucracy. She needs several witnesses to testify that she does not afford to pay. Then she must pay for a lawyer to verify that his client does not afford to pay for legal services.[381]

- **Introduced/strengthened free or low-cost health services for women and girls living in poverty**

The following are a few facts indicating the status of medical services provided to the general public in Iran. From this, one can conclude the situation of women and girls who are discriminated against and deprived of decent jobs and adequate income, and particularly those who live in poverty.
The government pays for only 20 percent of medical expenses of people and insurance companies pay for only 11 percent. As a result, people have to pay more than 60 percent of their medical expenses, something that pushes some 4 million people under the poverty line. Seven million people or nearly 10 percent of the populace have no form of insurance.[382]
The international average per capita expenses in the medical sector is $608, but in Iran this average comes down to $50, that is one-twelfth of the world's average.[383]
There are 380 Social Security medical centers and hospitals in Iran which are free of charge but provide only 25 percent of all medical services.[384]

---

[380] http://dadrah.ir/prices.php
[381] http://vekalate-online.com/%D9%88%DA%A9%DB%8C%D9%84-%D8%A7%D8%B1%D8%B2%D8%A7%D9%86/
[382] Shahabeddin Sadr, head of the National Medical System, Persian Deutsche Welle website, January 5, 2013
[383] Shahabeddin Sadr, head of the National Medical System, Persian Deutsche Welle website, January 5, 2013
[384] The state-run etemadonline.com, July 17, 2018

The budget for special patients, including cancer patients, has been cut from 234 billion tomans ($20 million) in 2017 to 216 billion tomans ($18.8 million) in 2018 to only 150 billion tomans ($13 million) in 2019.[385]

35 percent of AIDS patients in Iran are women who must afford to pay 4 billion tomans ($348,000) to receive treatment.[386]

Rural and nomad women have little access to specialist doctors and dentists. Many rural and nomad women die before reaching a medical center when they get sick.[387] In some places, like Hassanabad village, there are no adequate roads and patients must ride camels before they can get to normal roads where cars travel.[388]

Most tragic of all is the status of childbirth facilities as corruption has extended to public and private hospitals.

There are not enough midwives to care for women during labor.

Systematically, hospitals provide more facilities for Cesarean section than for natural child birth. And the government has turned a blind eye on this situation and even condones it.

A telling example is the case of a pregnant woman in the city of Salmas in West Azerbaijan Province, northwestern Iran, who should have had a C-section, but died during natural delivery because she couldn't pay for a C-section.[389]

---

[385] The state-run ISNA news agency, February 10, 2019
[386] Dr. Nowzar Nakhaii told a meeting of the working group of women and family in Kerman Province, asriran.com, May 29, 2019
[387] Parichehr Soltani, secretary of the working group on rural and nomad women living in underprivileged areas, the state-run ISNA news agency, October 5, 2016
[388] The state-run Asr-e Iran website, January 21, 2018
[389] The state-run salamatnews.com, website of the Ministry of Health, September 2, 2015

- **Other**

It should be stressed that poverty of women and its consequent social ailments are mainly and basically due to official policies and laws which discriminate against women. An expert told the press that the government is lagging with respect to economic indices, such as providing jobs and employment for women, mainly due to national policies. He said there are 22 women employed compared to every 100 men with employment. Women's employment rate in Iran is 12 percent, at best.[390]

A member of parliament said, "women with no guardians" (i.e. women heads of household) have the custody of their children, and due to financial poverty, unemployment, and their consequences, are subject to (social) harms. At the same time, the Welfare Organization cannot take appropriate measures to empower and create jobs for women heads of household, due to budget constraints.[391]

An official in Kermanshah admitted: "Often we witness women heads of household taking desperate measures and resorting to unconventional methods to provide the needs of their families including selling their kidneys!"[392]

A woman who has to provide for her three children but has no jobs and has already sold one of her kidneys, has no way but to sell her body.[393]

---

[390] Anoushirvan Mohseni Bandpay, head of the National Welfare Organization, the state-run Tabnak website, February 13, 2018. Bandpay is currently the governor of Tehran Province.
[391] Hassan Lotfi, a member of the Social Commission of the mullahs' parliament, May 2018
[392] The state-run Mehr news agency, October 8, 2015
[393] Shocking testimonies published on Aparat.com, October 19, 2016

Q 8-11 POVERTY ERADICATION, SOCIAL PROTECTION AND SOCIAL SERVICES

9. What actions has your country taken in the last five years to improve access to social protection for women and girls?

- Introduced or strengthened social protection for unemployed women (e.g. unemployment benefits, public works programs, social assistance)

As cited in previous sections, the Iranian regime spends the lion's share of its income on defense, security and propaganda. In other words, it spends the country's revenues to fund wars, terrorism and its proxy groups, and its nuclear and missile programs, an outlaw behavior which provoked international sanctions against it.

In addition, a large part of the country's wealth and revenues is embezzled by the mullahs' supreme leader, Ali Khamenei, the Revolutionary Guard Corps (IRGC), and all the hierarchy of officials. Little remains to pay the salaries of government employees, create jobs, and provide support to the vulnerable sectors such as women and youths.

Officials of the Presidential Directorate on Women and Family Affairs are boasting that they are going to receive 19% more budget in the new fiscal Persian year 1399 (March 2020-March 2021), amounting to 25 billion tomans ($2.17 million).[394] In the meantime, they acknowledge that this is a very small budget compared to other agencies and institutions.

One of the main criticisms to the 1399 budget bill is omission of the credits for insurance of women heads of households and women with bad guardians. The articles 19 and 22 of the 14th amendment to the 1398 bill which concerned credits for insurance of women heads of households and women with bad guardians have been omitted altogether.[395]

Again, the budget allocated to the policy-making council for women's seminaries, which is part of the regime's religious propaganda apparatus, is greater than the Directorate for Women and Family Affairs.

The Welfare Organization has acknowledged that it has 1 trillion tomans of deficit for implementation of the Women's Empowerment program.[396]

Also, the budget for Women's Social and Cultural Council has been cut by 18% because of omission of the plan for strategic researches without providing any clear reason.[397]

No credits have been allocated for insurance of women heads of households and women with bad guardians in the upcoming Persian year 1399.[398]

---

[394] Zahra Javaherian, deputy for planning and coordination in the Presidential Directorate on Women and Family Affairs, the state-run ISNA news agency, December 11, 2019: "The budget allocated this year to the presidential directorate on Women and Family Affairs is 25 billion tomans which shows a 19% growth compared to last year, which is of course very small in comparison to many other agencies and institutions."

[395] Zahra Javaherian, deputy for planning and coordination in the Presidential Directorate on Women and Family Affairs, the state-run ISNA news agency, December 11, 2019; Tayyebeh Saivoshi, member of the mullahs' parliament, the state-run javanonline.ir, January 2, 2020

[396] Derakhshani, member of the Social Directorate of the Welfare Organization, the state-run ICANA.ir, December 17, 2019

[397] Tayyebeh Saivoshi, member of the mullahs' parliament, the state-run javanonline.ir, January 2, 2020

[398] Zahra Javaherian, deputy for planning and coordination in the Presidential Directorate on Women and Family Affairs, the state-run ISNA news agency, December 11, 2019; Tayyebeh Saivoshi, member of the mullahs' parliament, the state-run javanonline.ir, January 2, 2020

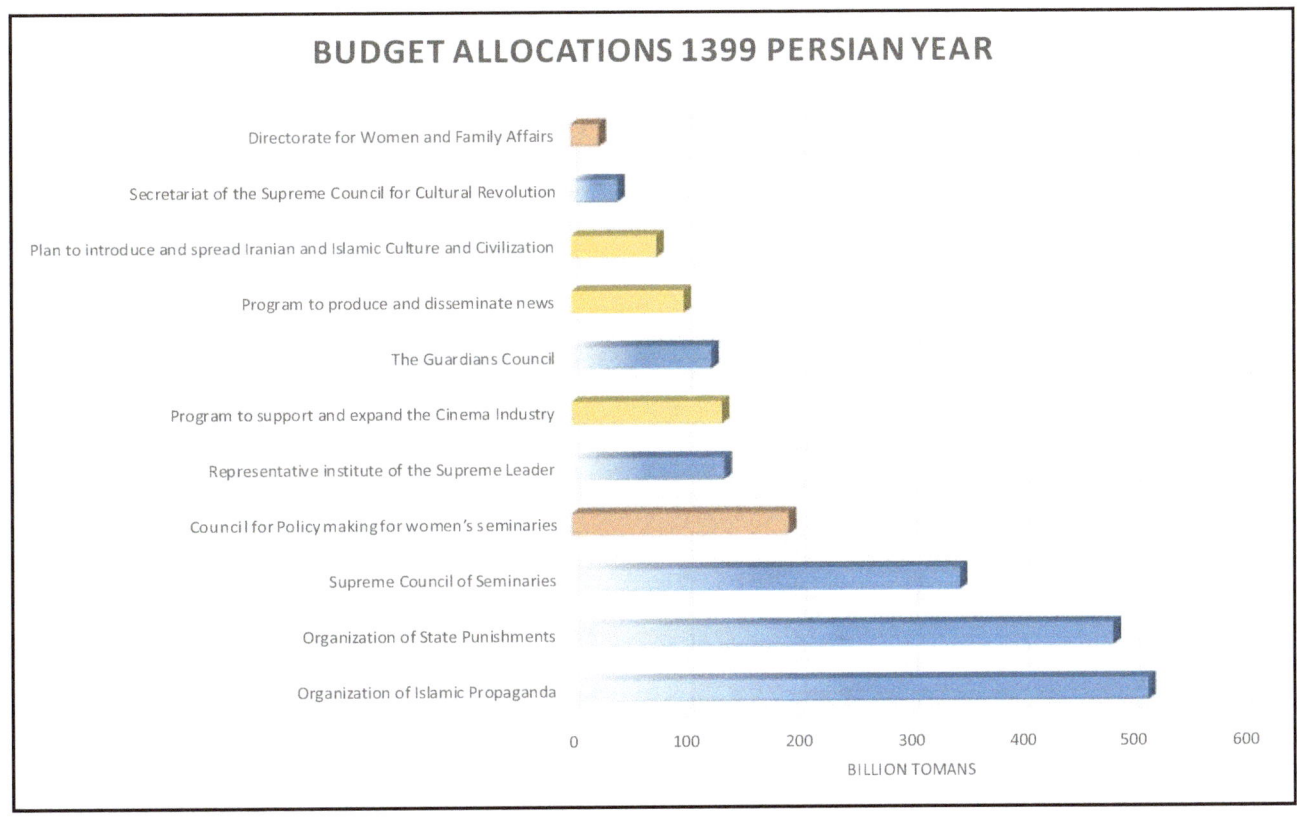

The Welfare Organization has no credits to provide support to 245,000 women heads of household, 60,000 families and 77,000 students who are on the Welfare Organization's waiting list.[399]

Again, let's compare the budget for various sectors in the fiscal year 1399 (March 2020-March 2021) compared to the 25 billion tomans allocated to the Directorate on Women and Family Affairs:[400]

Total budget for 1399 = 1988,000,000,000,000 tomans
Defense and Intelligence Affairs = 69,596,216,300,000 tomans
Ministry of Defense = 41,575,120,300,000 tomans
Martyrs' Foundation = 16,072,528,100,000 tomans
Parliament = 1,156,020,600,000 tomans
Ministry of Islamic Culture and Guidance = 1,879,008,000,000 tomans
The Paramilitary Bassij = 923,673,200,000 tomans
The Guardians Council = 124,358,500,000 tomans
Organization of Islamic Propaganda = 514,303,700,000 tomans
Organization of State Punishments = 483,580,400,000 tomans
Supreme Council of Seminaries = 345,000,000,000 tomans

---

[399] Ibid.
[400] The official IRNA news agency, December 9, 2019

Secretariat of the Supreme Council for Cultural Revolution =	41,010,000,000 tomans
Representative institute of the Supreme Leader =	135,540,600,000 tomans
Program to support & expand the Cinema Industry =	133,000,000,000 tomans
Plan to introduce and spread Iranian and Islamic Culture and Civilization =	76,052,200,000 tomans
Council for Policy making for women's seminaries =	192,000,000,000 tomans
Program to produce and disseminate news =	100,000,000,000 tomans

But what does this mean for the people of Iran and particularly for women?

It means that the government does not have the funds to pay its employees, nurses and hospital staff, teachers, factory workers, etc.

It does not have the funds to recruit more nurses badly needed in a country with shortage of 180,000 nurses. And obviously, it does not afford to provide social protection to anyone, particularly to women. This is why, sale of body organs, sale of infants, child labor, prostitution, addiction and suicides are of high rates in Iran.

There are at least 3.6 million women heads of household in Iran.[401] One of the Welfare Organization officials confessed that 82 percent of these women are unemployed and live under the "death line." Only 180,000 out of the 3 million in need receive small monthly pensions of around 10 dollars, not enough to pay for their expenses.[402]

The poverty line currently stands at 8 million tomans ($700).[403]

So, in real life, in the absence of any social protection, women have to take extreme measures, as a common practice, and sell their organs to provide for their families.

- **Introduced or strengthened non-contributory social pensions**

Women heads of household

One group of women who need to receive non-contributory social pensions and support from the government, are women heads of household. Currently, 3,600,000 women have been officially registered as women heads of household in Iran.[404] The number of women heads of household has more than doubled in a span of 20 years.[405]

The number of families headed by women has increased 58% compared to men over the past 10 years.[406]

---

[401] Massoumeh Ebtekar, Director of Women and Family Affairs, the official IRNA news agency, October 7, 2018

[402] Ebrahim Ghaffari, General Director of Welfare Organization of Golestan Province, the state-run Tasnim news agency, February 12, 2017

[403] Data compiled from the Iranian state media, April 2019

[404] Massoumeh Ebtekar, head of the presidential directorate on women and family affairs, interview with the official IRNA news agency, October 7, 2018

[405] Seyed Hassan Moussavi Chalak, chair of the Social Aid Association of Iran, the state-run Salamatnews.com, May 19, 2018

[406] The state-run ROKNA news agency, February 12, 2020

Only 18 percent of these women have some form of occupation, and over 3 million or 82% of women heads of household in Iran are unemployed.[407]

According to official figures, only 180,000 women heads of household are consistently receiving aid from the National Welfare Organization and another 100,000 receive social insurances. With regards to job loans to women without guardians or with bad guardians, however, the organization faces major challenges.[408]

Living conditions for women heads of household are described as being under the "death line" because even if these women receive pensions, it is only around 100 thousand tomans ($9) a month, while the poverty line is 8 million tomans ($700) for every family.

The number of women heads of household in Iran is steadily increasing but they face numerous problems due to the economic crisis in Iran and discrimination against women. Divorce, accidents, husband's disability, imprisonment and addiction are among the reasons contributing to the rising numbers of women heads of household.[409] At least 500,000 or 16% of women heads of household are under 20 years of age.[410] There are women heads of household as young as 14 and 15.[411]

According to a research, the three main problems women heads of household face in Iran are discrimination and inequality, unemployment, and lack of social security.[412]

Retired teachers

Another group of women eligible for social pensions, are retired teachers. One of the main demands of retired teachers is to raise their pensions to equal the salary of working teachers and improve their basic health care insurance.

A retired teacher said, "We object to the 2019 budget plan. It is not fair that only two billion tomans are considered for equalization of retirement pensions in the budget plan. Officials themselves say that they need at least 15 trillion tomans for equalization of liquidity."[413]

It should be noted that the monthly salary of working teachers is also below the poverty line.

---

[407] Massoumeh Ebetkar, speaking to a meeting of women members of the city and village councils in Semnan Province, the state-run ISNA news agency, July 7, 2018.

[408] Anoushirvan Mohseni Bandpay, head of the National Welfare Organization, the state-run Tabnak website, February 13, 2018.

[409] Fatemeh Zolqadr, member of the women's commission in the mullahs' parliament, the official IRNA news agency, July 2, 2019

[410] Fatemeh Zolqadr, member of the women's commission in the mullahs' parliament, the official IRNA news agency, July 2, 2019

[411] Zahra Rahimi, a civil rights activist and the Executive Director of a non-governmental organization, the state-run ROKNA news agency - February 12, 2020: "The age of women heads of household ranges between 18 and 60 years. However, in provinces where child marriages are common, girls as young as 14 or 15 are also taking care of the family."

[412] Susan Bastani, strategic studies deputy at the directorate for women and family affairs, the official IRNA news agency, May 4, 2019

[413] The state-run ILNA news agency, December 20, 2018

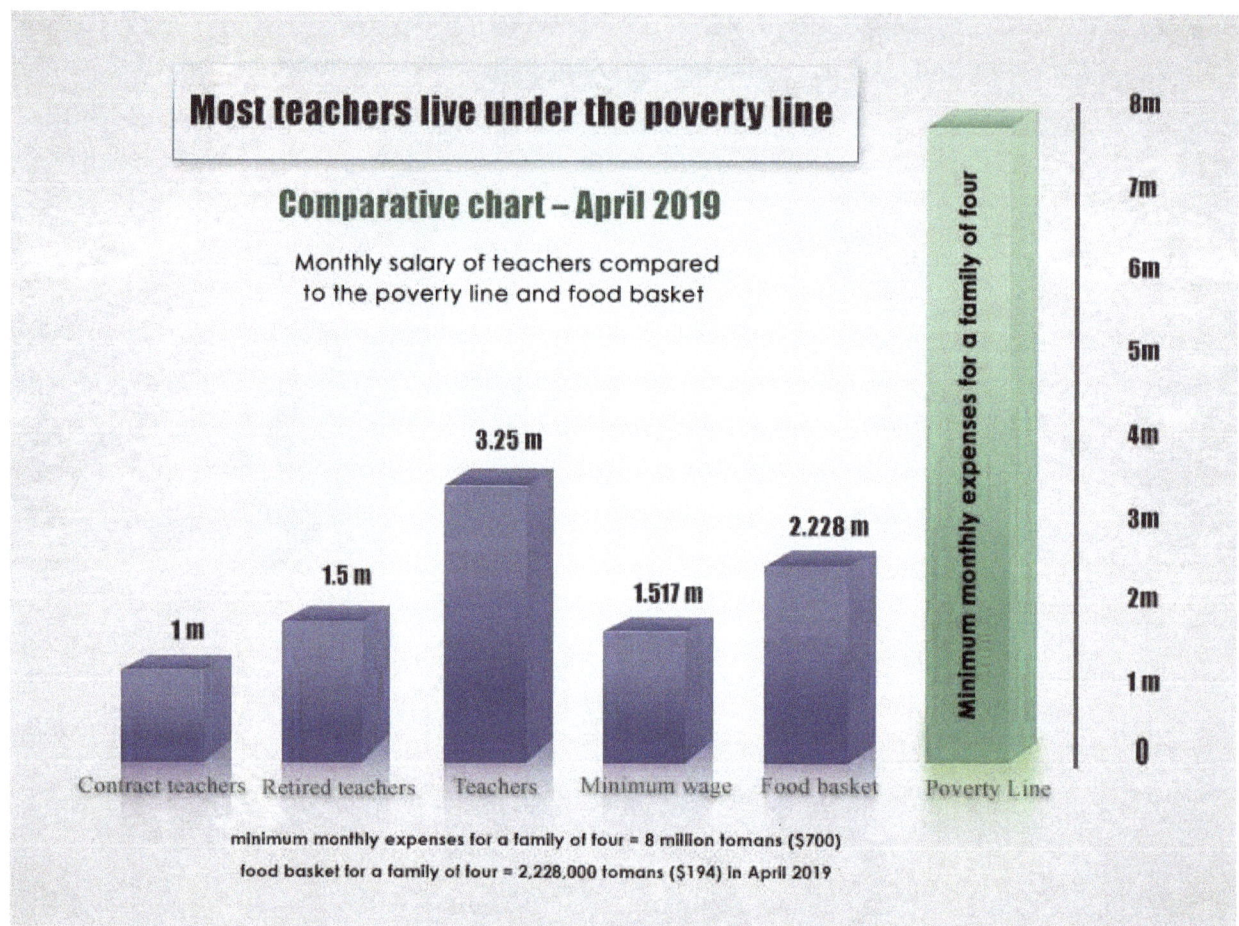

- Improved access to the above for specific populations (e.g. women in informal employment, including domestic workers; migrant and refugee women; women in humanitarian settings; women and girls with disabilities)

Women in informal employment

The majority of women heads of household who have jobs are involved in informal employment settings where workers do not receive any benefits or insurance.[414] They often earn their living with great difficulty. The occasional and insignificant support, such as loans and subsidies, or any aid from relatives or acquaintances, do little to improve the living conditions of women heads of household.

Only 18 percent of the 3.6 million women heads of household have jobs.

Most women heads of household are workers. They include divorced and widowed women who head low-income working families, women who have addicted husbands who are at home but do not work, women whose husbands are imprisoned, women who have children from

---

[414] Fatemeh Pourno, Secretary of the Union of Women Workers in Qazvin, the official IRNA news agency, May 3, 2018.

temporary marriages, women who are their family's breadwinner because of their husbands' disability, and girls who are their family's breadwinner.[415]

Only 180,000 women heads of household receive small aid of about $9 from the National Welfare Organization every month despite the poverty line standing at $700. Some 100,000 women heads of household receive insurance. The rest are left without any form of support.

Iranian officials admit that giving support to women heads of household has been long overdue despite being on the table for 35 years.[416]

Women in humanitarian settings

Another group of women who need to have access to social protection, are women living in disaster hit areas, where the population is hit by earthquake or floods. The Iranian regime has been very slow in attending to the immediate needs of the disaster-hit populations and has not attempted in any way to compensate for the damages.

The women who have been victims of earthquake or floods need access to non-contributory pensions, but there has been no sign of granting any form of aid to them.

- **Earthquake**
    - For example, two years after November 12, 2017, when the year's deadliest earthquake of 7.3 magnitude hit vast parts of Kermanshah Province in western Iran, residents of the afflicted areas continue to live in disastrous conditions. The earthquake damaged 10 cities and 1,930 villages, and destroyed more than 100,000 housing units, leaving at least 620 dead and 9,338 people wounded. The cities of Qasr-e Shirin, Sarpol-e Zahab and Salas-e Babajani were hit worst.
    - Five months after the earthquake, local officials said that some 60 per cent of the residents of affected areas had not received trailers and were living in tents. Even the trailers donated by private citizens had not been handed over to those in need. So, they had to live in tents or the ruins of their previous houses.
    - Lack of adequate shelter led to the deaths of a considerable number of children due to high fever, infection and other illnesses caused by the freezing cold of winter.[417]
    - After two years, many residents of Kermanshah Province are still living in makeshift homes. The Iranian regime has done almost nothing to restore the residents' housing, health and livelihood.

---

[415] The state-run ROKNA news agency, February 12, 2020
[416] Zohreh Ashtiani, secretary of the family faction of the mullahs' parliament. Interview with the state-run Shahrvand newspaper, July 10, 2018
[417] Five months on, earthquake survivors lack the minimums, website of the NCRI Women's Committee, April 19, 2018

- Mehdi Tahbaz, governor of Sarpol-e Zahab, announced that some 30 percent of those who lived in rented urban housings are now living in temporary arrangements on the streets.[418]
- The earthquake added to the number of women heads of household. Reports on the condition of women in these areas are scarce, but other news from these areas indicate that their situation is grim. A considerable number of married women with children have been committing suicide in these areas.[419]

- Floods
    - A similar situation is true with victims of the flashfloods of spring 2019, who lost their homes, and in the absence of any relief effort on behalf of the government have been relying on public's support and assistance to survive.[420]
    - Residents of flood-hit areas are angry at the regime for its failure to attend to their needs.
    - In Lorestan, women and little children had not eaten for several days after the floods.
    - They had not received any assistance. People had no place to go in the cold and slept in cars at night.[421]
    - In Khuzestan, 270 villages were evacuated, and 120,000 people were displaced. People lost everything and their farmlands were destroyed. In Bamdej, families lived in train wagons. Locals reported that instead of sheltering people, the Red Crescent of Khuzestan sold them tents for 500,000 tomans each.[422]

Homeless women

Another group of women in Iran who need access to social protection are homeless women.

There are various accounts on the number of homeless women in Tehran and other cities, but no official statistics are available on the overall number of homeless women in the country.

- In 2015, Shahindokht Molaverdi, former presidential deputy for women and family affairs, acknowledged that there are at least 5,000 women in Tehran who have no

---

[418] Mehdi Tahbaz, governor of Sarpol-e Zahab, the state-run ICANA news agency, November 7, 2018
[419] Suicides among women in Iran tops rates in the Middle East, website of the NCRI Women's Committee, September 9, 2019
[420] Devastating floods in Iran: problems of women in the absence of aid, website of NCRI Women's Committee, April 22, 2019
[421] Devastating floods in Iran: problems of women in the absence of aid, website of NCRI Women's Committee, April 22, 2019
[422] Devastating floods in Iran: problems of women in the absence of aid, website of NCRI Women's Committee, April 22, 2019

- place of residence and sleep in cardboard boxes in the streets.[423] Other sources indicated that the number was around 15,000.[424]
- The state-run media in Iran have also reported on the new phenomenon of "grave-dwellers." They reported of a woman by the name of Shahnaz living in a grave along with her 18-year-old son and 16-year-old twins.[425]
- According to one estimate, the average age of women who sleep in the streets is around 17 and 18.[426] Another report puts the average age at under 15 years.[427]
- A city official was cited as saying some 200 women including pregnant women, disabled women, elderly women, and girl children were living in 100 tents in south Tehran in the severe cold.[428]
- In Ahvaz, capital of the southwestern Province of Khuzestan, the number of women who have no place to sleep at nights is reported to be 2,700.[429]
- One of the ways for women to earn their living is resorting to trash beans to find food leftovers.[430]
- According to Ali Sadeghi, a social support deputy at the Tehran Municipality, the capacity of warm shelters in the city to hold homeless women sleeping in cardboard boxes is only 200. The number of homeless women sleeping in cardboard boxes in Tehran was estimated between 3,000 to 5,000.[431]
- A more recent report boasting of building shelters for homeless women in Tehran said there were only two shelters for women in the capital which could house between 400-500 women every night.[432] But homeless women need to show letters from the Judiciary to stay for limited hours in the shelter. There have also been reports of mistreatment and rape of women in these shelters.[433]
- No accurate updates have been provided on the number of homeless women in more recent years, but as the populace has become poorer in recent years and the poverty line risen from 3 million tomans in 2015 to 8 million tomans in 2019, it could be estimated that the actual number is far above these figures.

---

[423] The state-run ILNA news agency, July 11, 2015
[424] The state-run Arya news agency, May 30, 2015: "There are 15,000 women sleeping in the streets of Tehran every night."
[425] The state-run Tabnak website, December 27, 2016
[426] Jahangirifar, Deputy for social services in the Organization of Social Cooperation and Well-being , the state-run Alef website, May 9, 2016
[427] The state-run Tasnim news agency, September 27, 2017
[428] Head of the Social Committee of Tehran's City Council, the state-run Mizan news agency, January 3, 2017
[429] The state-run IRNA news agency, IRNA.ir/Khuzestan/, November 10, 2018
[430] Mousavi Chelek, deputy of Welfare Organization, the state-run ILNA news agency, October 8, 2016
[431] The semi-official Tabnak website, January 14, 2019
[432] The state-run Young Journalists Club, December 14, 2019
[433] The official IRNA news agency, November 10, 2018

Women and girls with disabilities

In December 2012, the elementary girls' school of Shinabad village caught fire due to malfunctioning of a kerosene heater. Thirty-seven (37) girls severely burned in the fire, leading to two deaths. Twelve (12) girls with serious injuries and their families were promised compensation which was never delivered by the authorities.

The girls were first promised to be sent abroad for treatment.[434] This promise was never fulfilled, and the girls were totally deprived of government assistance.[435]

The girls' lawyer explained, "The most important issue for these girls is that their treatment be expedited and improved. This must be done abroad. On the other hand, they must receive full compensation (from the government), which has not been paid to them (because they are girls). The girls must receive their full rights. Their mental problems must be attended to. They face problem in receiving their National Card and birth certificate. These problems must be resolved. These girls do not need mercy; they demand their rights."[436]

Shinabad was not the only fire incident inflicting serious injuries and disabilities on Iranian girl children.

A similar case came to light in April 2019, when six who had suffered burns in a fire incident at their school in Doroodzan, Fars Province, travelled to Tehran to hold a sit-in protest and demand assistance for their treatment and its high costs. Each of the six girls, now 20 years old, suffered more than 50% injuries in a fire incident 13 years ago at their school in the southern Fars Province. In their case, too, none of the promises for their treatment have been delivered.

---

[434] Rasoul Khezri, member of parliament from Piranshahr, the state-run Young Journalists Club, August 10, 2016
[435] Iran: Victims of fire in girls' school denied government support, the website of NCRI Women's Committee, August 12, 2016
[436] Hossein Ahmadi Niaz, the state-run ILNA news agency – March 4, 2018

Status of women with disabilities

Women account for **35%** of over **11million** disabled people in Iran

Disabled women are forced to accept and tolerate cruel behavior and relationships because of their physical and social limits.

- Other

Poverty, cause of various forms of social ills

Poverty is the source and cause of various social ills. Sale of body organs, addiction, prostitution, homelessness, sale of infants and unborn fetuses, and suicide are the most common forms of social ailments afflicting women in Iran.

Some Iranian regime officials have admitted that wrong policies and lack of proper planning in attending to the problems in rural areas have led to massive migrations to metropolises such as the capital, Tehran.[437] Most of the panhandlers, homeless people and inhabitants of slums and shanty towns are from among the population of migrants. Shanty towns are also the source of prostitution, addiction, and violence against women.[438]

Part of the petty sale of narcotic drugs is done by women who live in shanty towns because these women are at the disposal of their husbands. They gradually conclude that they need to earn money in order to be able to live and they resort to this venture. According to a sociologist, 63 per cent of women who are victims of violence live in shanty towns or in unofficial residences.[439]

a. Destitute women rent, sell and abandon their children

With the spread of poverty, more destitute Iranian women have been abandoning or selling their newborns.

Homeless pregnant women sell their unborn fetuses to earn some money to survive.[440]

Homeless women refer to hospitals in the south and center of the capital. After delivering their baby, they sell them for 100 to 200 thousand tomans ($US 9 to17).[441]

Women who sleep on cardboard boxes in the streets rent their children for 15,000 tomans ($1.30) a day for begging. Or they sell them for 2 million tomans ($174).[442]

Some parents sell their children. Infants are sold between 2 to 25 million tomans ($174 - $2174).[443]

Some women get pregnant with the aim of making money. Many of these infants and children are later taken advantage of in various crimes.[444]

---

[437] A member of Tehran's City Council said, "Many of those living in the slums and shanty towns, those sleeping on cardboard boxes in the streets and those who panhandle in various parts of Tehran, are people who originally owned lands in their cities and villages, but migrated to the capital and its outskirts because they did not have any jobs or assets." The state-run Shafaf website, October 9, 2017 http://www.shafaf.ir/fa/news/443373

[438] The state-run Mehrkhane website, November 9, 2016

[439] Ibid.

[440] The state-run Mehr news agency, August 22, 2015: "In continuation of the meeting, Dr. Chit Chian presented a plan to the governor's office and said: I have personally slept among those who sleep on cardboard boxes in the streets… Unfortunately, in these districts, I witnessed sale of kids. The conditions are so critical that they sell the fetus in the mother's womb before birth for 1 million or 750 thousand toumans."

[441] Tehran City Council's Fatemeh Daneshvar, the state-run ICANA news website, July 4, 2017

[442] Farahnaz Rafii, head of the Red Crescent Volunteers Organization, the state-run Young Journalists Club news agency, February 29, 2016

[443] Pathologist Majid Abhari, the state-run Fars news agency, May 3, 2016

[444] A member of Tehran's City Council, the state-run Shafaf website, October 9, 2017

The exact numbers of sale of unborn infants in their mothers' wombs and before they are born are not known but their numbers were large enough to make news.[445]

The Welfare Organization of Alborz Province announced, that 119 infants had been abandoned in the province in the period between March 2015 and December 2016.[446]

600 newborn infants were handed over to the Welfare Organization. The organization's social officer said these children and babies were being sold in some parts of the country.[447]

A one-day-old infant girl was found in the garbage bin of Khomein's hospital by the staff.[448]

b.1. Trafficking of infants of street women

Premature babies born from street women are smuggled out to be sold in other countries. Most of these infants are taken abroad to be sold to organs trafficking gangs, to families or to brothels. These gangs sell baby girls for a price higher than boys and send the babies to unknown destinations.[449]

b.2. Sale of organs

Following is an example of destitute women who have to sell their organs to provide for their family's expenses:

Donya, 28, has found no way but to sell one of her kidneys and part of her liver.[450]

Donya's mother had eight children when she got divorced 15 years ago. She works at a dairy factory in Neyshabur, northeastern Iran, and earns 820,000 tomans ($230) a month at best. Donya has a B.A. in physical training but has not found a suitable job. She works as a secretary at a doctor's office. Together with her mother, they earn 1.37 million tomans ($385) a month which is still 3 million tomans ($840) under the poverty line.

Since they are about to lose their housing and have no hope of saving any money, Donya has decided to sell one of her kidneys and part of her liver. It has been two months that Donya has posted an ad on the internet to sell her kidney, but has not found a suitable client.

c. Prostitution

Prostitution is often born in regions which are economically and culturally poor.[451]

Like many other issues, there are no statistics available on the number of prostitutes in Iran. The following information has been provided from one study involving 10,000 sex workers in Tehran which was quickly hushed up by the regime.

---

[445] Shahindokht Molaverdi, Rouhani's deputy for Women and Family Affairs, the state-run ILNA news agency, June 22, 2016
[446] The state-run ISNA news agency, January 14, 2017
[447] Habibollah Massoudi Farid, Social Affairs deputy to the Welfare Organization, the state-run ILNA news agency, August 17, 2017
[448] The state-run KhabarOnline.ir website, January 16, 2017
[449] Fatemeh Daneshvar, chair of the social committee of Tehran's City Council, the state-run Rokna.ir, March 8, 2017
[450] The state-run Salamatnews.com, December 12, 2017
[451] A sociologist, the state-run Mehrkhane website, November 9, 2016

At least 10,000 young women engage in prostitution in Tehran out of poverty. 35% of them are married. 30% of them have high school education and higher; 50% have not completed high school; only a small percentage are illiterate.[452]

The average price for these sex workers is 60,000 tomans ($18). Sixty per cent of these women are addicted or have some precedence of addiction. 30 per cent of them are women whose husbands are in jail and 15 per cent have been in jail, themselves. Many of these women who get pregnant either sell their infants, turn them in to welfare organizations or have abortions.[453]

Age of sex workers has dropped to 12.[454]

According to the National Welfare Organization of Iran, 50% of Iranian sex workers are married women who turn to such work because of economic problems.[455]

Homeless women have to sell their bodies to provide for very simple needs.[456] There are women who have to sell their body to provide for only one meal.

Soraya, a homeless woman in southern Tehran, due to hunger, went into a dark grave and gave herself up to three men for a falafel sandwich.[457]

Some girls sell their bodies to buy a pair of shoes or manteaux.[458]

There are cases when women have to sell their bodies for only 5,000 toumans ($1.5).[459]

d. Suicides

Under the clerical regime, suicides have been on the rise and Iran stands as the first record holder in the Middle East with regards to suicides among women.[460]

The rate of suicides among women in Iran increased by 66 percent during a five-year period from 2011 to 2015.[461]

The average international suicide rate is 8 per 100,000 persons. In some Iranian cities the average is much higher. For example, in Masjid Suleiman, the average suicide rate stands at 27.2 and in Kermanshah, at 26.2.[462]

---

[452] Mowj news agency, June 11, 2016
[453] Farahnaz Salimi, senior expert in psychology, the state-run aftabnews.ir, June 11, 2016
[454] Shahin Shams Mohammadi, a women's rights activist, the state-run salamatnews.ir, December 29, 2019
[455] The state-run salamatnews.ir, December 29, 2019
[456] The state-run vaghayedaily.ir, July 4, 2016
[457] The state-run ROKNA News Agency, December 17, 2019
[458] Shocking testimonies published on Aparat.com, October 19, 2016
[459] The state-run tebyan.net, June 15, 2016
[460] Suicide Of Young Women In Iran Indicates Pressure On Women, Girls, website of the NCRI Women's Committee, February 1, 2019
[461] A social pathologist, the state-run Khabar Online, November 3, 2017
[462] Saeed Madani, a social researcher and criminologist, the official IRNA news agency, January 21, 2018

Poverty main reason for prostitution of **10,000** sex workers in Tehran

not completed high school **50%**

high school education + **30%**

Small% illiterate

Average charge of a sex worker is **$18**

Age of sex workers down to **12**

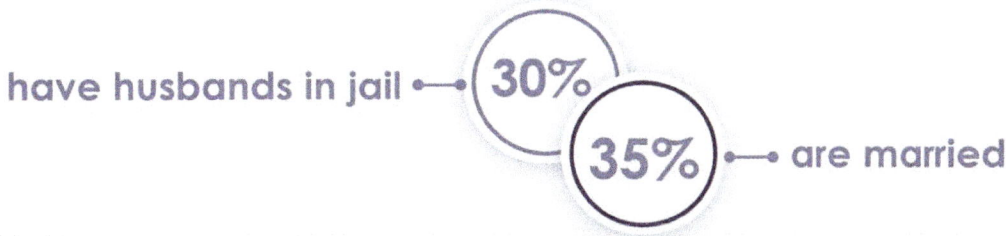

have husbands in jail — **30%**

35% — are married

If pregnant
- sell their infants
- turn them in to welfare organizations
- illegal/unsafe abortions

d.1. Poverty is among the main contributors to suicide among women in Iran

On numerous occasions, the regime's officials and experts have acknowledged that suicides are not fully reported and announced in Iran, and that the figures announced by the Coroner's Office and other government agencies must be considered as minimum.

The Iranian Journal of Forensic and Legal Medicine published the annual statistics on suicide in Iran in September 2018. According to this report, more than 1,365 women committed suicide in the Persian year 1396 (March 2017 - March 2018).

The number of women and girls who committed suicide due to poverty has increased in recent years. The large number of young mothers and pregnant women among victims is a new phenomenon caused by the immense pressure endured by poor and low-income families in Iran.[463]

- A mother and her 11-year-old daughter ended their lives by consuming aluminum phosphide on August 2, 2019, in Neyriz, Fars Province. The next day, the father of the family also killed himself in a deliberate accident with a semi-trailer truck.[464]
- Four members of a family committed suicide in Yazd on July 28, 2019. The mother of this family ended her life with high dose of insulin injections. Her three children also committed suicide by consuming aluminum phosphide, after informing the emergency, two of whom died. [465]
- In Urmia, a young mother of two who could not purchase meat for her children after months, hanged herself in front of them in mid-March 2019.
- A female municipality worker in Arak attempted self-immolation in protest over large deductions from salaries of employees. Her colleagues prevented her from doing so, but she was fired by the municipality of Arak.[466]
- Elaheh Amiri, the mother of a two-year-old, hanged herself on August 2, 2019, in a village in Saqqez, Iranian Kurdistan.
- A 34-year-old mother hugged her 6-year-old son and jumped from the fourth floor of a building in Tehran's Mehrabad district, ending their lives.[467]
- In Ilam, Mina Shahidi, 38, mother of three, killed herself due to the unbearable pressure of poverty on March 16.
- Parisa Nazari, 25, young mother of two, committed suicide on March 1, 2019 in Sarpol-e Zahab.
- Leila Ramezani, 24, pregnant mother of a one-year-old, committed suicide on March 3, 2019 in Salas-e Babajani.
- On February 20, 2019 Pershang Karimi, 22 and pregnant, hanged herself in Sarpol-e Zahab. Sarpol-e Zahab and Salas-e Babajani were both among the cities devastated by earthquake in November 2017 where people are still homeless and live in poverty.

---

[463] Young mothers, pregnant women among suicide victims in Iran, website of the NCRI Women's Committee, April 3, 2019
[464] Ibid.
[465] The state-run Fararu website - July 28, 2019
[466] The state-run ROKNA news agency – July 19, 2019
[467] The state-run ROKNA news agency, May 22, 2019

- Fereshteh Kahrarian, 30 and six-month pregnant, doused herself, husband and little child with kerosene and set themselves on fire on March 6, 2019 due to poverty. She subsequently died at a hospital in Kermanshah due to serious burns.
- Zahra Rahmati killed herself and her two young sons, 3 and 6, due to extreme poverty in a village in Kermanshah on February 10, 2019.
- A young woman, Nooshin Manavi, who had set herself ablaze on March 20, 2019, lost her life after two weeks on April 4, 2019, due to the extent and depth of burns. She had a young child.
- A 43-year-old mother who hugged her 14-month toddler and jumped off a building in Shahr-e Kord, capital of Chaharmahal and Bakhtiari Province in south central Iran on November 2, 2017.
- A 40-year-old woman committed suicide with her two children, a 10-year-old daughter and 5-month-old son, on December 25, 2017, in Rezvanshahr, Gilan Province, northern Iran. Eyewitnesses said the mother first threw her daughter off the fifth floor of the building where they lived. Then she jumped out with her 5-month-old son. The mother and her infant son died instantly, while the daughter hit the roof of a car and survived.

d.2. Poverty contributes to early marriages, and early marriages lead to suicides

Early marriage of girls under 18 is considered both violence against women and child abuse by international standards.

- Between 5 to 600,000 children get married every year (in Iran) according to the officially registered data. The main problem is that there are marriages taking place beyond those officially registered.[468]
- Some families force girls as young as 9 or 10 years old to get married with old men just to obtain some money to provide for the rest of the family's needs.[469]
- There are at least 15,000 young widows under 15 years of age in Iran, according to a report in 2018.[470]
- It often happens that young women commit suicide to escape forcible marriage.
- A 16-year-old young woman by the name of Ziba set herself on fire to evade her family's insistence that she marries an old man. The young woman was being forced into this marriage by her stepmother.[471]
- On June 5, 2019, in Baneh (western Iran), Souma Khedri, 19, ended her own life because of being compelled into forcible marriage against her own will.
- On May 31, 2019, in Piranshahr, Sara Esmaili, 17, who had been forced to marry a relative ended her own life.

---

[468] Ali Kazemi, advisor to the legal deputy of the Judiciary Branch, the state-run daily Entekhab – March 4, 2019
[469] Massoumeh Agha-Alishahi, member of the mullahs' parliament, the state-run ROKNA news agency, May 28, 2018
[470] Shahrbanou Imami, member of Tehran's City Council and former member of the mullahs' parliament, the state-run ILNA news agency, March 8, 2018
[471] The state-run Khorasan daily, August 26, 2019

- Delina Rahmani, 18, took her own life after being beaten by his father and the man she was being forced to marry. She shot herself on April 21, 2019.

Child abuse

Child abuse, domestic violence against women, abuse of the elderly and suicides are the first four social harms in Iran.[472]

Some sociologists believe that the surge in child abuse is due to economic problems and compulsory early marriages. But there are other reasons as well.

The bill on the rights of children has been stalled in the parliament for 10 years.

The bill to increase the age of marriage for girl children in Iran was rejected in December 2018.

Civil and Penal codes do not clarify limits on physical punishment by parents.

Fathers are not punished even for killing their daughters, because they are considered owner of their children's blood.

The Iranian Law to Protect Children and Adolescents (2002) does not protest against physical abuse; no mention of sexual abuse.

A bill called the Law to Support Disadvantaged, Defenseless and Abandoned Children was passed by the Iranian regime's Parliament on September 22, 2013, which sanctions marriage between the child and her guardian (stepfather), with the approval of a court. According to this law, fathers and grandfathers are considered owners of their children and their blood and they are not punished if they kill their children.[473]

- Fifty-two percent of the abused children are girls, and 57% of the abusers are their fathers.[474]
- In a shocking report on rape of young women by their first-degree relatives namely their fathers and brothers, head of the Social Ills Association in Tehran revealed that there were 5,200 incest cases filed with the Justice Ministry. According to this official, the figure does not include cases of rape by uncles, father-in-laws, and other instances of sexual exploitation and assault.[475]

---

[472] Reza Jafari, the head of Social Emergency, the state-run Fars news agency, April 14, 2019
[473] Article 301 of the Islamic Punishment Code
[474] The state-run Salamatnews.com, October 4, 2018
[475] The state-run Young Journalists Club, August 1, 2016

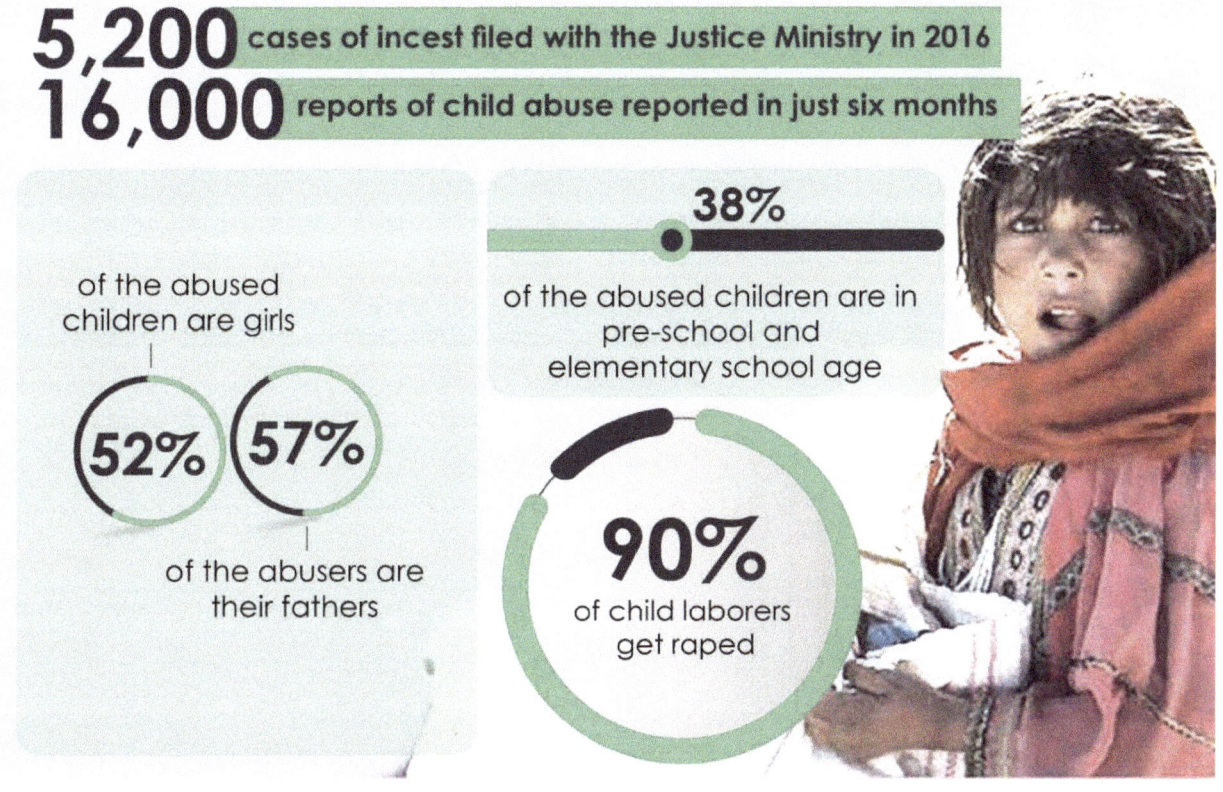

- The incumbent advisor to Khuzestan's Governor revealed that from among 18 girls aging between 12 and 14, who had complained to the Governor's women's office about rape by their fathers and brothers, 12 were under 14 years old. According to the official, the average age of girls raped by their fathers was between 10 and 12, and the age of those raped by their brothers was between 15 and 16.[476]
- A woman sued her husband for torturing and raping their daughter, now 20 years old. The girl, Elmira, said she had been constantly tortured and raped by her father since she was eight years old.[477]
- Following a research done on 400 child laborers, the executive director of the Organization of Social Services in Tehran's Municipality said, "We are going to prove that 90 per cent of child laborers get raped."[478]
- Sexual abuse is the greatest ailment among young scavenger children.[479]
- 21% of street children in Tehran have experienced sexual relations.[480]
- Rana, 19, who has been engaged in dangerous and harmful jobs such as making spare parts for cars and working with acid since she was 11. Rana's father is an

---

[476] The state-run ISNA news agency, November 2003
[477] The state-run Fararu website, June 2, 2019
[478] The state-run Salamatnews.com, November 8, 2017
[479] Elham Fakhari, member of Tehran's City Council, the state-run Salamatnews.com, November 8, 2017
[480] Ebrahim Ghafari, the social deputy of the Iranian regime's Welfare Organization, October 13, 2015

addict and used to sexually assault her four daughters. The girls were also victimized by other men in the community.[481]

- There have been 16,000 reports of child abuse in just six months. 38% of the abused children are in pre-school and elementary school age, and 12 percent are older.[482]
- More than 13,000 cases of child abuse were reported to and registered by the Social Emergency Room of West Azerbaijan Province (northwestern Iran), during the Persian year 1396 (March 2017- March 2018). The high statistics include only the reported cases.[483]
- Child abuse rose 10 per cent in North Khorasan Province in the course of one year targeting mostly girls.[484]
- A 12-year-old girl and her 7-year-old brother who had been stabbed by their father, died on April 27, 2019, shortly after they were taken to hospital in Fardis, one of Karaj counties.[485]
- A seven-year-old girl, Atena Aslani, became victim of sexual violence and murder in Parsabad on June 19, 2017. Atena's father was a street peddler who sold clothes. The state media identified the suspect as Ismail, a local businessman selling paint.
- A 5-year-old girl in Mashhad suffered brain after being battered by her stepfather. Multiple scars of injury were evident on the girl's abdomen, head, and face upon admission to hospital. After clinical examinations, it became clear that she suffered broken legs, hip, and brain damage.[486]
- A three-year-old girl child went into coma after being beaten by her addicted father. The little girl was taken to a medical center by residents of the village near Marand, in East Azerbaijan Province.[487]
- Three children, including two girl children, were found in the backyard of their house in hot weather being tortured by their father and stepmother. Fatemeh, 12, Omolbanin, 8, and their five-year-old brother, Ali Akbar, were tortured physically and psychologically by an ax, a hammer, hot iron rods, etc. in their home in Taleghan, near Mahshahr, in Khuzestan Province.[488]

---

[481] The state-run Salamatnews.com, November 8, 2017
[482] Reza Jafari, head of Social Emergency Room, the state-run ILNA news agency, February 25, 2018
[483] Mehrdad Motalebi, a sociologist acting as deputy for Social Affairs in the Welfare Organization of West Azerbaijan Province, the state-run uromnews.ir, August 7, 2018
[484] Ali Akbar Sahranavard, the social deputy of the General Welfare Department of North Khorasan Province, the state-run ISNA news agency, April 16, 2019: "Child abuse in 1397 (March 2018- March 2019) has targeted kids between 5 and 11 years old, showing a 10 per cent increase compared to the previous year. Girl children made up the majority of victims of child abuse."
[485] The state-run ISNA news agency, April 27, 2019
[486] The state-run IRNA news agency, May 3, 2017
[487] The state-run ISNA news agency, May 27, 2019
[488] The state-run Asriran.com, April 24, 2018

10. What actions has your country taken in the last five years to improve health outcomes for women and girls in your country?

- **Promoted women's access to health services through expansion of universal health coverage or public health services**

Access to health services is a major problem for the people of Iran due to shortages of hospitals, clinics, doctors, and nurses as well as the high fees charged for medical services.
Since many people do not have insurance, they cannot afford to pay for the high cost of their treatment. The increase in hospital accommodation in the current situation is such that 40% of the beds of private hospitals in the country are vacant due to high prices.[489]
The clerical regime with its irresponsible policies has no intention nor the ability to resolve this crisis. The health budget for the year 2018 was only increased by 6.4% compared to the prior year, while the Ministry of Health had a deficit of 15 trillion tomans ($1.1 million).[490]
The situation is even worse for women due to their special needs, and there has been no considerable measures reported on improvement or expansion of women's access to health services and coverage. This issue has been dealt with in length in a previous section in answer to question 5 on gender-responsive social protection floors to ensure that all women have access to essential health care, childcare facilities and income security. However, we will briefly review some examples of women's lack of access to medical and health services in this section, too.

Rural areas

In underdeveloped rural areas, poverty, malnutrition, and heavy work contribute to health problems among inhabitants, especially women and children.
- There is one medical center for every 3 to 4 villages and most villagers have problems receiving medical care.[491]
- Rural and nomad women have little access to specialist doctors and dentists. Many rural and nomad women die before reaching a medical center when they get sick.[492]
- For 105,000 women living in the cities of Farouj and Shirvan in North Khorasan Province, there is only one mammography machine in Shirvan's hospital. Occasionally, the women of two other cities are also added to the clients.[493]

---

[489] The state-run taadolnewspaper.ir, January 17, 2019
[490] The state-run Bartarinha website, January 27, 2018
[491] Moussa Reza Servati, member of the Social Committee of the Parliament, the state-run Mehr news agency, December 31, 2016
[492] Parichehr Soltani, secretary of the working group on rural and nomad women living in underprivileged areas, the state-run ISNA news agency, October 5, 2016
[493] The official IRNA news agency, August 21, 2019

Urban areas
There is not an acceptable situation in the urban areas, either.
- Urmia is the capital of West Azerbaijan Province in northwestern Iran with more than 73,000 inhabitants.[494] Kowthar Gynecology and Obstetrics Hospital in Urmia is the only specialized maternity hospital in this city.
- It has only 62 beds and lacks the necessary medical facilities for pregnant women. The situation in this hospital is the same as it was 30 years ago, and pregnant women face lots of difficulties at the time of delivery due to lack of facilities and low sanitation in this hospital.[495]
- This case found its way to the media, but it should be considered that the same situation is true for many hospitals in all small cities and towns.

Women in humanitarian settings
Reports from earthquake-hit areas show that many deaths are caused by lack of access to hospitals, medical clinics and health services.
- At least four women and girls were killed after a 5.9-magnitude earthquake struck northwestern Iran on November 8, 2019. One of the victims was the ten-year-old Zahra Abedi who lived in Varnakesh village. Her father, Asghar Abedi, says, "Zahra was trapped under the rubble. Immediately, we pulled her out from under the rubble. My daughter was unconscious, but she was breathing. I quickly took her to (the nearby) Chaldoran. The electricity was cut off there and no one could help Zahra. We could not save her."[496]
- Doctors visit Varankesh village in East Azerbaijan Province two days a week. On the night of the earthquake, no doctor was in the village. So, Zahra's father had to take her to the nearby town of Turkmanchay, but there was also a power outage and, consequently, Zahra died.
- One of the villagers said, "If we had a doctor, maybe Zahra would still be alive with us today."
- Another villager who lost his wife and niece in this earthquake, said his niece, 12, died on the way to hospital. "If there were a hospital, no one would have died."[497]

---

[494] The state-run Tasnim news agency, July 7, 2018
[495] [Kowthar Maternity Hospital in Orumieh lacks minimum medical facilities](), website of the NCRI Women's Committee, July 7, 2018
[496] The state-run Young Journalists Club, November 10, 2019
[497] The state-run ISNA news agency, November 8, 2019

There were similar examples in the earthquake in Kermanshah on November 12, 2017:
- Sanitation was literally non-existent in the areas affected by the earthquake.
- Pregnant women faced the most difficult conditions. The number of miscarriages surged. Most of them also suffered infection due to the difficult conditions of living in tents for months.
- In the first month after the earthquake, 11 pregnant women and 39 pre-school children died in the quake-stricken areas of Kermanshah Province.[498]
- The state-run news agencies published a story on January 24, 2018, reporting the death of a two-year-old girl in Kermanshah, western Iran. Sarina died on January 18, 2018, after catching the flu.[499] More than 70 days after the earthquake, her father says the authorities failed to provide his family a trailer or any form of shelter and the little Sarina died due to the freezing winter cold.
- Sarina's father, Mr. Zahabi, explained, "High fever and repeated seizures worsened Sarina's condition and the clinic in Sarpol-e Zahab did not have a specialist doctor. On January 17, she lost consciousness and we took her to the city's hospital, but they did not have adequate facilities and doctors and they could not do anything for Sarina. They told me to take her to a hospital in Kermanshah."[500]
- Most of the earthquake survivors do not have access to clean potable water due to broken pipelines. In some areas, water is contaminated, and shortage of chlorine is a major problem.
- Most areas are not drained of wastewater and their garbage is not collected. As a result, the areas surrounding the temporary residences of earthquake survivors are extremely contaminated.
- Strong odor, insects and rodents take over the areas and snakes and scorpions are prevalent in the ruins of the buildings, jeopardizing the survivors' health and safety.
- Local officials say some 30 per cent of the live stocks were killed in the earthquake. No action was taken to remove the corpses of animals and the garbage. Many sewage structures were damaged and there was a threat of dangerous diseases spreading.

---

[498] Ibrahim Shakiba, head of the Health Center of Kermanshah, the state-run ISNA news agency, December 5, 2017
[499] Iran: Toddler earthquake victim dies due to freezing cold, website of the NCRI Women's Committee, January 25, 2018
[500] The state-run Tasnim news agency, January 24, 2018

- Expanded specific health services for women and adolescent girls, including sexual and reproductive health services, mental, maternal health, HIV services

Reproductive health

In May 2014, the mullahs' supreme leader Ali Khamenei announced the general population policies:[501]

- Promotion of dynamism, growth and youthfulness of the population by increasing the fertility rate.
- Removal of obstacles to marriage, facilitating and promoting marriage and having more children, lowering the legal age for marriage, etc.

Subsequently, the parliament passed a bill banning any surgery intending to permanently prevent pregnancy and vowing to punish perpetrators.[502]

The parliament also passed another bill in late April 2014 to "increase fertility rate and prevent population decline." According to this bill, all measures related to abortion and vasectomy and all advertisements for birth control and reduction of pregnancy were banned and their perpetrators punished.[503]

The abovementioned laws stripped Iranian women of their fundamental rights to make choices about their own bodies and lives and viewed them as baby-making machines.

Infant mortality

Infant mortality rate in Iran is five times greater than in developed countries. Every year, 15,000 infants and some 300 mothers die during delivery.[504]

A considerable part of infant mortality occurs in underprivileged areas and villages, because there rarely are any medical centers in these areas.[505]

These figures must be considered as being the minimum due to lack of an effective data collection system in Iran and lack of transparency on the part of the government.

AIDS

The number of AIDs victims among women has increased ten folds in the past two years.[506]

47 percent of the 70,000 HIV positive patients in Iran are women. The population of addicted women or women involved with narcotic drugs has tripled over the past several years.[507]

The age of AIDS patients has dropped to 16 in recent years, and the rising trend of contraction of this disease had inclined towards women and teenage girls.[508]

---

[501] Khamenei.ir, May 20, 2014
[502] The state-run ICANA news agency, August 10, 2014
[503] The state-run Kayhan daily newspaper, April 13, 2014
[504] Ali Akbar Sayyari, deputy Minister of Health, the state-run Asr-e Iran website, January 21, 2018
[505] Iraj Khosronia, head of the GI Specialists' Association, the state-run Tabnak website, February 2, 2017
[506] Minoo Mohraz, head of the AIDs Research Center, the state-run khabaronline.ir, May 19, 2018)
[507] Reza Mahboubi, deputy director of the Interior Ministry's Social Affairs Organization, the state-run ISNA news agency – August 20, 2019
[508] Massoud Mardani, member of the National AIDS Committee, the state-run Shafaqna.ir, July 30, 2015

Regime experts have explicitly confessed that official statistics must be multiplied by 5 and sometimes by 7, to find the actual number of AIDS victims. For women, the numbers must be multiplied by 10 because many women are unaware of this virus.

All women suffering from AIDS complain from lack of special medical centers. For example, there are not enough dental clinics or gynecologists. These patients have problem receiving medical treatment for mouth and dental illnesses, and for gynecology and childbirth. A number of them speak of being mistreated by the medical community. Patients say doctors rarely accept them, so they have to conceal their illness.[509]

In October 2019, at least 300 residents of a village including hundreds of women, children and infants contracted AIDs.[510]
Residents of Chenar Mahmoudi village say that a health clinic agent used disposable syringes multiple times to take diabetes test from them. This led to the sudden outburst of HIV virus and contraction of the disease by so many people. Some residents say as many as 500 people have been affected. Some residents refused to have the test fearing they would also contract the disease. One of the victims was a six-month baby who contracted a skin disease after being injected. Her lips chapped and her mouth foamed.[511]

- **Ensured access to prevention, treatment, and palliative care for non-communicable diseases (heart disease, chronic respiratory diseases, diabetes, and cancers)?**

The cost of treatment for heart disease, chronic respiratory disease, diabetes, and cancer are far beyond what most Iranian women can afford since they are not covered by insurance:
- The cost of changing a heart valve has increased from 3 to 12 million tomans. This while insurance companies do not cover this operation.[512]
- The cost of heart surgery in Iran is the world's highest.[513]
- The monthly expenses for the medications for CF patients are 4.5 million tomans.[514]
- The yearly expenses for treatment of Asthma is between 1.8 and 2.4 million tomans.[515]
- The cost for the treatment of a diabetic patient is 2 million tomans a year.[516]
- Every year, some 13,000 women suffer breast cancer, the cost of whose treatment is on the rise, while there is no screening system in the country to detect and prevent cancer.[517]

---

[509] The state-run Tasnim news agency, February 21, 2018
[510] The state-run ROKNA news agency, October 2, 2019
[511] [Hundreds including women, children infected with HIV in Chenar Mahmoudi](#), website of the NCRI Women's Committee, October 4, 2019
[512] The state-run salamatnews.com, January 2014
[513] The state-run Mehr news agency, December 23, 2008
[514] The official IRNA news agency, October 13, 2018; the official IRNA news agency, October 13, 2018
[515] The state-run ISNA news agency, May 3, 2014; the state-run Fars news agency, May 3, 2015
[516] Ali Rabbani, the state-run ILNA news agency, August 14, 2018
[517] Salem Khabar website, October 13, 2019

In the meantime, there is no ensured access to medical care for anyone in Iran. There are numerous cases where people are not admitted to hospital for treatment or not released until they pay for hospital expenses.

- A 35-year-old woman from Mashhad had a natural delivery which is free according to the law, but she and her newborn were held for five days by the hospital until her husband, a seasonal worker, paid the hospital's expenses.[518] They charged the poor couple 1.2 million tomans, i.e. 380,000 tomans for every day of stay at hospital.
- A homeless woman, 22, was hospitalized for a severe case of influenza. The hospital refused to dismiss her because she could not pay for the hospital fees. The hospital charged the homeless woman for 5.5 million rials ($153) and another 1.7 million rials ($50) for pharmaceuticals.[519]

- **Strengthened comprehensive sexuality education in schools or through community programs**

The Iranian regime does not allow sexual education in schools or through community programs. This was one of the reasons, they opposed the United Nations Education 2030 agenda.[520]

- **Gathered data on the health status of marginalized groups of women such as women with disabilities, lesbian, bisexual and transgender women, ethnic minorities, indigenous women, etc.**

According to statistics released by the mullahs' parliament in 2017, more than 11 million disabled people live in Iran, with women accounting for 35% of this population. The number of disabled women who have to earn their living was 39,372, almost twice as much as disabled men in the same situation.[521] Annually, 100,000 people are added to the number of disabled persons in Iran.[522]

Disabled people make up about 3-5% of the population of unemployed in each region. The number of unemployed disabled women is twice the number of men. Only one-sixth of women with disabilities might have an opportunity in the job market. While others cannot even afford to pay for their own transportation. This situation also makes them incapacitated for their medical and healthcare expenses which is an immediate basic necessity for any person with disabilities.[523]

---

[518] The state-run ROKNA news agency, January 24, 2018
[519] Iran: Homeless woman forced to stay in hospital until she pays for fees, website of the NCRI Women's Committee, December 22, 2015
[520] Education 2030 Framework for Action (SDG4) and Iranian officials' hysteric reactions to it, website of the NCRI Women's Committee, Special Report, June 2017
[521] Disabled women disregarded under inhumane policies in Iran, website of the NCRI Women's Committee, December 1, 2018
[522] The state-run fararu.com, October 18, 2019
[523] Iran: Unemployment of disabled women is twice as much as men's, website of the NCRI Women's Committee, December 16, 2016

Women with disabilities are 1.5 times more likely to suffer violence, harassment, abuse and discrimination than men with disabilities.[524] Disabled women are forced to accept and tolerate cruel behavior and relationships because of their physical and social limits.

Poverty of the family, lack of decent homes, lack of urban services and appropriate transportation services for the disabled, and lack of educational facilities required for the disabled contribute to exclusion of people with disabilities from society.[525]

In 2004, the Iranian regime passed a law entitled 'Disabled Persons' Rights' that remained unimplemented. In 2017, a general bill on this issue was again passed by the mullahs' parliament, the implementation of which was made contingent on the adequacy of the government budget and, therefore, was not enforced.

- **Provided post-abortion care services and decriminalized abortion**

Abortion is essentially illegal in Iran, unless it is done for medical purpose to save the life of mother when the fetus is less than 19 weeks old.[526]

A Health Ministry official said between 300 to 500 thousand illegal abortions are carried out in Iran, every year, adding that from the 1,000 abortions that are carried out in Iran every day, only ten are legal.[527]

There are also numerous reports on the arrest and imprisonment of the doctors, nurses and midwives involved in illegal abortions.

- **Other**

Depression

Depression is one of the widespread health problems in Iran. Again, there are no accurate statistics available.

According to one source, some 13.5 per cent of the Iranian population suffer from depression. (This amounts to over 10 million people.) 16% of Iranian women and about 10 per cent of Iranian men have been reported to be depressed.[528]

The regime's Health Minister, however, stated that 6.4 million people are depressed in Iran, and women have a greater share of depression.[529]

---

[524] Iran: Mentally retarded woman raped in a government center, website of the NCRI Women's Committee, September 7, 2017

[525] Iran: Disabled woman has to feed from the trash bin, website of the NCRI Women's Committee, September 25, 2017

[526] The state-run Tasnim news agency, July 21, 2013; the state-run salamatnews.com, August 30, 2016

[527] Mohammad Baqer Larijani, educational deputy to the Health Minister, the state-run Fars news agency, August 20, 2019

[528] Arash Mirabzadeh, secretary of the Scientific Association of Psychiatrists, the state-run ILNA News Agency – September 19, 2017

[529] The state-run hamshahrionline.ir, April 9, 2017

Suicides

Under the clerical regime, suicides have been on the rise and Iran stands as the first record holder in the Middle East with regards to suicides among women.

Increasing pressure and restrictions imposed on Iranian women in addition to various obstacles to their employment and social activities, the marriage laws and widespread poverty, are some of the main causes of growing depression and despair among women in Iran, leading to a growing rate of suicides among women.

- Mohammad Mehdi Tondgouyan, deputy youths' affairs in the Ministry of Sports and Youths, for the first time revealed the figures on suicide in Iran on August 19, 2018. He said 4,992 persons had committed suicide in Iran from March 2017 to March 2018, adding, "Two-thirds of those inclined to commit suicide are women and one-third are men."
- Tondgooyan added that the Greater Tehran Province had the highest rate of suicide in the country. He said that on the average, most suicides occur in the age ranges of 25-34, and 35 and above, but that under-17 suicides have been occurring for several years. "According to the latest figures, 212 youngsters under the age of 17 committed suicide."[530]
- The Iranian Journal of Forensic and Legal Medicine published the annual statistics on suicide in Iran in September 2018. According to this report, more than 1,365 women committed suicide in the Persian year 1396 (March 2017 - March 2018).
- Maryam Abbassi Nejad, head of the Health Ministry's Plan to Prevent Suicides, said 100,000 suicides were registered in Iran during the Persian Year 1397 (March 2018- March 2019)
- In recent years, a shocking number of young mothers and pregnant women are committing suicide in Iran due to growing poverty among the populace.[531]

---

[530] The state-run ILNA news agency – August 19, 2018
[531] Suicides among women in Iran tops rates in Middle East, website of the NCRI Women's Committee, September 9, 2019

Suicides of women in Iran

Top record holder in the Middle East

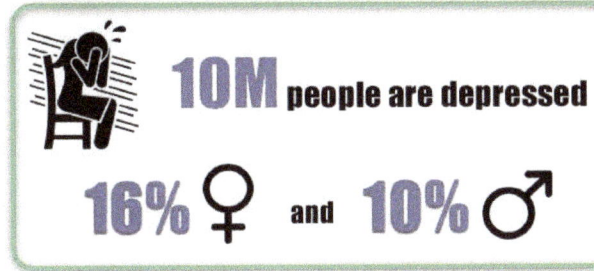
10M people are depressed
16% ♀ and 10% ♂

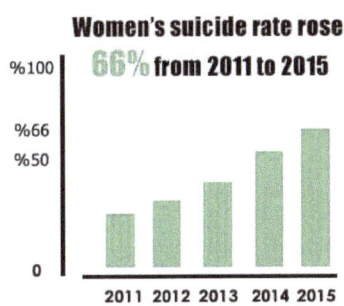
Women's suicide rate rose 66% from 2011 to 2015

100,000 suicides registered (March 2018-March 2019)

---

11. What actions has your country taken in the last five years to improve education outcomes and skills for women and girls?

• Undertake constitutional amendments and/or other appropriate legislative action to ensure the protection and enforcement of the rights of girls and women to, within and through education and throughout the life cycle

Principle 30 of the Iranian Constitution stipulates: "The government is obliged to provide free elementary and high school education for all members of the nation and facilitate free higher education for all until the country is self-sufficient."
But education in Iran is neither free nor mandatory.[532]
Schools and universities are formally asking for tuition from students, which further contributes to school drop outs since more than 80 percent of the populace are living below the poverty line. 37 percent of Iranian students drop out of school before getting their diploma, and only 7 percent of high school graduates are admitted to universities.[533]
More girls are deprived of education compared to boys.[534]

---

[532] Ali Bagherzadeh, deputy Minister of Education and head of the Literacy Movement Organization, the state-run Salamatnews.com, April 25, 2018
[533] The head of the Association of Skills Training Schools, the state-run Fars news agency, November 4, 2017
[534] Shahindokht Molaverdi, former director of the presidential directorate on Women and Family Affairs, October 2016

The number of girls deprived of education in Iran is three to four time greater than boys.[535] What is meant by "deprived of education" is any girl or boy between 6 and 18 years of age who is not present in the national education cycle.[536]

In many border provinces, high schools cover only 50 per cent of girls in high school level. This means that between 40 to 50 per cent of girl students remain out of school.[537]

Early marriages contribute to girls dropping out of school. However, the bill to increase the age of marriage for girl children in Iran was rejected in December 2018 by the Legal and Judicial Committee of the parliament for containing "religious and social deficiencies" and for contradicting "the teachings of Islam."[538]

The Iranian regime has not undertaken any constitutional amendment or legislative action to ensure the protection and enforcement of the rights of girls and women to, within and through education and throughout the life cycle.

- **Taken measures to increase girls' access to, retention in and completion of education, technical and vocational education and training (TVET) and skills development programs.**

The latest estimates put the number of illiterates in Iran around 11 million, i.e. 13 per cent of the population, two-thirds of whom are women and girls.[539]

This shows 1.5-million increase in seven years considering the figure of 9,483,028 in 2011, announced by the National Statistics Center (NSC). Approximately two-thirds of this illiterate population are women and girls.

The growing number of illiterates in Iran is unfortunately a good indication that the ruling regime has not taken any measures to increase girls' access to, retention in and completion of education, technical and vocational education and training (TVET) and skills development programs.

There are more than 15 million school-age children and youths in Iran, but the student population is only 13 million. This means that at least 2 million Iranian students, including a large number of girls, have not been able to go to school and are deprived of the basic education.[540]

A total of 4.23 per cent of students dropped out of school in 2017-2018 academic year. Girl students constituted 4.17 per cent of it, meaning that there is a whopping gap between girls' and boys' drop outs. Girls are more vulnerable relative to boys.[541]

---

[535] Massoumeh Ebtekar, director of the presidential directorate on Women and Family Affairs, the official IRNA news agency, September 16, 2019

[536] Massoumeh Ebtekar, director of the presidential directorate on Women and Family Affairs, the state-run ANA news agency, September 17, 2019

[537] Rezvan Hakimzadeh, the Education Ministry's deputy for elementary schools, The state-run ILNA news agency, September 9, 2017

[538] Allahyar Malekshahi, chair of the Legal and Judicial Committee of the mullahs' parliament, the state-run Fars news agency, December 23, 2018

[539] The state-run salamatnews.com, September 26, 2018

[540] The state-run salamatnews.com, September 26, 2018

[541] Abbas Soltanian, deputy for mid-level education in the Ministry of Education, the state-run ILNA news agency, June 25, 2018

In some Iranian provinces, the percentage of illiteracy is over 30 per cent and a considerable number of children under 17 do not have the opportunity to continue their education.

Drop-out of girls older than 6 years of age is widespread in the provinces of Sistan and Baluchestan, Khuzestan, Western Azerbaijan, and Eastern Azerbaijan, comprising the country's highest rates of illiteracy.[542]

More than 98 percent of girls in Kurdish villages and other parts of Iran drop out of school and stay home after finishing elementary education without having any professional or artistic plans or activities.

Many rural families bring their daughters out of school because they do not afford to pay for their tuition.[543]

In November 2017, all the girl students in the Zilaii region in Boyer Ahmad, had to quit their school because there was no separate school for girls and their families did not afford to pay for their transportation to a segregated school in another place.[544]

Shortage of resources leads to Iran's nomad students dropping out of school. Between 46 to 50 per cent of nomad students drop out of school after finishing their elementary education. Factors such as living in distant places, severe cold, and lack of transportation to school, make education conditions extremely difficult for nomad girls especially in Sistan and Baluchestan Province (southeastern Iran) and in some instances lead to the students dropping out of school.[545]

At least 25,000 school-aged children in Tehran, are working instead of attending school.[546]

- **Strengthened educational curricula to increase gender-responsiveness and eliminate bias, at all levels of education**

Gender bias is inherent to the educational system in Iran and is promoted by the government and religious authorities. Iranian leaders and officials opposed signing on to the Education 2030 Framework of Action (SDG4) because it seeks gender equality and equal opportunities for girls and future women of Iran.[547]

Women are systematically deprived of studying in at least 77 fields of study and accordingly deprived of working in the related fields.[548]

Not only are there all-women universities, banning young women from enrolling in certain fields, but there were even attempts by some officials to segregate kindergartens and pre-schools,[549] and separate textbooks for grade schoolgirls and boys.[550]

---

[542] The state-run Khabaronline website, November 18, 2015
[543] The state-run IRNA news agency, December 25, 2016
[544] The state-run Tnews website, November 12, 2017
[545] Mohammad Reza Seifi, director of the Office of Nomads' Education, the state-run Mizan news agency, January 28, 2018
[546] Director-general of Tehran's Department of Education, the state-run ANA news agency, October 2015
[547] Education 2030 Framework of Action and Iranian officials' hysteric reactions to it, website of the NCRI Women's Committee, July 2017
[548] Countless obstacles before women's education and employment, Special Report, February 2016, website of the NCRI Women's Committee, women.ncr-iran.org
[549] Habibollah John-Nessari, acting commander of the State Security Force Special Units, the state-run Aftabnews.ir - October 2, 2019: "Why is it that today, in the kindergartens of the capital, our mothers and sisters

- Revised and developed non-stereotypical educational curricula, textbooks and teaching materials to eliminate traditional gender stereotypes, address gender-based violence against women and girls

70 percent of the textbooks in the elementary schools in Iran are male-oriented including the images, names, roles, tools, etc.[551]

There is no law preventing teaching of violence in children's books. As it can be seen in the picture below, a shepherd has hanged the dog protecting the herd for his complicity with the wolf. In another picture, the mice have handcuffed and hanged a cat. Such pictures teach and promote use of violence, animal abuse and suicide.[552]

As such, there are no grounds for revising or developing non-stereotypical educational curricula, textbooks and teaching materials to eliminate traditional gender stereotypes, address gender-based violence against women and girls.

---

put the hand of a 5-year-old girl in the hand of a boy, and under the excuse of having a party, they play music and have the kids dance together? We must know that today the enemy has targeted our religion."

[550] Habibollah John-Nessari, acting commander of the State Security Force Special Units, the state-run Aftabnews.ir – October 2, 2019

[551] Seyed Javad Hosseini, caretaker Minister of Education, the state-run ISNA news agency, July 31, 2019

[552] The state-run ILNA news agency, May 24, 2016

- Provided gender equality and human rights training for teachers and other education professionals

The Iranian regime considers gender equality and human rights as western ideas. As a result, they have not attempted and would never do to provide for teaching such taboos at schools, or train the teachers and other education professionals.

- Integrated age-appropriate education on women's human rights, gender equality and peace education into school curricula at all levels

The following example clearly shows what the regime has done towards integrating women's human rights, gender equality and peace education into school curricula at all levels:
In the months leading to the Iranian regime's presidential elections in spring 2017, Education 2030 document turned into an issue of wrangling among the regime's internal factions. Finally, on June 13, 2017, the Supreme Council of Cultural Revolution (SCCR) meeting presided by the mullahs' president Hassan Rouhani decided to stop implementation of the agenda in education and instead consider the Fundamental Reform Document of Education (FRDE) adopted under Mahmoud Ahmadinejad in December 2011, as the benchmark for all educational affairs in the country.
In a meeting with teachers on May 7, 2017, Khamenei blasted the Agenda 2030 and said, "The UNESCO 2030 education agenda and the like are not agendas that the Islamic Republic of Iran should have to surrender and submit to."[553]
The reason for such opposition to the UN Agenda 2030 on education was vividly expressed in an article published by the state-run Tasnim news agency which wrote:
"In the (Education) 2030 Framework for Action, there are references to terms such as global citizenship and gender equality… the adoption and implementation of this document would transform national education in many ways. Among them, one can point to the omission of sexual stereotypes, teaching of sex education to children, and omission of some Quranic concepts and values from textbooks to promote peace and non-violence."[554]
Not only the Fundamental Reform Document of Education (FRDE) devised and implemented by Iranian regime does not attempt to eliminate inequalities, create a culture of tolerance, or promote peace and non-violence, it seeks to preserve and enhance the fundamentalist views of the ruling regime, promoting war, violence and terrorism as well as gender, religious and ethnic discriminations.[555]
Under the pretext of "modesty," the FRDE seeks to enforce the veil, gender segregation and regulations against women by frequently repeating this term in its articles.[556]

---

[553] Khamenei.ir website, May 7, 2017
[554] The state-run Tasnim news agency, May 7, 2017
[555] Education 2030 Framework for Action (SDG4) and Iranian officials' hysteric reactions to it, website of the NCRI Women's Committee, Special Report, June 2017
[556] Ibid.

- Promoted safe, harassment-free and inclusive educational environments for women and girls, including use of technology and internet

Inclusive educational environments for women and girls

In some mixed-gender schools or girls' schools with male teachers, schoolgirls are deprived of physical education. In deprived regions, girls play in a corner during the physical education hour.[557]

Girls do not have access to secondary educational centers. This is while the secondary educational centers like libraries, cultural centers, and the centers for the education of children and youths have been designed for use by both sexes.[558]

- Increased access to skills and training in new and emerging fields, especially STEM (science, technology, engineering and math) and digital fluency and literacy

Access to skills and training in new and emerging fields, especially STEM (science, technology, engineering and math) and digital fluency and literacy has not increased in any way. On the contrary, there have been numerous reports indicating restriction of women's access to basic education and existing fields, along with demands for tuition which deprive students from low-income families from continuing their education.

Restriction of education fields for women

The efforts by the Iranian regime to eliminate women from higher education were intensified in 2012, when women were officially banned from studying in 77 fields of study.[559]

- Women were deprived of most of mathematical and technical sciences with 36 fields.
- In 2013, on the order of the Minister of Education, gender segregation was intensified and the number of universities with only male or female students increased to 29. [560]
- In 2014, some 47 universities rejected female students in various fields. Gender-based quotas strongly favored male students. The number of gender-based majors reached 215, as a result of government policies.[561]
- In 2018, about 60 percent of those who enrolled for the national university entrance exam were female. In the same year's master's test, about 51 percent of volunteers were men and 49 percent women, and in the doctoral exam, about 57 percent were male and only 43 percent women.[562]

---

[557] Minister of Education Mohammad Bat'haii, the state-run ISNA news agency, September 17, 2017
[558] Minister of Education Mohammad Bat'haii, the state-run ISNA news agency, September 17, 2017
[559] The state-run Tabnak website, August 9, 2012; the state-run khabaronline website, August 7, 2012
[560] The state-run khabaronline website, August 14, 2012; the state-run Tasnim news agency, April 16, 2013
[561] Daneshjoonews.com and the state-run Tabnak website, August 6, 2014
[562] The state-run Tabnak.ir, August 2, 2018

Failure to provide access to skills and training

Under the clerical rule, the quality of education has deteriorated, and students constantly protest the low quality of education and lack of labs and equipment to advance their studies. Instead of attending to the labs and equipment, university authorities spend their time, energy and funds on monitoring the outfits and head covering of female students.

- Girl students of the University of Qom expressed their protest on October 18, 2016, against discriminations and deprivations in the university policies.[563]
  They said all the educational accommodations at the Technical School of Massoumiyeh are exclusively at the disposal of male students and even on special occasions, the school's main educational services are granted to male students. They also complained of the extremely low quality of education at the Technical School.
- On April 23, 2018, young women participated in an act of protest at the College of Environment in Karaj, to protest transformation of the college into a training center for environmental protection guards.[564]
- Students of Jondishapur School of Dentistry in Ahvaz (southwestern Iran) held a protest rally on September 26, 2017 against lack of educational space.
- Girl students of the Medical School of Azad University in Shahrood (northeastern Iran) refused to attend their exam on July 24, 2017 and protested against bad educational conditions.

Iranian students have been also protesting universities' demand for tuition which deprives students from low-income families from continuing their education.

- Students of Tehran's Allameh Tabatabaii University staged a protest on April 29, 2018 and spoke out against the policy of Rouhani's government to obtain tuitions from college students. They held placards which read, "No to college tuitions", "Allameh U is an economic firm", etc.
- Masters students of the University of Urmia held a three-day protest, February 14-17, 2018, against the policy of demanding tuition from students.
- Students of Tehran's University of Art also held a protest on February 17, 2018, against the policy of receiving tuition from students.
- On May 9, 2018, the students of Urmia University spread empty table cloths on the ground in protest to a plan for charging students for course units.

---

[563] Monthly report of the NCRI Women's Committee, October 2016
[564] The state-run Mehr news agency – April 22, 2018

- **Ensured access to safe water and sanitation services and facilitated menstrual hygiene management, especially in schools and other education/training settings**

Three young girls drowned while drinking water from a *Hootag* (water ditch). The tragic incident took place in Chabahar, in the deprived Sistan and Baluchestan Province, on May 29, 2019.[565]
In the absence of pipelines and even tankers, people in this region dig ditches to collect rain as a water reservoir for both humans and animals. Monireh Khedmati, Maryam Khedmati and Sierra Delshab were studying in the second and third grade.
In the rural areas, most girls drop out of school before reaching the age of menstruation.

- **Strengthened measures to prevent adolescent pregnancies and to enable adolescent girls to continue their education in the case of pregnancy and/or motherhood**

Adolescent pregnancies out of marriage are considered a taboo in Iran and under the prevalent culture. So, if a teenage girl gets pregnant out of marriage, it is considered the end of life for her. If not killed by her brother or father, she would be rejected by her family and community, let alone continuing her education. This is a cultural issue which has been further promoted and strengthened under the ruling clerical regime under the pretext of Islam.
Likewise, sex education and measures to prevent adolescent pregnancies are not applicable.

But adolescent and teenage pregnancies are widespread due to large number of early marriages which are the main cause of girls' leaving school and discontinuing their education. The number of early marriages of girl children in Iran has seen a delirious rise in recent years.
Ali Kazemi, advisor for the legal deputy of the Judiciary Branch, announced on March 4, 2019, that in the course of just one year (March 2018-March 2019), some 5 to 600,000 child marriages had taken place in Iran.[566]
According to article 1210, the age of maturity for a girl is 9 lunar years and for a boy 15 lunar years. In addition, article 1041 of the Civil Code sanctions marriage of girl children under 13 years of age with the consent of father.
If schools find out that a girl has got married, they expel her from school and she can only continue her education in night classes with adults.[567]

- **Ensure women's participation in management of educational institutions**

Principally, women's participation is not ensured in any field including management, economy and politics. As far as women's participation in management of educational institutions is concerned, there are no specific data and information available.
However, in 2016, a government official acknowledged that 2 million girls had graduated from Iran's universities in the past 20 years, comprising over 60 percent of college graduates, but unemployment rate among women had increased.[568]

---

[565] The official IRNA news agency, May 29, 2019
[566] The state-run ILNA news agency, March 5, 2019
[567] The state-run Taghrib news agency, December 17, 2018

Likewise, the advisor to the Minister of Science, Research and Technology in women's affairs, said only 16% of the faculty members of universities are women while 40% of Ph.D. graduates were female.[569]

- **Other**

The education system in Iran is sick

Seyyed Mohammad Javad Abtahi, member of the Education and Research Committee of the mullahs' parliament, declared on September 25, 2018, that the number of illiterates in Iran had reached 11 million, a figure which indicates "numerous flaws in the country's educational system."

Abtahi said, "We should be ashamed that the average age of social crimes has dropped to 11 or 12."

"There is no doubt that the educational system in Iran is sick and is threading away from standard education," he added.[570]

---

[568] Sussan Bastani, deputy for strategic studies in Rouhani's presidential directorate for Women and Family Affairs, interview with the state-run ISNA news agency, February 13, 2016
[569] Elaheh Hejazi, advisor to the Minister of Science and Higher Education in women's affairs, the state-run ANA news agency, January 29, 2017
[570] The state-run salamatnews.com, September 26, 2018

FREEDOM FROM VIOLENCE, STIGMA AND STEREOTYPES

12. In the last five years, which forms of violence against women and girls has your country prioritized for action?

The ruling regime in Iran has no priority for dealing with violence against women. As a matter of fact, they have been foot dragging for nearly a decade in the adoption of the bill on violence against women. As a result, violence against women has spread and intensified without being criminalized, to the extent that the regime's experts and officials have had to acknowledge the gravity of the situation. Here are some statements:

Iran has one of the highest rates of violence against women

After road accidents and street fights, the main reason for women referring to the Coroner's Office in Tehran is being battered by their husbands

Violence against Women is institutionalized in Iran

- %66 of Iranian women experience domestic violence
- Domestic violence against women saw a %20 rise (March 2017 - March 2018)
- Over 35,000 women were battered and bloodied (March 2018 – March 2019)
- Most victims are between 20 and 35

- Iran has one of the highest statistics on violence against women.[571]
- Today, we see that violence (against women) has become institutionalized.[572]
- Domestic violence against women is pervasive in society. Clearly, we see many forms of violence against women in society.[573]
- Domestic violence against women in Iran saw a 20% rise from March 2017 to March 2018.[574]
- 66 per cent of Iranian women experience domestic violence in their lifetime.[575] (Although the given figure is double the world average of one-in-every-three women (or 33%), it must be considered a blatant mitigation of the reality.)
- Violence against wives ranks second only after violence against children in Iran.[576]
- After road accidents and street fights, the main reason for women referring to the Coroner's Office in Tehran is being battered by their husbands.[577]
- Most victims of domestic violence are women between 20 and 35 years of age.[578]

Of course, when the regime's experts and officials speak about violence against women, they focus on domestic violence. While in Iran, the main forms of violence against women are carried out by state agents and sponsored by the state.

- **Violence perpetrated by state actors**

Enforcing the mandatory *Hijab*
The most common and widespread form of violence against women in Iran is the state-sponsored measures to force Iranian women to observe their *Hijab*.
- A report by the Office of Cultural Studies of the Research Center of the mullahs' parliament (Majlis), published in July 2018, indicated that some 70% of Iranian women do not believe in the mandatory dress-code, namely the head-to-toe black veil or *Chador*, imposed by the regime.[579]
- The report confirms that Iranian women observe the veil only through coercion and harsh restrictions.[580]

---

[571] VAW expert Parastoo Sarmadi, the state-run ILNA news agency, September 18, 2018

[572] Parvaneh Salahshouri, member of the mullahs' parliament, the state-run ILNA news agency, September 18, 2018

[573] Parvaneh Salahshouri, head of women's faction in the mullahs' parliament, the state-run IRNA news agency, November 25, 2017

[574] Reza Jafari, head of the Social Emergencies, interview with the official IRNA news agency, July 18, 2018

[575] Fatemeh Ghassempour, head of the Research Center on Women and Family in Tehran, the state-run ISNA news agency, November 16, 2018

[576] Kamel Delpasand, sociologist and a researcher in social sciences, interview with the official IRNA news agency, July 18, 2018

[577] Tehran's forensic officials, January 2017

[578] Ali Hadizadegan, head of the Coroner's Office of Mashhad, The state-run Fars news agency, November 23, 2017

[579] The official website of the clerical regime's parliament, ICANA.com, July 2018

[580] The compulsory veil in Iran – regime admits most women defy, website of NCRI Women's Committee, July 31, 2018

- The Iranian regime spends exorbitant sums of money to pay for 26 government and state agencies as well as 301 associations in charge of enforcing the veil and monitoring Iranian women's observance of the mandatory *Hijab* or veil.[581]
- One of the regime's top officials revealed that the Assembly to Promote Virtue and Forbid Evil has 30,000 members in 26 provinces who send their reports every six months directly to the supreme leader.[582]
- The Commander of the State Security Force (SSF), Hossein Ashtari, announced in September 2016 that, "Some 2000 women who wear improper clothing are arrested every day in Tehran and some other provinces."[583]

Obviously, these arrests are not peaceful. The video clips substantiating violent treatment of women on the streets by guidance patrols and SSF agents, bring to life the horror Iranian women experience and watch for in every moment of their lives.

- Maryam Shariatmadari, 32, a student of Computer Sciences at Tehran's Amir Kabir University, was pushed off a telecoms box by a State Security Force officer and hurt in the knee on February 23, 2018, when she was protesting mandatory *Hijab* by removing her shawl.
- On April 18, 2018, at least four SSF Guidance Patrols attacked four young women in a park, beating and shoving them around for improper veiling. One of the young women who had a heart condition went unconscious as a result of the beatings.[584]
  - In response to the public outrage, Hossein Rahimi, Tehran's Chief of Police, declared, "We powerfully defend our agents."
  - On April 30, 2018, SSF Commander Hossein Ashtari announced that the officer involved had been granted a plaque and honored at the SSF command headquarters.
  - Finally, in November, the Prosecutor of the Armed Forces' Judiciary Organization turned down the complaint filed by two of the victims, saying their evidence for incriminating the officers was insufficient.
- Another case was reported on June 26, 2019, when a young woman, 15, was violently arrested by SSF plainclothes agents in a park in Tehran for not observing the veil during a water-gun game with her friends.[585]
- In late October 2019, a young woman walking without the veil in a park in Shahr-e Ray was brutalized by an SSF agent. The video clip of this incident was posted on the internet.[586]

---

[581] A Network of 26 Agencies Charged with Clamping Down on Women in Iran, website of NCRI Women's Committee, September 19, 2016
[582] Mostafa Izadi, one of Khamenei's deputies in the General Staff of the Armed Forces, the official IRNA news agency – September 30, 2019
[583] The state-run Tasnim news agency, September 29, 2016
[584] Young woman badly brutalized in Tehran by Guidance Patrols, website of NCRI Women's Committee, April 21, 2018
[585] Violent arrest of a young woman by plainclothes agents causes outrage, website of NCRI Women's Committee, June 26, 2019

These are just a few examples which were filmed and documented. In thousands of cases every day, the State Security forces brutalize women out of the public eye.

Death penalty

Iran is the only country in the world that executes so many women.

105 women have been executed during Rouhani's tenure since August 2013.[587]

The majority of the women executed are themselves victims of domestic violence and discriminatory family laws. Many act in self-defense against mistreatment by their husbands and a system that miserably fails to protect them.[588]

The death sentences are issued at the end of unfair, closed-door trials coupled with torture to force prisoners into making confessions.

In a letter published on July 27, 2019, political prisoner Golrokh Ebrahimi Iraee, addressed the issue of women convicted of murder and sentenced to death:

"In meeting women convicted of murder, I learned that a large percentage of them had murdered their husbands ---instantly or based on a pre-meditated plan—after years of being humiliated, insulted, battered and even tortured by them and because of being deprived of their right to divorce. Although, they consider themselves criminals but are convinced that if any of their repeated appeals for divorce had been granted, they would not have committed such a crime."[589]

---

[586] Security Force beats up young woman walking without the compulsory veil, website of NCRI Women's Committee, October 30, 2019

[587] List of women executed under Rouhani, website of NCRI Women's Committee

[588] Eleven women imprisoned on death row held in Qarchak Prison, website of the NCRI Women's Committee, October 24, 2018

[589] Mounting repression of women in Iran, in step with growing discontent, Monthly Report NCRI Women's Committee, July 2019

Mistreatment of political prisoners
Political prisoners are systematically brutalized and mistreated to be forced into making false confessions, cooperating with the regime, or giving their information.

- On January 24, 2018, political prisoners Golrokh Ebrahimi Iraee and Atena Daemi were brutalized and forcibly transferred from Evin Prison to the Qarchak Prison in Varamin (a.k.a. Shahr-e Ray), in breach of the principle of separation of prisoners of different categories.
- In June 2019, it was reported that political prisoner Ameneh Zaheri Sari was brutalized in the notorious Sepidar Prison of Ahvaz.
- Saba Kord Afshari, 20, was arrested and imprisoned on June 1, 2019, and tortured for months to cooperate with the regime. IRGC interrogators even arrested her mother to further pressure her. Once they failed, they gave her a prison sentence

of 24 years for removing her veil while walking in public. Her sentence was later commuted to 9 years.[590]
- Kurdish activist Zahra Mohammadi was violently arrested in Sanandaj on May 23, 2019 and tortured for months to force her into making false confessions against herself. She was temporarily freed on December 2, 2019 on a heavy bail of 700 million tomans ($61,000) until her verdict is issued.
- The regime also handed down many flogging sentences of 74 to 148 lashes for women activists in 2019, including for Atefeh Rangriz, Parisa Rafii, Nahid Khodajoo, Marzieh Amiri, Nasrin Javadi, Sepideh Farhan, Nasrin Sotoudeh, among others.[591]
- At least in one case, 74 lashes were carried out for Sufi woman Elham Ahmadi before releasing her from prison, on August 13, 2019.[592]

There have been several reports on women activists being brutalized in their prison cells.

- Labor activist Neda Naji was beaten up in Qarchak Prison at least once on July 6, 2019, and a second time along with three other inmates, Yasaman Aryani, Atefeh Rangriz and Sepideh Qolian, on July 26, 2019.[593]
- In another case on February 8 and 9, 2019, all prisoners of wards 1 and 2 of Qarchak Prison were brutalized, pepper gassed and deprived of food and water for demanding medical treatment for a sick inmate.[594]

Violent arbitrary arrests

The arrest and imprisonment of people for their political or religious beliefs is contrary to the international law. Article 18 of the Universal Declaration of Human Rights stipulates: "Everyone has the right to freedom of thought, conscience and religion."

The clerical regime ruling Iran, however, has numerous agencies to clamp down on the public, each of which acts independently to arrest anyone who opposes the regime. The State Security Force (SSF), the Islamic Revolutionary Guard Corps (IRGC), the paramilitary Bassij, and even the disciplinary committees at the universities are components of a vast network that cracks down on the Iranian people's freedom of thought, expression and gathering.

These agencies arrest women in public or at home, often without presenting legal warrants and by use of brute force and violence.

In the majority of cases, including those of political prisoners Atena Daemi and Golrokh Ebrahimi, the IRGC Sarallah Corps filed complaints as complainant. Then it sent a team of its own agents to make the arrest and then interrogate and determine the charges in subsequent stages. This organ also influences the stage of issuing verdicts without any effort to conceal its role.

---

[590] Saba Kord Afshari sentenced to 24 years for refusing video confessions, website of NCRI Women's Committee, August 27, 2019
[591] Monthly Report of the NCRI Women's Committee, August 2019
[592] Ibid.
[593] Monthly Report of the NCRI Women's Committee, July 2019
[594] Qarchak Prison Guards Attack and Injure Female Prisoners, website of the NCRI Women's Committee, February 8, 2019

Political prisoner Atena Daemi who is currently incarcerated in Evin prison for her activities in defense of human rights and against the death penalty, shared part of her arrest experience.[595] In part of a letter leaked out of prison, she wrote, "They attacked our house today, November 26, 2016... Three agents who arrest women on the streets for being mal-veiled, invaded my privacy and watched me while I was not wearing a veil!

"According to the law, they must have sent me a subpoena and waited at least five days for me to report in to the prison. Even if I did not go, prison agents or agents of the Directorate of Implementation of Sentences were the ones who could come and arrest me, not the Revolutionary Guards' Sarallah Corps...

"We opened the door and asked to see their written warrant; they did not show any but roamed into the house... Again, I asked them to show their warrant, but they attacked me. A woman started beating me and when my younger sister intervened, she pounded her in the chest. A male guard used pepper gas against an unarmed and defenseless woman. They arrested me without letting me call and say goodbye to my parents who were on a trip.

"They took me away, to the Evin, blindfolded and handcuffed. On the way, they kept threatening me that they would file spurious charges against me. They said, 'We will cook up some soup for you (a Persian proverb) so that you would forget thinking about coming out of prison!'"

Court orders for flogging, blinding and stoning

- The Supreme Court ruled on February 3, 2017, that a woman must be blinded in one eye. The unidentified woman was found guilty of splashing acid two years before in the face of another woman in Kohgiluyeh.[596]
- The Criminal Court of Lorestan Province sentenced a man and a woman to stoning on February 3, 2017. The woman was identified as S.M.[597]
  The verdict was issued for their public dissemination of a video clip showing the illicit relationship between a clergy and a woman in Gerab, Koohdasht.
- More than 30 young men and women were arrested at a graduation party in Qazvin and subsequently punished with 99 lashes. The General Prosecutor of Qazvin sentenced each of the youths to 99 lashes and the verdicts were carried out on the same day.[598]
- The Criminal Court of Gorgan (northern Iran) issued flogging sentences for 20 people, including eight women, for attending a private mixed-gender yoga class. Each of the participants were sentenced to 50 lashes.[599]

---

[595] Letter by Atena Daemi from the Women's Ward of the Evin Prison, November 26, 2016; Atena's voice cannot be silenced with oppression and injustice, website of the NCRI Women's Committee, December 1, 2016
[596] The state-run Tasnim news agency – February 3, 2017
[597] The state-run Kashkan website, February 3, 2017
[598] The state-ran Alef website – May 26, 2016
[599] The state-run ROKNA news agency – September 30, 2019

- Intimate partner violence/domestic violence, including sexual violence and marital rape

Obscure statistics

The figures presented by various officials and agencies on violence against women vary and are at times, conflicting. At the same time, they show the gravity of the situation.

- In January 2017, Tehran's forensic officials announced that an average of 52 women refer to the Coroner's Office every day.[600]
- In September 2017, Tehran's Coroner's Office announced that it had registered the names of 12,159 women, victims of violence, in only four months from March to July 2017.[601]

This is an average of 101 referrals by women per day and almost double the figure announced nine months earlier by the same agency.

- In March 2017, an official of the National Welfare Organization said they had registered 11,000 women as victims of domestic violence.[602]

It is not clear whether they are talking about Tehran or the whole country and over what span of time. Nevertheless, it can be assumed that these are not the same women who referred to the Coroner's Office in Tehran.

- In June 2017, the Coroner's Office of Khorasan Razavi Province announced 7,000 women had been battered by their husbands in one year.[603]

Again, this number must be added to the previous numbers.

- In February 2018, a Social Emergencies official announced 14,599 cases of violence against spouses had been reported in six months.[604]

It could be assumed that he is talking about the period from August 2017 to January 2018, which is an average referral of 40 women per day.

- In June 2018, Tehran's Chief Coroner announced that most of the medical examinations done at the Coroner's Office were related to family quarrels and most of those who went for medical examination were women.
- In 2016, the number of such clients was 77,280 (including 74,180 women and 3,100 men) and in 2017, this number reached 81,729 (including 77,059 women and 4,670 men).[605]

---

[600] Tehran's forensic officials, January 2017
[601] The Coroner's Office in Tehran, the state-run Mehr news agency – September 23, 2017
[602] Habibollah Massoudi Farid, the state-run khabaronline.ir, March 4, 2017
[603] The state-run Mashreq news website, June 26, 2017
[604] Reza Jafari, interview with the state-run ILNA news agency, February 25, 2018
[605] Chief Coroner Shojaii, the official IRNA news agency - June 9, 2018

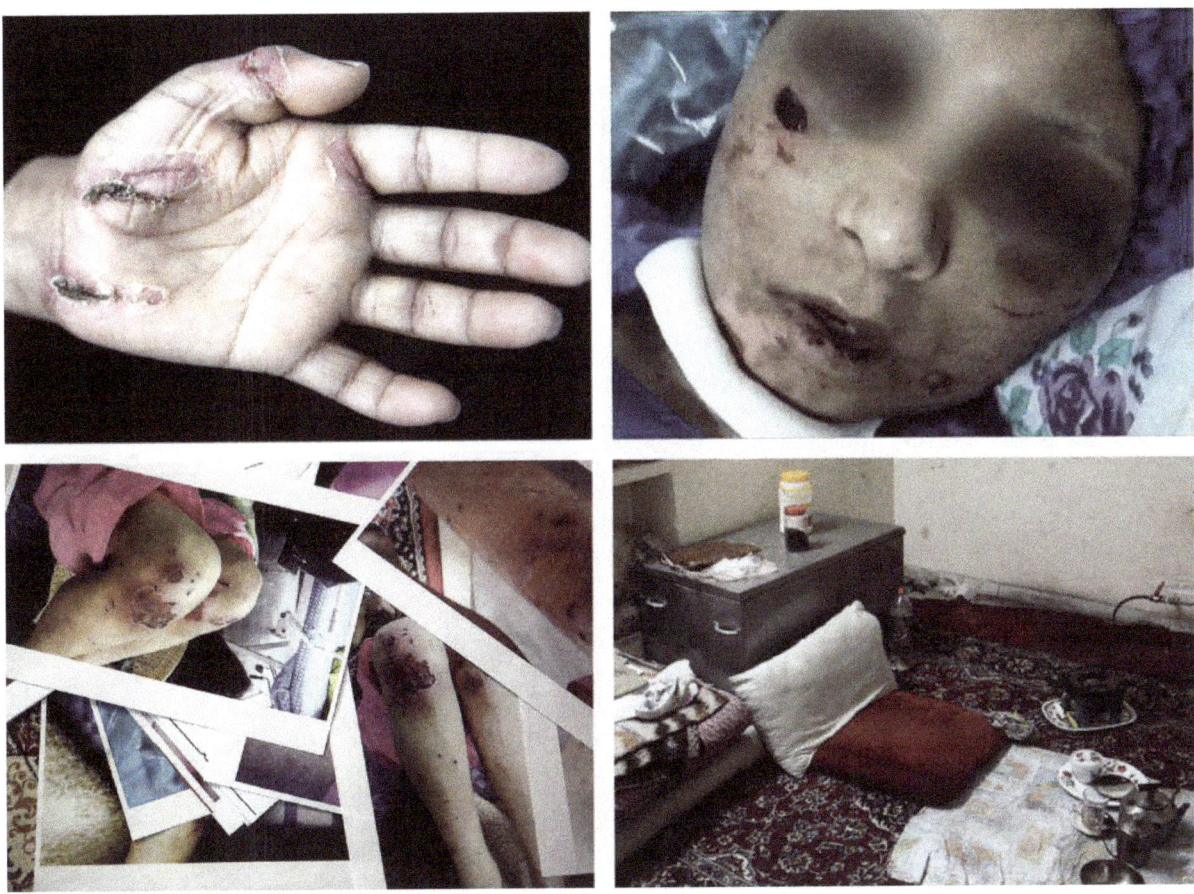

Azam's condition when found at her home in Mashhad

Here, we see that the daily average of referrals by women to Tehran's Coroner's Office is 206 for 2016, and the average daily referrals by women in 2017 is 214, which are four times the 52 referrals announced 1.5 years earlier for the same period.

- In the Persian year 1397 (March 2018-March 2019), 35411 women referred to the Coroner's Office of Tehran Province. That's an average of 100 women every day.[606]
- A 2015 study on violence against pregnant women showed that the prevalence of domestic violence against pregnant women was 48%.[607]
- The number of women who filed complaints against domestic violence rose 5.8% in 2017 compared to 3.2% increase in the preceding year.[608]

---

[606] The state-run ROKNA news agency, April 24, 2019
[607] VAW expert Parastoo Sarmadi, the state-run ILNA news agency, September 18, 2018
[608] Chief Coroner Shojaii, The official IRNA news agency - June 9, 2018

Domestic violence

Women who are victims of rape are punished by the regime. Since legal testimony by women is regarded only half the weight accorded to the testimony by men, victims of rape and sexual abuse are deprived of access to justice, and furthermore subjected to prosecution for adultery, which is defined as sexual relations outside of marriage.

- As a case example, a 32-year-old woman by the name of Nahid was sentenced to 15 years in prison and 99 lashes on the charge of "illicit relations" with a man who drugged, raped, filmed and blackmailed her in 2011.[609]
Ironically, Nahid's husband, who cut off the man's head, was cleared of murder charges and freed on the grounds that the man who had raped his wife was punishable by death, anyway.

In other cases, when a woman complains to the court and local judiciary officials against being abused by her husband, the authorities advise her to go back home, without investigating the case or providing any form of social protection for the abused woman.

- Example: Neighbors in Mashhad accidentally discovered a 30-year-old woman, Azam, and her two daughters, 5 and 8 years old, and rescued them.[610] They had been tortured for 21 days by their husband and father while being deprived of food and water. Azam's husband had broken her nose and cut her rectum with a knife. He confessed that he had intended to kill his wife and children, throw them into a well, and burn them in fire.
It was later revealed that the woman had repeatedly complained to judicial authorities to seek help but every time she had been sent back to her abusive husband.[611]

As a result of patriarchal policies of the ruling regime in Iran, their common practice of the death penalty even in public, and regarding men as owner of their wives, violence against women by their intimate partners has led to horrific crimes. There have been numerous reports of husbands murdering their wives. Here are a few examples:

- A young woman who had been hanged by her husband died in hospital after 24 hours in coma on March 2, 2019.[612]
- Monireh Abu (Mehrnia), 35 and eight months pregnant, was hanged by her husband, Mohammad Mahmoudi during a family quarrel. The 8-month-old embryo also died while Monireh died in a health center after one day in coma.
Monireh Abu Mehrnia had previously left her husband but returned home only three months earlier. Her husband fled after hanging his wife.
- A man hanged his wife in Sonqor, Kermanshah Province, on March 7, 2019. The young woman, Maryam Mohebi, had two children. After returning home, Maryam

---

[609] The state-run Rokna.ir, February 18, 2017
[610] The state-run ISNA news agency, April 23, 2016
[611] Legal gaps and lack of support for women led to torture, website of NCRI Women's Committee, April 27, 2016
[612] Innocent young woman hanged by her husband dies in hospital, website of NCRI Women's Committee, March 5, 2019

encountered her husband's insults, harassment, and abuse as to why she was late and subsequently she was hanged by her husband only because she was late.[613]

- **Sexual harassment and violence in public places, educational settings and in employment**

Sexual harassment and violence at the workplace

Iranian women face widespread sexual violence and harassment at their workplace. This is not a cultural issue, but the direct result of the misogynistic dictatorship of the mullahs' regime in Iran. Widespread poverty and unemployment of Iranian women and lack of any social and legal support as well as the state's imposition of various sexual discriminations and segregations are the main causes contributing to abuse of women at the workplace.

While the system tries to keep women away from participating in and influencing the society, employers take advantage of the situation and try to benefit from this cheap and defenseless labor force in the worst possible way. In most cases, the violence is exerted by employers or influential people and the victim has to keep silent fearing to lose her job.

- In Iran, there is no special law on sexual harassment especially at the workplace and even Article 637 in the old Penal Code, where the offender could pay the victim a fine for the offense, was removed from the latest legislation.[614]
- The Iranian regime's laws criminalize men only for the highest degree of sexual abuse, i.e. rape. But on the basis of these laws, if a woman can prove sexual harassment or aggression, she will most likely be fired if the aggressor is the employer or the superior. There is no protection for the victim under the misogynist laws of the mullahs' regime.
- On the other hand, if the woman fails to prove her claim, she is also considered to be a criminal offender for the charge.
- In a limited survey carried out on 82 working women in Tehran, sexual harassment at work environment was calculated to be 75%.[615] Prevention of sexual harassment at work environment is generally the duty of the employer but in Iran, by using the anti-women laws, employers deliberately criminalize victims. In the best-case scenario, the law enforcement and judicial institutions evade from their duties and throw the responsibility of proving the crime on the shoulder of victims.
- According to a recent finding, 40 percent of working women in Iran are sexually harassed at the workplace. The same research indicates that 90 percent of Iranian women have experienced some form of sexual harassment during their lifetime.[616]
- According to a survey done with 59 female reporters, 90% of them have been sexually harassed at least once while doing their job.[617]

---

[613] Acid attack, honor killing, and suicides take toll on Iranian women, website of NCRI Women's Committee, March 16, 2019
[614] The state-run Tabnak.ir, June 28, 2018
[615] The www.bbc.com/persian, October 11, 2017
[616] Aliyeh Shekarbeigi, sociologist and head of the Association of Sociologists, Meidaan.com, October 1, 2019
[617] Abbas Abdi, head of the journalists' Association of Tehran Province, Iran daily, February 7, 2020

Another issue is the lack of supervision in this regard. In Iran, the smaller the factories, the more violent, intense and widespread is the violence.

In manufacturing workshops, which are mostly enclosed and inadequate in underground spaces, the risk of sexual harassment and violence against women is higher, while these manufacturing workshops are the main places for women to be employed.

In addition, the lower the level of professionalism and job position of women in different occupations and the less family support they have, they are more likely to be subjected to harassment at the workplace.

Sexual harassment of women in the workplace is to such an extent that they even leak into the state-run media and show that even young women and girls who work at medical offices and large companies are harassed by their employers and fearful of losing their jobs they are inevitably forced to remain silent and obey.

Girl child laborers

Based on the reports and video clips posted on social media in February 2019, girl child laborers who work in the streets to earn meager amounts of money, are physically and sexually abused by municipality agents.[618] The population of child laborers is estimated to be 7 million.[619]

- A social worker said the girl child laborers are sexually abused in addition to being brutalized. "Two of the labor child girls who work at the intersection, were forced into a car by municipal agents. One of the agents told one of the girls to unbutton her clothes. This girl even told us that when she was taken to the police station, she was separated from other kids and forced to take off her clothes." [620]
- One of the girl child laborers talked about sexual abuse of her friend by municipal agents. She said, "One day, when I saw Sara, I asked her, 'Why are you upset?' She said municipal agents caught me and mistreated me… They pulled my scarf and touched me. When I screamed, he stepped away. But when I went to the office of the municipality and told my story, they did not believe me. They said I was making up the story so that they would let me go."[621]
- A research done on 400 child laborers, it was revealed by an official of Social Services in Tehran's Municipality that some 90% of child laborers are sexually abused.[622]

---

[618] Girl child laborers among the most innocent victims of mullahs in Iran, website of the NCRI Women's Committee, June 12, 2019
[619] The state-run Tasnim news agency, September 27, 2017; Power and wealth monopoly behind plight of Iran's child laborers, IranNewsWire.org, December 26, 2018
[620] Labor child girls are physically and sexually abused by city agents, the website of NCRI Women's Committee, February 6, 2019
[621] Ibid.
[622] The executive director of the Organization of Social Services in Tehran's Municipality, the state-run Salamatnews.com – November 8, 2017; Iran state media confess to rape of girl child laborers, the website of the NCRI Women's Committee, November 9, 2017

Rape in public places
An increasing number of rape accounts kept mushrooming in different parts of Iran, including the rape and murders of 6 and 7-year-old girl children.

- A seven-year-old girl became victim of sexual violence and murder in Parsabad. Parsabad is a city in Ardabil Province, in northwestern Iran.[623]
- Atena Aslani went missing on June 19, 2017. Atena's father was a street peddler who sold clothes. On the day of the incident, Atena left her father as he was talking to a customer, and never returned.
- Atena's life-less body was found on July 10, 2017, in a parking lot inside a plastic barrel. She had been raped before being murdered. The state media identified the suspect as Ismail, a local businessman selling paint.
- Setayesh Ghoreishi, 6, was raped and killed by acid on April 10, 2016 in Kheirabad village in Varamin.
- A nine-year-old girl was molested and raped by her teacher, a married 30-year-old man with two children. This happened in Ghareh Mohammad village in Zanjan Province.[624]
- The dean of students at the University of Zanjan was caught while sexually assaulting one of the girl students in this university.[625]
- In December 2018, news broke out on the molestation of at least four students in a school in Isfahan.[626]

Rapes in Sistan and Baluchestan
The rapes of 41 women and girls in Iranshahr, in southeastern province of Sistan and Baluchestan, was the most horrific case stirring controversy across the country in June 2018. The victims were between 18 and 30 years of age assaulted by a gang of four men, linked to the city's wealthy and influential families, the Bassij and IRGC.

Rape of mentally disabled
There was also the case of repeated rape of a mentally disabled woman at a government-run welfare center in Tehran which shocked and outraged the public.[627]
The 30-year-old woman had been living in the welfare center for several years. An aid worker revealed that she had been repeatedly raped by one of the workers at the facility. It was also found out that this was not the first case of rape by the assailant but he had also assaulted two other mentally disabled women in the center.[628]

---

[623] Seven-year-old girl, victim of sexual assault and murder, website of the NCRI Women's Committee, July 24, 2017
[624] The state-run ROKNA news agency, January 30, 2016
[625] The state-run Fararu website, June 15, 2008
[626] The state-run Tabnak.ir, December 3, 2018
[627] The state-run Mehr news agency – September 3, 2017
[628] Mentally retarded woman raped in a government center, the website of the NCRI Women's Committee, September 7, 2017

Violence against nurses and students

Violence against women and girl children is not limited to sexual harassment but also include physical punishment and abuse. Here are some examples:

- Studies on violence against women at the workplace, show that 72.6% of nurses faced violence at their jobs.[629]
- In October 2016, school authorities in the southern Iranian village of Mokhtarabad in South Roodbar, Kerman, struck eight lashes to at least 10 girl students and expelled them from school because their parents did not afford to pay 30,000 toumans (approx. $8.5) demanded by the school's principal.[630]

- ### Child, early and forced marriages

Early marriages of girls under 18 is considered both violence against women and child abuse by international standards.

The law in Iran, however, sets the legal age of marriage for girls at 13 and sanctions marriage under 13 years of age with the consent of father and confirmation of maturity by a court judge. As a result of this law and particularly because of widespread poverty of the people, early and forced marriage of girl children has become common in Iran.

Here are acknowledgements by state officials and experts:

- New data released by the Iranian census organization indicates that 234,000 marriages of girl children under 15 years of age were officially registered from March 2017 to March 2018 (Persian year 1396). 194 of these were marriages of girl children under 10 years old.[631]
- Another official admitted that between 5 to 600,000 children get married every year (in Iran) according to the officially registered data. The problem is that more marriages are taking place without being officially registered. [632]
  Early marriages are on the rise due to the regime's new policy of granting a larger number of marriage loans, girls are literally being sold under the name of marriage, and the number of early marriages is growing by the day. Based on the data obtained from the Central Bank, in the six-month period from March to September 2019, the number of early marriages of girls under 15 years of age increased four folds compared to the same period in the previous year.[633]

---

[629] VAW expert Parastoo Sarmadi, the state-run ILNA news agency, September 18, 2018
[630] Girl children whipped at school, website of NCRI Women's Committee, October 12, 2016
[631] The state-run Iran daily newspaper – October 30, 2019
[632] Ali Kazemi, advisor to the legal deputy of the Judiciary Branch, the state-run daily Entekhab – March 4, 2019
[633] Mohammad Mehdi Tondgouyan, deputy Minister of Sports and Youths, the state-run Mehr news agency, December 30, 2019

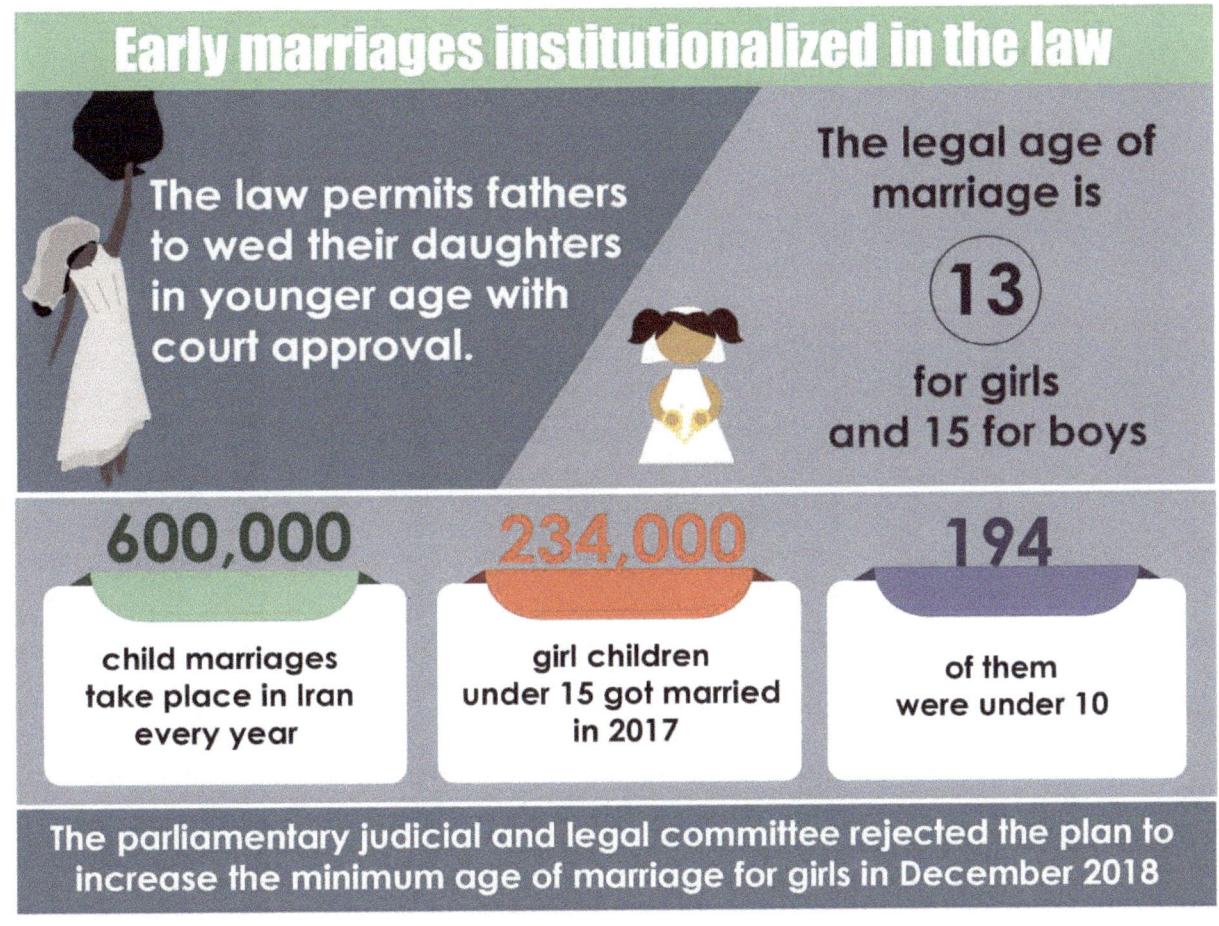

These new figures are considerably higher than what had been announced by various government officials and experts in previous years:

- 180,000 early marriages take place in Iran every year.[634]
- Some 37,000 girl children under 15 years of age got married from March 2017 to March 2018.[635]
- Some 43,000 girls under 15 were married in the Persian year 1396, from March 2017 to March 2018.[636]
- Based on the statistics of the National Statistics Center, last year (March 2016-March 2017) there were 36,422 marriages of girls under 15 years of age.[637]
- The largest number of registered marriages of 10-14 girl children was in 2014 which amounted to 40,229.[638]

---

[634] Batool Salimi Manesh, a social researcher, the official IRNA news agency, August 5, 2018
[635] Parvaneh Salahshouri, head of the women's faction in the mullahs' parliament, the state-run IRNA news agency - May 8, 2018
[636] The statistics and monitoring director of the Social and Cultural Council of Women and Family, the state-run salamatnews.com, July 24, 2018
[637] Zahra Ayatollahi, the state-run ISNA news agency – March 10, 2018
[638] Batool Salimi Manesh, a social researcher, the official IRNA news agency, August 5, 2018

The Razavi Khorasan Province (eastern Iran) has the largest number of early marriages, while East Azerbaijan Province (northwestern Iran) ranks second.[639]

They are followed by the provinces of Sistan and Baluchestan, West Azerbaijan, and Kermanshah which are national record holders with around 4,000 marriages of girl children under 15 per year.[640]

Early marriages are also common practice in the province of Ardabil. Out of a total of 12,000 marriages in 2018 in this province, 37 percent (i.e. 4,400) have been from among girls between 10 to 14 years of age. This is while 42 percent of the total number of marriages in this province were from among women under 19 years of age.[641]

The most tragic consequence of the regime's law on girls' marriage is the marriage of girls under 13 years of age. Following are official acknowledgements in this regard:
- The number of girl children under 10 who have gotten married was 220 in 2011; 187 in 2012; 201 in 2013; 176 in 2014; and 179 in 2015. These figures are probably higher because of unregistered marriages. [642]
- The average marriage age for girl children in Zaweh village is 11.[643]
- The marriage age for girls in Zainub village is under 10.[644]
- Some families force girls as young as 9 or 10 years old to get married with old men just to obtain some money to provide for the rest of the family's needs.[645]

Another tragic outcome is the phenomenon of child widows. According to official statements:
- There are some 24,000 widows under 18 years of age in Iran, and most of the early marriages end up in divorce.[646]
- There are 15,000 young widows under 15 years of age in Iran.[647]

---

[639] The official IRNA news agency, August 5, 2018
[640] The state-run website of Young Journalists Club, July 5, 2018
[641] Behzad Sattari, general director of the Welfare Organization in Ardabil, the state-run daily Entekhab – March 4, 2019
[642] Batool Salimi Manesh, a social researcher, the official IRNA news agency, August 5, 2018
[643] Ali Baghdar Delgosha, advisor in youths' affairs to the Governor of Razavi Khorasan Province, told a meeting at the School of Literature of Ferdowsi University of Mashhad on May 14, 2018. Zaweh is located in Razavi Khorasan Province in northeastern Iran.
[644] Amir Taghizadeh, cultural and youth affairs deputy in the General Department of Youths and Sports in East Azerbaijan Province, the state-run ISNA news agency, May 24, 2018
[645] Massoumeh Agha-Alishahi, member of the mullahs' parliament, the state-run ROKNA news agency, May 28, 2018
[646] Ibid.
[647] Shahrbanou Imami, member of Tehran's City Council and former member of the mullahs' parliament, the state-run ILNA news agency, March 8, 2018

13. What actions has your country prioritized in the last five years to address violence against women and girls?

- Introduced or strengthened violence against women laws, and their enforcement and implementation

Obstruction of the bill to eliminate violence against women

After eight years of obstructions and procrastination by the mullahs' parliament and Judiciary preventing adoption of a proposed bill to eliminate violence against women, the Iranian Judiciary eventually finalized and passed a bill to the government on September 17, 2019.[648]
A member of parliament said the government had taken no action and the bill was not going to be passed to the current parliament before the elections in February 2020.[649]

Background

It has not been mentioned exactly when, but the bill was reportedly proposed for the first time in 2011.[650] Called "Elimination of Violence Against Women," the bill had 92 articles and 5 principles and sought to provide protection and support to all women over 18 and married women over 13.
But the parliamentary Committee on Bills found some faults with the bill, deliberations on the bill were brought to halt, and ultimately it was pushed out of the agenda with the termination of presidency of Mahmoud Ahmadinejad.
In step with surge in violence against women, the bill was again activated in 2015.
"The bill initially called, 'Elimination of Violence Against Women', was first renamed as 'Provision of Security for Women (PSW).' For two and a half years, the bill was supposed to come back to the parliament, but it got stuck in a labyrinth incomparable to any other bill or plan."[651]
In 2017, the bill was renamed, "Provision of Security for Women." 41 of its 92 articles were removed ostensibly because they ran parallel to the articles of the Islamic Punishment Code and the Penal Prosecution Procedure. And even then, the mullahs' parliament rejected the bill.
On August 24, 2017, Zabihollah Khoda'ian, legal deputy to the Judiciary, expressed his opposition to the adoption of the PSW bill because 70 percent of the articles of the bill were "criminalizing" and "setting prison sentences for even the slightest tensions between couples."[652]
The Judiciary's cultural deputy, Hadi Sadeqi, also asserted, "The PSW bill against violence is apparently drafted to support women, but in essence it strikes the greatest blow to women and

---

[648] [Provision of Security for Women bill finalized by Judiciary after 8 years](#), website of the NCRI Women's Committee, September 19, 2019
[649] Fatemeh Zolqadr, member of the Cultural Committee of the mullahs' parliament: "The bill has been sent from the judiciary and returned to the government, but we do not know why it has remained silent in the government... A month ago, at a meeting with Massoumeh Ebtekar, the issue was raised that the bill was being considered by the Government Committee to make the final amendments, but so far nothing has been reported and it is unlikely it will reach the parliament this year." The state-run ROKNA news agency, December 27, 2019
[650] Ashraf Geramizadegan, a legal advisor to the presidential directorate on Women and Family Affairs, interview with the state-run ISNA news agency, April 15, 2018
[651] Parvaneh Salahshouri, member of parliament, the official IRNA news agency, September 18, 2018
[652] The official IRNA news agency, August 26, 2017

families. When a woman sends her husband to jail, then that man can never be a husband for her again, and the woman must accept the risk of getting divorced in advance."[653]

These remarks and others by Iranian Judiciary officials indicate that they do not take it seriously that domestic violence and violence against women have a destructive impact on the foundations of families which will in turn lead to drastic social ailments.

A glance on cases of death-row female prisoners, women's suicide, runaway girls and growing divorce rates in Iran which have already jeopardized the foundations of the family shows that in the majority of cases, these women were initially victims of violence and domestic violence.

In the next round of deliberations on the PSW bill, Gholam-Hossein Mohseni Eje'ii, first deputy minister and spokesman of the mullahs' Judiciary Branch, said the bill had too many faults, it could not be reformed, but had to be completely overhauled and re-written.[654]

Explaining the reason for rejection of the bill and the need for re-writing it, it was said that the bill would "weaken the authority of men in the family."[655]

In September 2019, the Judiciary passed the bill to the government. The overhauled bill was renamed as "Protection, Dignity and Provision of Security for Ladies Against Violence." Another 15 articles of the bill were removed and its objective and focus totally changed, rendering it ineffective in preventing and eliminating violence against women.

In the first place, the final bill revised by the Judiciary does not present any basic definition of violence against women. Consequently, it does not criminalize violence against women. The deterrent mechanisms and the punishments for committing violence against women have not been defined, and the bill instead contains some articles of the Punishment Law.

The Judiciary's re-written bill has changed the term "violence" to "misdemeanor," thus eliminating the focus of the original bill on crimes involving violence against women in order to protect them against violence in all public and private places including the family, school, university, work place, streets, and even on the cyberspace. Parts of the articles dealing with these issues have been removed.[656]

Articles 26-30 in the previous bill which dealt with sexual crimes, including sexual exploitation of women, rape and sexual violence have been totally removed.[657]

A good number of the articles in this bill do not concern violence against women, but focus on the mullahs' religious interpretations, some punishing women who are victims of violence.

Article 48, for example, states: "Anyone committing behavior which, contrary to the regulations, leads to forcible removal of a woman's veil is going to be sentenced to the sixth-degree (maximum) imprisonment or payment of cash fine."[658]

---

[653] The state-run Tasnim news agency, June 27, 2018
[654] The official IRNA news agency, February 17, 2019
[655] Ashraf Geramizadegan, a legal advisor to the presidential directorate on Women and Family Affairs, the state-run ILNA news agency, September 18, 2018
[656] Shima Qusheh, jurist and women's rights activist, the state-run rouydad24.ir, September 30, 2019
[657] Ibid.
[658] Articles 45-50 of the bill for the "Protection, Dignity and Provision of Security for Mesdames Against Violence" concerns religious precepts such as any deliberate touch in public between a man and a woman's bodies, proposing sexual relations out of marriage, inviting women to mixed-gender parties, etc. none of which are considered violence against women.

The original bill intended to facilitate filing complaints by women who are victims of violence; the Judiciary's bill again requires the victim to go through the difficult judicial process to prove her claim.[659]

The bill contains "general, ambiguous, abstract, and vague terms and statements which are open to interpretation" thus creating "the opportunity for personal interpretation and analyses."[660]

Another controversial part of the bill is using the term "ladies" instead of "women," excluding single women, young girls, victims of social harms, vulnerable women, run-away girls, victims of human trafficking, etc. from any protection that this bill could presumably provide.[661]

In addition, the spokesman for the Judiciary asserted that the bill only protects the rights of women who abide by the law, regulations and religious values, excluding the respectable married women who oppose the regime's numerous restrictions on women.[662]

Most of the text of the bill has been devoted to a series of general statements, like "educating people" and "building the culture," which are ambiguous terms producing no concrete guarantees and no deadlines for practical enforcement and implementation of the bill, and does not specify the duties of those in charge of this.[663]

Furthermore, no financial investments have been considered in the bill to prevent violence or build shelters for victims of violence.

The National Committee of Protection, Dignity and Provision of Security for Ladies Against Violence is in charge of implementing the bill. All members of the committee are men except for Massoumeh Ebtekar who is the director of the Presidential Directorate for Women and Family Affairs. In addition to government officials, three members of the NGOs and two members of the Seminary of Qom are also members of this committee.

And yet the government has not passed this totally overhauled bill to the mullahs' parliament for adoption.

Bill to increase the legal age of marriage for girls

Child marriage has been institutionalized by the mullahs' regime in Iran by setting the legal age of marriage for girls at 13.

Early marriages take place while persons under 18 years of age are not permitted to do any business.

Poverty is the most important factor leading to early marriages.[664]

The parliamentary women's faction first proposed the bill to increase the age of marriage in December 2016.[665] According to the drafted bill, Article 1401 of the Civil Code on the minimum age of marriage had to be amended, banning all marriages under the age of 13 for girls and 16 for boys. The legal age of marriage was proposed to be raised to 16 for girls and 18 for boys.[666]

---

[659] Shima Qusheh, jurist and women's rights activist, the state-run rouydad24.ir, September 30, 2019
[660] Shahindokht Molaverdi, presidential deputy on citizens' rights affairs, the state-run jamaran.ir, October 2, 2019
[661] Ibid.
[662] Ibid.
[663] Ibid.
[664] Farshid Yazdani, one of the officers in charge of the associations supporting children, the state-run Iran daily newspaper – October 30, 2019
[665] The state-run Mehr news agency, January 23, 2019
[666] The state-run ISNA news agency, March 11, 2019

The parliamentary judicial and legal committee rejected the plan in December 2018. The committee's chair said, "Raising the legal age of marriage is contrary to the general policies of the state."[667] Mohammad Dehghani, a member of this committee, had already declared, "The plan is being deliberated by the Committee, and we are opposed to it because we cannot oppose the sacred Islamic law."[668]

The Iranian census organization has released new statistics on early marriages in Iran. According to the new data, 234,000 marriages of girl children under 15 years of age were officially registered by this organization from March 2017 to March 2018 (Persian year 1396). 194 of these were marriages of girl children under 10 years old.[669]

Ali Kazemi, advisor to the legal deputy of the Judiciary Branch, announced in March 2019, that between 5 to 600,000 girl children get married every year (in Iran). This figure relates to officially registered marriages and does not include those which were not officially registered.[670]

The latest news is that after the Iranian regime facilitated granting marriage loans, the applicants for these loans increased 90 folds in the first five months of the year compared to the same period in the previous year.[671]

A government expert asserted that poor families are literally selling their daughters, and according to the Central Bank's figures, the number of early marriages of girls under 15 in six months increased four times the under-15 marriages throughout the previous year.[672]

The plan for punishment for acid attacks

On May 13 and 20, 2019, the Iranian regime's parliament adopted a plan on punishment for acid attacks and giving support to the victims, without limiting or banning the sale and purchase of acid, itself.

According to this bill, the person who commits the crime of splashing acid is sentenced to execution or retribution in kind. The accomplices in this crime are sentenced to imprisonment between 5 and 25 years. If the assailants are not arrested, the government must pay compensations to the victims but when the assailant is arrested, the victim has the right to ask for retribution.[673]

Experts say the act is incomplete without imposing a total ban or limit on sale and purchase of acid, because like other cold arms, acid can destroy and burn.[674]

In October 2014, a wave of acid attacks was carried out against women in Tehran and Isfahan after incitement by Friday prayer leaders and took toll on dozens of women. The assailants were never arrested and punished, and acid attack became a common practice for personal revenge.

---

[667] Allahyar Malekshahi, Chairman of the parliamentary Judicial and Legal Committee, interview with the state-run Fars News Agency, November 26, 2018
[668] Mohammad Dehghani, member of the judicial and legal committee of the mullahs' parliament, the state-run Fars news agency, November 27, 2018
[669] The state-run IRNA news agency, January 6, 2019
[670] The state-run daily Entekhab, March 4, 2019
[671] Tayyebeh Siavoshi, a member of the mullahs' parliament, the state-run Sarpoosh.com, December 29, 2019
[672] Mohammad Mehdi Tondguyan, deputy Minister of Sports and Youths, the state-run Sarpoosh.com, December 29, 2019
[673] The official IRNA news agency – May 20, 2019
[674] The state-run Salamatnews.com - May 20, 2019

Sigal Mandelker, the Under Secretary for Terrorism and Financial Intelligence at the U.S. Treasury Department, said the Ansar-e Hezbollah, which is a state-backed institute, attacks and persecutes the Iranian people and has been linked to the acid attacks against women in Isfahan.[675]

- **Monitored violence against women seeking asylum, being a refugee, internally displaced or stateless, widowhood, migration status, heading households, living with HIV/AIDS, being deprived of liberty, and being trafficked or in prostitution, women in situations of armed conflict, geographical remoteness and human rights defenders.**

Violence against human rights defenders

Human rights defenders are one of the groups of women who constantly face state-sponsored violence.

- The United Nations released a World Report on the Situation of Human Rights Defenders in December 2018, by Mr. Michel Forst, UN Special Rapporteur on Human Rights Defenders. [676]
- The report emphasized that "since December 2017, the situation for human rights defenders in Iran has become significantly more dangerous, as scores of protestors were arrested, detained, charged and even killed in anti-government protests which swept across the country."
- The report added that Iran "has also intensified its crackdown on women."
- "Scores of women defenders are persecuted for their legitimate work. Hoda Amid, Najmeh Vahedi and Rezvaneh Mohammadi were arrested and arbitrarily detained in unknown locations in September 2018 in retaliation for their involvement in workshops on equal marriage rights and other peaceful activities related to women's rights. Atena Daemi and Golrokh Ebrahimi Iraee are detained for fighting for women's rights, opposing child labour, and opposing the death penalty. They are being kept in 'quarantine' and have restricted contact with the outside world.
- "The State views human rights defenders as threats to national security. Therefore, there is no national law or policy to protect human rights defenders, and the rights of the Declaration are not respected."
- The report also mentions that "defenders have been subjected to torture, including mock executions, beatings, sleep deprivation and denial of access to adequate medical care; arbitrary arrest and detainment followed by unfair trials; violent dispersal of peaceful protests; travel bans and harassment of human rights defenders' family members including their children."
- Amnesty International issued a statement on September 3, 2018, warning that the arrests of lawyers and women's rights activists in Iran signal intensifying crackdown on civil society.[677]

---

[675] USAdarFarsi, June 7, 2018
[676] World Report on the Situation of Human Rights Defenders, December 2018
[677] Iran arrests of lawyers and women's rights activists signal intensifying crackdown on civil society, Amnesty International, September 3, 2018

- AI wrote, "These latest arrests are a blatant attempt to silence those advocating for human rights in Iran… The arrests of human rights lawyers are part of an attempt by the authorities to prevent them from being able to defend their clients, who are often human rights defenders or individuals who face the death penalty, including for crimes committed as a child."
- At least 104 women were arrested from March 2016 to February 2017 for participating in protest gatherings and other peaceful activities in defense of fundamental human rights.[678]
- At least 600 women activists, dissidents and opponents were arrested and detained in Iran from January 2017 to February 2018, an estimated 500 during the uprising in January and afterwards.[679]
- At least 40 women were arrested from March 2018 to February 2019, and prison sentences were issued for at least 50 other women.[680]

- **Introduced or strengthened measures to increase women's access to justice (e.g. establishment of specialist courts, training for the judiciary and police, protection orders, redress and reparations, including for femicide cases, enforcement and combating impunity, improving criminal evidence system to enhance prosecution quality and integrity of eventual judicial decisions, possibility of ex officio/victimless prosecution, clarity on jurisdictions in countries with pluralistic legal systems)**

Women's access to justice

Political prisoners and prisoners of conscience and many ordinary prisoners in Iran are deprived of due process of law and do not have access to justice. Judicial proceedings do not conform to the regime's own laws, let alone international laws.

The prisoner is confined to a solitary cell after being arrested to be forced under pressure and torture to make confessions against herself. During this period, the prisoner has no contact with the outside world to inform her family of her arrest and place of detention. Under such circumstances, it is totally impossible for the prisoner to have a defense attorney.

On numerous occasions, prisoners have resorted to hunger strike as a last resort and refused food and endangered their health in order to reach their rightful demands.[681]

Following are a few examples of unfair sentences and unjust treatment of prisoners:

---

[678] Annual Report of the Women's Committee of the National Council of Resistance of Iran, March 2017
[679] Annual Report of the Women's Committee of the National Council of Resistance of Iran, March 2018
[680] Annual Report of the Women's Committee of the National Council of Resistance of Iran, March 2019
[681] Women in Pursuit of Justice, Arbitrary trends and illegal proceedings victimizing female political prisoners in Iran, A Special Report by the NCRI Women's Committee, January 2019

Maryam Akbari Monfared

Maryam Akbari Monfared, 43, with three daughters, was arrested in late December 2009, after contacting her siblings who are members of the opposition People's Mojahedin Organization of Iran (PMOI/MEK). She was arrested and charged with *Moharebeh* or waging war on God. Maryam Akbari was deprived of access to legal counsel throughout her legal proceedings and was sentenced to 15 years in prison in a 5-minute trial.

The verdict issued for Maryam Akbari contradicts not only international standards of justice but the laws of the Iranian regime.

According to Articles 19 and 288 of the Punishment Law in Iran, the punishment for *Moharebeh* is between 10 to 15 years or a maximum amount of 550 million rials in cash fine.

The same law defines *Moharebeh* as "using weapons to target one's life, property or family or terrify in a way that makes the social setting insecure."

Maryam Akbari has never taken up arms and has never been a member of the People's Mojahedin Organization of Iran.

Moreover, Article 141 of the Punishment Law states that "penal responsibility is personal." But Maryam Akbari was told by the judge that she is "paying the price of her sister and brothers."

Maryam Akbari has served ten years of her sentence in Qarchak Prison of Varamin, Gohardasht Prison of Karaj, and the Metadon Ward of the Evin Prison without any furloughs. Presently, she is incarcerated in the Women's Ward of the Evin Prison.

Her family paid 11.5 billion rials as bail, but prison officials have refused to grant her leave for medical treatment.

Zeinab Jalalian

Zeinab Jalalian is sentenced to life in prison and detained in the Prison of Khoy.

But in the first place, it had been illegal to charge her with *Moharebeh* (waging war on God) according to the Iranian regime's laws.

Chapter 8, Article 279, of the Punishment Law defines *Moharebeh* as the following: "*Moharebeh* (or waging war on God) is using weapons to target one's life, property or family or terrify them in a way that makes the social setting insecure."

Whenever someone, with personal motive, aims a gun at one or more specific persons and their act does not target the public, also if a person aims a gun on people, but does not cause insecurity due to inability, the person is not considered a *Mohareb*.

Zeinab Jalalian did not have any guns at her disposal at the time of arrest or any other time.

Article 288 of the same law states, "Whenever members of an outlaw group are arrested before confrontation and use of arms, they are sentenced to third-degree imprisonment if that organization and its central committee exists. If the organization and its central committee were already dissolved, they are sentenced to fifth-degree imprisonment."

Based on this law, the third-degree imprisonment is between 10 to 15 years. While the sentence for Zeinab Jalalian was initially the death penalty later commuted to life imprisonment despite the fact that she did not carry any weapons.

The Iranian regime's officials who are aware of the illegal nature of their sentences, have repeatedly pressured Ms. Jalalian to do television interviews and make confessions against herself. They have even made her medical leave contingent on such interviews while one of her eyes has become blind due to torture and lack of treatment, and the other is going blind, as well.

Fatemeh Mossanna

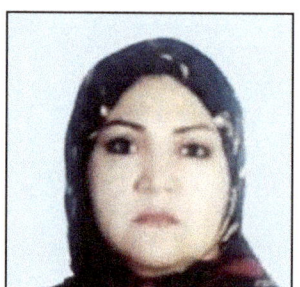

Fatemeh Mossanna is charged with waging war on God through collaboration with the PMOI and sentenced to 15 years in prison in Evin Prison.

Based on Article 288 of the Punishment Law, Fatemeh Mossanna has been handed down a sentence of 15 years in prison which is the maximum sentence that could be issued for a member of an outlaw group.

Fatemeh Mossanna and her husband, Hassan Sadeghi, were simultaneously imprisoned for holding a funeral ceremony for Mr. Sadeghi's father who was a member of the PMOI/MEK. This is despite Article 141 of the Punishment Law which underscores that "penal responsibility is personal."

Ms. Mossanna also suffers from chronic rupture of her leg tendon due to lack of medical care in prison.

In addition to such blatant violation of the law, the family's business, the only source of the family's income, has been shut down and confiscated by the regime. The authorities also intend to confiscate their house where Ms. Mossanna's mother and children presently live.

Fatemeh Mossanna's two brothers were executed in the 1980s. Ms. Mossanna was 13 at the time when she was incarcerated along with her mother who was imprisoned for supporting the PMOI/MEK.

Golrokh Ebrahimi Iraee

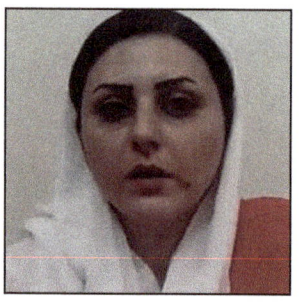

A writer and a human rights activist, Golrokh Iraee went on an 81-day hunger strike, in protest to her unlawful exile on January 24, 2018 to the notorious Qarchak Prison in breach of the principle of separation of prisoners' categories, demanding to be returned to the women's ward in Evin Prison.

Qarchak (Shahr-e Ray) Prison of Varamin is a disused chicken farm used as a detention center for ordinary and dangerous women criminals. Political prisoners are transferred there to experience more physical and mental torture.

Golrokh Iraee and her fellow inmate Atena Daemi started their hunger strike on February 3, and switched to dry hunger strike on February 10 for one week.

Ms. Iraee and Ms. Daemi were deprived of contacting their families and could call them only once a week in the presence of prison guards. They were held in conditions similar to solitary confinement. They were not allowed to leave the ward and no one had permission to visit them. In the final days of her hunger strike, Golrokh Iraee was no longer able to talk, walk or stand up and had lost 22 kilograms. She ended her hunger strike on April 24, 2018, upon the appeals of some 1,000 human rights advocates and families of execution victims and political prisoners.

In light of Ms. Iraee's resistance and perseverance and the wave of domestic and international solidarity with her, the clerical regime finally returned Golrokh Iraee and Atena Daemi to Evin on May 10, 2018.

Ms. Iraee was released on bail from Evin Prison on April 8, 2019, after serving half of the six-year sentence she had been serving since 2016.

Tehran's Revolutionary Court examined a new case filed against Golrokh Ebrahimi Iraee and Atena Daemi on June 18, 2019, sentencing them to three years and seven months for protesting while in detention, against the unfair executions of three Kurdish dissidents.

Golrokh Ebrahimi Iraee was apprehended at home again on Saturday, November 9, 2019, by 10 male security agents who did not show their arrest warrant.

On Monday, November 11, 2019, Ms. Iraee was taken back home where security agents ransacked her apartment, confiscating her personal belongings. Then she was driven to Qarchak Prison in a vehicle mounted with a prisoner's cage.

Ms. Iraee's husband, Arash Sadeghi, is presently incarcerated in poor health in Gohardasht (a.k.a. Rajai Shahr) Prison. He is serving a 19-year sentence for his peaceful activities. He suffers from bone cancer (chondrosarcoma) and underwent an operation last year but was returned to prison before completing his chemotherapy and other essential treatment.[682]

Atena Daemi

Atena Daemi, 30, a human rights and child rights activist, was violently arrested at home at 8 a.m. on November 26, 2016, in an unwarranted raid by agents of the IRGC Sarallah Corps. She was brutalized, intimidated and taken to Evin Prison. Her sisters were also beaten up at the time of the raid.

On March 13, 2017, the three Daemi sisters (Atena, Ensieh and Hanieh) were falsely accused of beating IRGC agents and sentenced each to 91 days of imprisonment for "preventing implementation of the verdict" and "insulting public officers on duty."

In protest to the unfair prison sentences issued for her sisters, Atena Daemi started a hunger strike on April 8, 2017 to prevent security agencies from manipulating her family as a tool for further psychological torture and for terrorizing the society.

During her hunger strike which lasted 54 days, Atena fought back several times despite poor health and numerous complications caused by hunger strike.

On May 31, 2017 the Revision Court revoked the prison sentences for Ensieh and Haniyeh Daemi and political prisoner Atena Daemi ended her hunger strike.

Again, Evin Prison officials not only failed to provide adequate treatment and medical care for Ms. Daemi but accused her of making false pretenses of illness.

Atena Daemi went on another hunger strike on February 3, 2018 for 12 days when her condition had become fatally dangerous.

---

[682] Imprisoned Civil Activist Arash Sadeghi is in Critical Condition, Iranhr.net, June 28, 2019

Nargess Mohammadi

Nargess Mohammadi was arrested in a violent raid on her residence on May 5, 2015 and taken to the Women's Ward of Evin Prison in Tehran. Nargess Mohammadi suffers from emboli in the lungs and muscular paralysis. She had been previously arrested in July 2012 but released on a court verdict indicating that she could not endure detention because of her illnesses.

Prison officials have hampered her treatment despite her dangerous physical conditions which requires her to consume 23 medications every day. As a consequence, she has been suffering from heart palpitations and high blood pressure. In December 2015, prison guards transferred Ms. Mohammadi to hospital without removing her handcuffs and did not leave the room when she had to "change her clothes," to be examined.

Ms. Mohammadi's demand for her rights was a new pretext for intelligence officials to initiate a new case against her and request the maximum penalty, as a result of which her prison sentence was increased to 16 years in January 2016.

Nargess Mohammadi has young twins who live abroad but she is not allowed to contact them. In protest to this situation, Ms. Mohammadi went on hunger strike in June 2016. Her hunger strike forced the regime to back off after 18 days and grant her permission to contact her children from prison.

On December 3, 2019, Nargess Mohammadi was brutalized and sent to exile to the Prison of Zanjan.

Nasrin Sotoudeh

Human rights lawyer Nasrin Sotoudeh was arrested on June 13, 2018, to serve a five-year sentence issued for her in absentia in 2016 on the charge of association and collusion with the intent of sabotaging national security, by citing a sit-in outside the Justice Ministry's Lawyers Guild.

While she was in prison, a new file was opened for her which included seven more charges. Her case was examined in December 2018 and again on February 4, 2019, by Tehran's Revolutionary Court in her absence and while the lawyer of her own choosing was also prevented from attending the trials and handling her case.

On March 11, 2019, Nasrin Sotoudeh's husband informed the public that another 34 years and 148 lashes had been issued for her, adding up to a total of 38.5 years plus 148 lashes of the whip.

This is the second time Ms. Sotoudeh has been arrested. She was first arrested and imprisoned on September 4, 2010, for defending a number of protesters arrested during the 2009 uprising and activists defending women's and children's rights who faced the death penalty. She served three years in prison during which time she went on three hunger strikes for a total of 122 days.

Sepideh Moradi

Sepideh Moradi was arrested on February 20, 2018 during a protest by Gonabadi dervishes in Tehran. She was charged with disruption of public order, assembly and collusion against national security and sentenced to 5 years in Shahr-e Ray (Qarchak) Prison, plus a 2-year ban on leaving the country, membership in any political party, group or association and any activity on the internet.
Sepideh Moradi was sentenced in absentia on August 9, 2018 by the Revolutionary Court of Tehran presided by Judge Salavati. Neither her, nor her lawyer were present in the trial.
She had been summoned on July 14, 2018 by the 15th Branch of the Revolutionary Court of Tehran but did not report in, in protest to the Sufi prisoners' being denied their inalienable legal rights such as having access to lawyer.

Rouhiyeh Nariman

Rouhiyeh Nariman and her husband were arrested on October 8, 2018 for their faith and for teaching their pre-school child and several other Baha'i children at home. They were sentenced to 2.5 years in prison in prison of Shiraz.
The Baha'i couple asked the court to have their sentences implemented consecutively so that their child could stay with one of the parents, their request was turned down. On July 21, 2018, they were ordered to report in to the Directorate for Implementation of Sentences in Shiraz to begin serving their sentences.
Simultaneous imprisonment of both parents of a young child is carried out in accordance with the clerical regime's Constitution which has outlawed the Baha'i community in Iran in contrast to the Universal Declaration of Human Rights which recognizes freedom of religion and belief as basic human rights.

Holding prisoners under undecided status

Another common practice by the Iranian regime to pressure female political prisoners is holding them under undecided status.
A prisoner with undecided status is someone whose interrogation has been completed and the Ministry of Intelligence has filed suit against her but her trial has not been held. Sometimes, her court convenes but no sentence is issued for a long time.
Detaining a prisoner in undecided status gives her interrogators an open hand to make any decision at any time on her fate or harass her by any conceivable method.
This practice has been rejected by the Universal Declaration of Human Rights, the International Covenant on Civil and Political Rights, and many other international laws.
Some of the prisoners who have been detained in an undecided status are:

Marjan Davari

Marjan Davari arrested on September 24, 2015, was detained for almost two years in undecided status.

Ms. Davari, 50, a researcher, translator and writer, was first interrogated at the Intelligence Ministry Ward 209 of the Evin Prison for three months and held in solitary confinement without having access to legal counsel.

She was subsequently transferred to the women's general ward in Evin on January 3, 2016. In February 2017, she was transferred to the Shahr-e Ray Prison, a.k.a. Qarchak Prison, in Varamin.

Marjan Davari was sentenced to death on March 12, 2017, by the 15th branch of the Revolutionary Court in Tehran. Her death sentence was commuted to life imprisonment on January 6, 2018, by the Supreme Court. She is still detained in Qarchak Prison on charges of "spreading corruption on Earth," "collusion and complicity against the state," and insulting the mullahs' supreme leader, among others.

She was finally sentenced to 75 years' imprisonment in mid-February 2020.

Sepideh Farhan Farahabadi

Sepideh Farhan Farahabadi was a graduate student of architecture and a civil activist who was arrested by security forces in January 2018. Agents of the Ministry of Intelligence (MOIS) took her to Ward 209 of Evin Prison where they could keep her under their own watch. For about one month, Ms. Farhan was detained and mistreated under interrogation without having access to lawyer. On February 17, 2018, she was freed from Evin on a 250-million toman bail, but this was just the beginning.

On July 7, 2018, when she had been called to report to the court, Sepideh Farhan found out that she had been tried in absentia on June 24, 2018, by Branch 26 of the Revolutionary Court and sentenced to 74 lashes and six years in prison. The young student had been sentenced to one year in prison and 74 lashes on the charge of "disrupting public order by participating in unlawful gatherings." She was sentenced to another 5 years on the charge of "association and collusion to take actions against national security."

Sepideh Farhan Farahabadi was transferred to Evin Prison on January 1, 2020, to serve her sentence.

Atefeh Rangriz

Atefeh Rangriz, a graduate student of sociology and a labor activist, was arrested during a Labor Day demonstration in Tehran on May 1, 2019. She was sentenced to 11 years and six months in prison and 74 lashes. Her sentence was later commuted to 5 years.

Atefeh Rangriz started a hunger strike in the notorious Qarchak Prison of Varamin on October 16, 2019, to protest her unjust treatment in prison. In an open letter on the first day of her hunger strike, she wrote from prison:

"I was arrested on May 1, 2019, during the International Labor Day gathering. After four days, I could be freed on a 30-million-toman bail, but my release was prevented.
"For 28 days, I was being transferred back and forth between Qarchak and Evin prisons and interrogated. Although I had repeatedly told them in my answers that my activities had been completely legal, and I could not understand any of their questions, I finally faced charges which were utterly fake and fabricated...
"I have repeatedly objected to the illegal proceeding of my case, including the rejection of my bail bond, and the authorities' failure to observe the principle of separation of prisoners' categories. Outside the prison, my family did not receive any response for their inquiries, neither did I from inside..."
Ms. Rangriz was temporarily released on October 26, 2019.

Neda Yousefi
Neda Yousefi was arrested during the uprisings of January 2018 in the city of Shazand in Arak. She was released on bail but was later sentenced to one year in prison and 74 lashes by the 102nd branch of the Penal Court 2 of Arak in a trial presided by Judge Mohammad Reza Abdollahi.

- **Introduced or strengthened free and quality services for survivors of violence (e.g. shelters, help lines, dedicated health services, legal, justice service, counselling, housing)**

The Iranian regime occasionally provides data on the number of people who have called their helplines in the case of emergencies, suicides, etc. It is not clear, however, if they are for survivors of violence. Neither are there reports on shelters and services for survivors of violence. However, the case of one of the victims of violence was published in the press.

Azam, the woman who was accidentally found by neighbors after being tortured 21 days by her husband, was transferred along with her two daughters to a government welfare center.
The Welfare Organization's social affairs deputy in the Khorasan Razavi Province said the two daughters of Azam will stay with their mother in this center until they reach a better psychological condition. Then, they are going to be transferred to a children's house where they can stay, permanently if they want. Azam, however, will not be permitted to stay in such centers, permanently.[683]
This is while Azam's husband who had tortured her to the verge of death was released easily on a petty 20-million-toman bail (approx. $1,740) and could hurt her again.[684]
This incident is a vivid testimony to the lack of social protection for vulnerable women in Iran and the absence of any laws to provide them protection and to punish perpetrators of violence against women.

---

[683] The state-run ISNA news agency, April 25, 2016
[684] Tortured woman to stay without social protection, website of the NCRI Women's Committee, April 26, 2016

- **Introduced or strengthened strategies to prevent violence against women and girls (e.g. in the education sector, in the media, community mobilization, work with men and boys)**

A number of Iranian sociologists and social researchers have underscored the escalation of domestic violence against women in Iranian society, indicating that poverty and class differences, and discrimination are among the most important factors contributing to violence against women. Some say the legal, judicial and disciplinary structures are such that they allow men to use force against women.

- Reza Jafari, head of the Social Emergencies, told the media in May 2018 that domestic violence against women had seen a 20% growth in the period spanning from March 2017 to March 2018.
- Ahmad Bokharaii, director of social damages group affiliated with the Sociology Association, says, "Regardless of the existing cultural backgrounds promoting male domination (under the mullahs' rule), the legal, judicial and disciplinary structures are such that men allow themselves to imply force and commit violence against women…

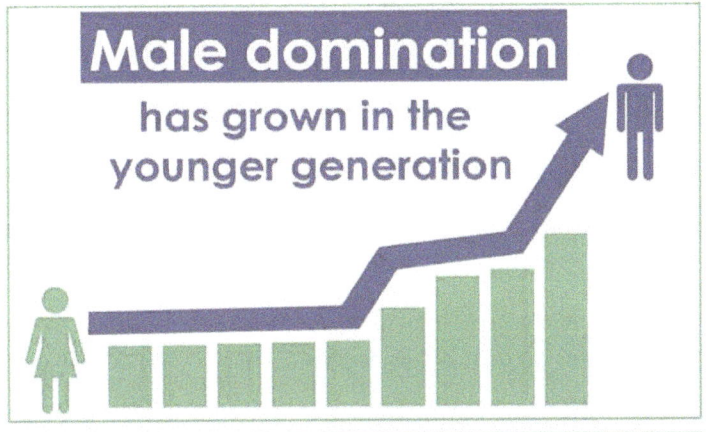

Between March 2017 and March 2018, there were 300 media reports on murders within the family and the statistics show that more than 80 percent of the victims were women."[685]

- Another social expert said male domination and its relevant prejudices have grown in the younger generation and based on the culture promoted (under the mullahs' misogynous rule), men consider domestic violence against women as a right they are entitled to.[686]

- **Monitoring and evaluation of impact, including evidence generation and data collection, including regarding particular groups of women and girls**

Data collection
The Iranian regime does not have an accountable census and data collection system. Furthermore, the regime is not transparent in providing the data. Officials usually speak by percentages without mentioning exact figures.
On rare occasions when they provide figures, the figures are insufficient or conflicting. The remarks made by a few officials are helpful in getting a picture of the situation:

- The last national survey on violence against women in Iran was conducted in 2000... Since then, no national research on violence against women has been carried out. If done, the results have been kept confidential and not publicly announced.[687]
- Domestic violence is not clearly seen in society because unfortunately a woman who is subjected to such violence, rarely speaks out about it. This is why many women suffer from it.[688]
- Many women who are subjected to violence do not file complaints for different reasons. Nevertheless, they lose their living skills due to the violence inflicted on them, to the extent that sometimes they lose their sanity and commit suicide... Women and mothers who are subjected to violence or are constantly brutalized cannot manage their families, properly.[689]
- Statistics on domestic violence against women is not reported, registered or published in the media, so there is nowhere you can find the exact data.[690]

---

[685] The official IRNA news agency - July 18, 2018
[686] The official IRNA news agency - July 18, 2018
[687] In 2014, the presidential deputy on women and family affairs, Shahindokht Molaverdi revealed that 32 volumes of books containing the outcome of a national research done on domestic violence against women "have been lost" and no copies of them can be found "in the Ministry of Interior or the directorate for women and family affairs."
[688] Parvaneh Salahshouri, head of women's faction in the mullahs' parliament, the state-run IRNA news agency, November 25, 2017
[689] Tayyebeh Siavoshi, member of the women's faction of the mullahs' parliament, the state-run donya-e-eqtesad.com, July 17, 2018
[690] Kamel Delpasand, sociologist and a researcher in social sciences, interview with the official IRNA news agency, July 18, 2018

- Women generally do not complain about the violence they experience and the government's data does not accurately reflect the reality.[691]

14. What strategies has your country used in the last five years to prevent violence against women and girls?

- Public awareness raising and changing of attitudes and behaviours
- Work in primary and secondary education, including comprehensive sexuality education
- Grassroots and community-level mobilization
- Changing the representation of women and girls in the media
- Working with men and boys
- Perpetrator programs

Perpetrator programs

The Iranian regime does not have any perpetrator programs. The assailants are rarely arrested, and in the case of government officials, they are granted impunity.

In the meantime, the regime's officials and clerical authorities often incite violence against women. One of the most vivid examples of this was in the case of chain acid attacks on women in 2014.

Zahra Navidpour

On January 6, 2019 the lifeless body of Zahra Navidpour was found in her mother's residence in Malekan, a small city in East Azerbaijan Province. Zahra had been raped repeatedly by the city's deputy. Her death was initially announced as suicide, but the circumstances were suspicious.

Zahra Navidpour, 28, was looking for a job after her father's death, when she was offered a job by Salman Khodadadi, the city's deputy in the parliament, and lured into his office in Tehran where she was raped.

Holding audio recordings and other incriminating documents at hand, Zahra filed a suit against Khodadadi but due to the latter's collusions with the court, she faced an unfair trial and a presiding judge who was intent to incriminate her.

In a verbal encounter in the parliament building, Khodadadi threatened to kill Zahra and her family "overnight without anyone knowing."

Zahra's death projected as suicide seemed suspicious, so the coroner's office was supposed to perform autopsy on her, but security forces stole and secretly buried her body in a village before the autopsy.

---

[691] Ali Hadizadegan, Chief Coroner of Mashhad, The state-run Fars news agency, November 23, 2017

In the wake of Zahra's death, Tehran Province's Criminal Court convicted Salman Khodadadi of adultery "without use of violence" and sentenced him to 99 lashes in addition to two years of internal exile and deprivation of holding elected or appointed positions.

Khodadadi objected the verdict and his case was undertaken by one of the branches of the Tehran Supreme Court.

Later, in October 2019, Tehran's Supreme Court branch accepted the convict's objection. While rejecting the charge of "rape," the Supreme Court did not uphold the preliminary ruling because Khodadadi suffers from diabetes and injects insulin. The case was turned back to the Criminal Court of Tehran to be re-examined.[692]

Farinaz Khosravani

On May 4, 2015, a young woman by the name of Farinaz Khosravani threw herself off the fourth floor of Tara Hotel in Mahabad, Iranian Kurdistan, to escape rape by an agent of the Intelligence Department, Morteza Hashemivand.[693]

Khosravani was 26 and lived in Mahabad. She had a Bachelor's degree in Computer Sciences but worked in a hotel to provide for her family's expenses.

The lawyer of Khosravani family announced, "To this day, the result of Farinaz's case has remained unclear and no convictions have been ordered by the court."

Then on June 22, 2015, the Ministry of Interior announced that the "Mahabad incident" had been closed.[694]

Reyhaneh Jabbari

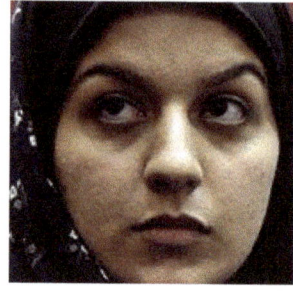

Reyhaneh Jabbari, 26, was executed at dawn on October 25, 2014 in Gohardasht Prison in Karaj, west of Tehran. She had already spent 7 years in prison.[695]

Jabbari, a decorator, was 19-years old when charged with murdering Morteza Sarbandi, a 47-year old married doctor who had three children and was a former employee of the Ministry of Intelligence (MOIS). Jabbari defended herself against the MOIS employee's attempt to rape her.

Ahmad Shaheed, the United Nations Special Rapporteur on Human Rights in Iran, had at the time described her death sentence as inadmissible and unfair. He cited credible documents that proved Jabbari was innocent of premeditated murder charges. The UN Special Rapporteur emphasized if Jabbari's claims are true, she is twice a victim: once by the individual who intended to rape her; and second, by the judicial system that must protect individuals against sexual and physical aggression.

---

[692] The state-run Fararu website – October 15, 2019
[693] Girl commits suicide to save herself from rape, another crime against women by mullahs, website of the NCRI Women's Committee, May 8, 2015
[694] Case of Farinaz Khosravani remains under legal consideration, website of the NCRI Women's Committee, June 22, 2015
[695] Special report: Reyhaneh Jabbari's execution, website of NCRI Women's Committee, November 26, 2014

Incitements provoking acid attacks

In 2014, where a systematic wave of acid attacks on women in Tehran and Isfahan left dozens of women disfigured for the rest of their lives, the Iranian police and judiciary failed to arrest any perpetrators.

A stark reality is that the Iranian authorities are the ones who incite such attacks against women. Following are a number of their remarks preceding the acid attacks:

- Ahmad Khatami, member of the Assembly of Experts' board of directors: "Blood must be spilled in order to resolve the issue of hijab."[696]
- Yousef Tabatabai-Nejad, Friday prayer leader of Isfahan: "To confront 'mal-veiling' we must raise a 'wet stick' and resort to force."[697]
- MesbahYazdi, a high-ranking mullah in Bojnourd close to Khamenei, said: "Prohibiting vice cannot be established with kindness." [698]
- Mullah Ahmad Alam ol-Hoda, Mashhad Friday prayer leader: "Mal-veiled women are vicious as wolves. The sin of improper veiling is worse than theft and murder."[699]

17. Has your country taken any action in the last five years to address violence against specific groups of women facing multiple forms of discrimination?
YES/NO

No. Not only the Iranian regime has not addressed violence against specific groups of women facing multiple forms of discrimination, but has systematically used violence against them.

Sufi women

Eleven Gonabadi dervish women were taken to Qarchak Prison. Shokoufeh Yadollahi, Sepideh Moradi, Maryam Farsiabi, Nazila Noori, Sima Entesari, Shima Entesari, Shahnaz Kiani, Maryam Barakouhi, Elham Ahmadi, Avisha Jalaledin and Sedigheh Safabakht were brutalized during the crackdown on the dervishes' protest gathering in Tehran on the night of February 19 which carried through morning of February 20, 2018.

They were detained since under inhumane conditions, without access to their lawyers. Some needed urgent medical care for injuries sustained from beatings at the time of arrest.

These women have suffered a range of health problems in custody, due to ill-treatment by security forces, including head injuries, broken arms and vaginal bleeding. They also have been denied adequate treatment for pre-existing medical conditions such as asthma, diabetes and high blood pressure.

---

[696] The state-run Aftab daily, May 6, 2011 http://aftabnews.ir/vdcgzn9qtak9xu4.rpra.html
[697] The state-run Asr-e Iran daily, November 23, 2011 http://www.asriran.com/fa/news/191466/
[698] The state-run Fars news agency, October 23, 2014 http://www.farsnews.com/newstext.php?nn=1
[699] Ahmad Alam al-Hoda's personal blog http://omolbnin4.blogfa.com/post/169/

- Shokoufeh Yadollahi was badly brutalized during arrest and subsequently under torture as a result of which she lost her sense of smell and needs to be treated urgently. A six-month denial of medical care led to an increase in the level of infection in her blood and endangered her life.
- Shima Entesari, who suffers from asthma, experienced severe breathing difficulties requiring supplemental oxygen.
- Dr. Nazilla Noori who had been through vicious torture, was hospitalized but deprived of having a company, receiving visitors or phone calls.
- Sepideh Moradi suffered injuries in the hand, elbow and fingers while being arrested during the Sufis' protest in Tehran. Her legs got burnt due to security forces' use of tear gas. Ms. Moradi was denied medical care.
- Ms. Shahnaz Kian Asl (Kiani) was transferred to the dispensary of Qarchak Prison of Varamin on May 19, 2018 upon insistence of inmates, but was returned to the ward without receiving medical care. She suffered from diabetes and her symptoms had aggravated due to mal-nutrition. A new mass had appeared in her chest area and she contracted ulcer and GI inflammation, but had not been cared for at the dispensary.
- "Women prisoners of conscience from Iran's Gonabadi Dervish religious community are being subjected to verbal abuse, including sexual slurs, and denied proper medical treatment by doctors and other health professionals at Shahr-e Rey prison on the outskirts of Tehran," Amnesty International said in a statement issued on May 25, 2018.

Philip Luther, Amnesty International's Research and Advocacy Director for the Middle East and North Africa, asserted, "Deliberately denying medical treatment to any prisoner is unlawful, cruel and inhuman and can amount to torture. These women from Iran's Gonabadi Dervish community should not even be imprisoned in the first place. It is deplorable that the Iranian authorities are seeking to intimidate and torment them further."

- Sufi women went on hunger strike for 16 days from June 17, 2018, in the wake of their being attacked and beaten up by special prison guards using batons and shockers on June 13.
- The Revolutionary Court sentenced Nazilla Noori, Avisha Jalaleddin, Sima Entessari, Shima Entessari, Elham Ahmadi and Sedigheh Safabakht each to five years in prison.
- Maryam Farsiabi was tried and sentenced to a six-month jail and a two-year ban from traveling abroad.
- Sepideh Moradi was sentenced to five years' imprisonment in absentia on August 8, 2018 by Tehran's Revolutionary Court. She was also banned from leaving the country for two years, and from engaging in any social or political party or group or any activity in the social media.
- Shokoufeh Yadollahi was sentenced to five years in jail. She was in critical conditions due to lack of medical treatment in prison.
- Ms. Shahnaz Kian Asl due to her dire health conditions and Ms. Massoumeh Barakoohi on the orders of the 15th Branch of the Revolutionary Court, were released.

Bahai's

Followers of the Baha'i faith are systematically harassed and persecuted under the clerical regime in Iran. They are denied equitable access to employment, education, political office and exercise of their economic, social and cultural rights.

Dozens of Baha'i students are expelled from universities and deprived of continuing their education every year.

In the time span from March 2017 to February 2018, at least 47 Baha'i women were arrested.[700]
At least 16 Baha'i female students were denied admission to universities in 2019 despite successfully passing the competitive National University Exam with high marks.[701]
After being arrested in November 2018, Shahrzad Nazifi, a Baha'i citizen and motocross champion and trainer in Iran, has been deprived along with her family of participating in any competition or training others in this field without any official judicial verdict.[702]
Ms. Nazifi's daughter, Nora Naraghi, who is also a top moto-crosser, has been deprived of any athletic activities along with her mother because of her faith.

Mazdak Etemadzadeh, an attorney at law who has represented some Baha'is issued a short report on the conditions of Baha'i women's detention and prosecution.[703]

---

[700] Annual Report 2018, the website of the NCRI Women's Committee, March 2018
[701] Annual Report 2020, the website of the NCRI Women's Committee, March 2020
[702] Ibid.
[703] Open letter by Mazdak Etemadzadeh, AdianCommittee.wordpress.com, July 16, 2016

According to the report, every defendant has only 4 minutes to defend herself in the court which is a violation of the legal procedures. The defendants are charged with proselytizing Baha'ism. According to Etemadzadeh,

- Sheida Ghodousi from Gorgan, was sentenced to 11 years in prison;
- Farah Tebianian, Pouneh Sanaii, Mona Amri Hessari, Parisa Shahidi, Mojdeh Zohouri, Parivash Shojaii, Tina Mohebati and Hana Aghighian from Gorgan as well as Bita Hedayati and Hana Koushki from Gonbad-Kavous were sentenced each to 9 years in prison;
- Rofia Pakzadan, Soudabeh Mehdinejad, Mitra Nouri, Shiva Rohani, Maryam Dehghan and Nazi Khalkhi from Gorgan as well as Shohreh Samimi and Kameli Bideli from Minoudasht were each sentenced to 6 years in prison.
- The report also indicated that Baha'is are tortured because of their faith. The tortures include: suspension (by hands from ceiling), dragging on the ground while handcuffed, keeping the prisoner under rain for a long period, interrogations during the night, threatening to harass young girls and accusing them of illicit relationships, aggressive body search during transfer to the detention center, and severe beatings.[704]

Christians

Christian converts from Islam are seriously discriminated against. Considering that the Christian population in Iran is 300,000 at most, they experience disproportionate levels of arrests and detention, and high levels of harassment and surveillance.

- Fatemeh Mohammadi (Mary), a Christian convert and student at Azad University of North-Tehran, was banned from attending school on December 21, 2019. She was previously beaten by the guidance patrol in Tehran on July 9, 2019 and sentenced to six months in prison on the charge of Christian activity.
  She was arrested again on January 12, 2020, after she participated in a ceremony commemorating victims of the Ukrainian plane shot down by the IRGC.
  She was transferred to Tehran's Vozara Detention Center and subjected to physical and sexual torture. She was sent to the courtyard and forced to sit on the asphalt floor in front of the toilets in the freezing cold weather.
  She was then questioned by three male interrogators.
  Mary Mohammadi was denied food during the first 24 hours of her detention.
  In addition to beating her, female officers conducted a physical examination and forced Mary to remove all her clothing, and do repeated squats. The officers threatened to strip her by force if she did not do it herself.
  She is presently detained in Qarchak Prison.
- On July 1, 2019, four Christian women, along with their spouses, were arrested by agents of the Ministry of Intelligence. Maryam Fallahi, 35, Marjan Fallahi, 33, Khatoun Fathollahzadeh, 61, and Fatemeh Talebi, 27, were arrested along with their husbands.

---

[704] Ibid.

- On January 6, 2018, a court in Tehran issued a five-year prison sentence for Ms. Shamiram Essavi on the charge of acting against national security for launching home churches.
- Two Christian women, Shima and Shokufeh Zanganeh, were both arrested at their homes by the Ministry of Intelligence agents on December 2, 2018. Thirteen plainclothes agents raided and inspected the homes of these two Christian women and seized some of their personal documents and transferred them to an unknown location.
- Christian Kurdish woman, Massoumeh Taqinejad, 30, from Kermanshah in western Iran, was arrested and detained along with her son, Artin, in a raid by intelligence forces on her residence in Karaj, on July 2, 2018. This Christian Kurdish woman was charged with "proselytizing Christianity" on the internet.
- On September 11, 2017, Sara Nemati and Mehrdad Houshmand, a Christian couple, were arrested for participating in a funeral in Behesht-e Zahra, in which they practiced Christian rituals.
- Anousheh (Veronica) Rezabakhsh and her son were arrested on February 20, 2017, and taken to a detention center in Urmia, capital of West Azerbaijan Province.

Kurds

Kurdish women activists are systematically imprisoned and tortured.
Kurdish activist women have been arrested and imprisoned throughout 2018 and 2019.
In the time span from March 2017 to February 2018, at least 47 Kurdish women were arrested.[705]

- Shetaw Faroughi from Marivan was transferred to the Central Prison of Sanandaj on March 24, 2018. She was arrested with her two children on March 3, 2018, at Tabriz Airport, upon return from Istanbul where she had visited her husband. Her children, 12 and 5, were released after three days.[706]
- Zeinab Jalalian sentenced to life imprisonment remains in Khoy Prison.
- Zahra Mohammadi, 29, was arrested on May 23, 2019, when agents of the Intelligence Department of Sanandaj raided her residence. She was a member of Nojin Social and Cultural Association in Sanandaj which is active in protection of the environment in Kurdistan. Zahra holds an M.S. degree in geopolitics from the University of Birjand.
  She was temporarily released on December 2, 2019 on a heavy bail of 700 million tomans ($166K).
- A Kurdish woman activist, Parvin Advaii, was arrested at home during a raid by agents of the Intelligence Department of Marivan, Iranian Kurdistan, on July 27, 2019.
- Civil activist Iran Rahpaykar continues to remain in limbo in the detention center of Sanandaj, capital of the Iranian Kurdistan Province, despite passage of 1.5 months

---

[705] Annual Report 2018, the website of the NCRI Women's Committee, March 2018
[706] Wife, two children of Kurdish activist arrested, website of the NCRI Women's Committee, March 9, 2018

since her arrest. She has been taken to the Department of Intelligence for interrogation several times.
- Sara Zahmatkesh, 24, a women's rights activist and a social sciences expert from Paveh, was arrested on April 21, 2019, by agents of the intelligence department of Paveh and taken to an unknown location. No information is available on her fate. Ms. Zahmatkesh headed the Jiar-Tin Women's Association.
- Sahar Kazemi, a Kurdish civil rights and environmental activist and a sports coach from Sanandaj, was arrested at her home in Sanandaj, on August 9, 2018. She was sentenced to five years in prison in mid-February 2019.
- Sorayya Khedri was arrested in Sanandaj on September 13, 2018.
- Kurdish activist woman, Ronak Aghaii, was taken to the Prison of Mahabad on April 4, 2018, to serve her jail sentence of six months.

PARTICIPATION, ACCOUNTABILITY AND GENDER-RESPONSIVE INSTITUTIONS

18. What actions and measures has your country taken in the last five years to promote women's participation in public life and decision-making?

The Iranian regime is not an advocate of women's participation in public life and decision-making. Even when it speaks of women's participation, it is in response to public and international pressure.
Therefore, the policies of the Iranian regime are not devised to promote women's participation, eliminate discrimination against women in government or non-government institutions, compensate for their underrepresentation in trade unions, or implement capacity building, skills development for women.
At the same time, for a regime that persecutes religious and ethnic minorities it is inconceivable to encourage participation of minority and young women in public life and decision making.

- **Reformed constitution, laws and regulations that promote women's participation in politics, especially at decision-making level, including electoral system reform**

According to the Constitution of the clerical regime, women cannot be elected as the president, cannot be judges, or employed in the army and in the main branches of the police force.
From the regime's religious perspective, women can only guide women, therefore women cannot be appointed to the high assembly of experts. Heads of the three government branches should also be elected from among men.[707]
These laws have not been reformed to this date.

Article 115 of the Iranian Constitution states: The President of the Republic must be elected from among the religious and political *Rejal*.[708]
The Guardians Council has reiterated that the word *Rejal* refers exclusively to men and no woman can be elected as President.[709]
As recent as the 12th presidential elections in 2017, all the 137 women who had registered as candidates were disqualified.[710] Subsequently, Interior Minister Abdul Reza Rahmani Fazli announced that women are not included among presidential candidates and that the Council of Guardians had turned down all registration requests.[711]

---

[707] The state-run Javanonline newspaper, November 4, 2015
[708] Constitution of the Islamic Republic of Iran, Research Center of the parliament, http://rc.majlis.ir/fa/content/iran_constitution
[709] Why the Iranian regime does not join the CEDAW? website of the NCRI Women's Committee, March 5, 2016
[710] Disqualification of female candidates went unheeded, Shahindokht Molaverdi, presidential deputy for women and family affairs, May 3, 2017
[711] Disqualification of female candidates went unheeded, website of the NCRI Women's Committee, May 5, 2017

Similarly, membership of the Assembly of Experts is exclusively for men. Although this has not been written out clearly in the law, it is implied, and no woman has been appointed to the assembly in the past 40 years.

All 16 women who had signed up as candidates for the Assembly of Experts election on January 26, 2016, were disqualified.[712]

According to Articles 105 and 109 of the Constitution, women cannot be leaders, either. In addition, according to Article 20 on women's political rights, leadership is a duty that is only granted to men.

- **Adoption of temporary special measures, such as quotas, reserved seats, benchmarks and targets to promote women's participation in public life and decision making**

Despite a 2012 instruction by the Islamic Countries' Inter-Parliamentary Union Conference for Iran to consider a 25% quota for women in the parliament to compensate for women's small presence,[713] the Iranian regime has refused to do so.

In fact, Iran ranks embarrassingly low even in the Middle East with regards to women's political participation. It ranks 14 among 16 Middle East countries[714] and 180 among 191 countries in the world. Only Nigeria, Thailand, Sri Lanka, Lebanon, Maldives, Kuwait, Haiti, Oman, Yemen and Guinea rank lower.[715]

The average number of seats allocated to women in the Iranian regime's parliament stands at 5.9 percent in 2019 compared to the world's average of 24.3%.[716]

In April 2019, the Iranian parliament voted down a proposal to allocate a one-sixth quota of parliamentary seats to women by a vote of 110 to 79 on April 16, 2019.

Ironically, one of the MPs said in the debate that setting a quota for women would be against Article 9 of Principle 3 of the Constitution against discrimination.[717]

---

[712] The state-run Aftabnews website, January 26, 2016
[713] Shahnaz Sajjadi, member of the Ministry of Justice's central Lawyers Guild, The state-run ISNA news agency, October 21, 2015
[714] Shahnaz Sajjadi, member of the Ministry of Justice's central Lawyers Guild, The state-run ISNA news agency, October 21, 2015
[715] Parvaneh Mafi, a female member of the mullahs' parliament, the state-run Iran daily, April 17, 2019
[716] Ibid.
[717] Shahab Naderi, member of the mullahs' parliament, the state-run ICANA news agency, April 17, 2019

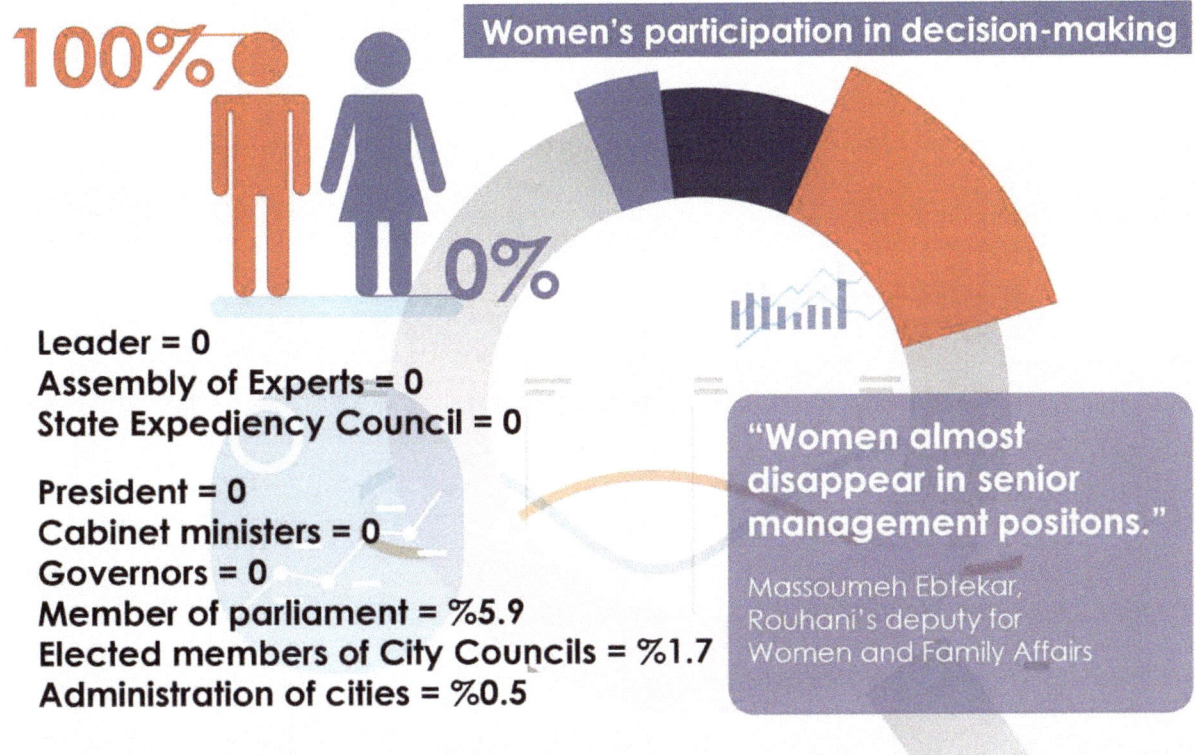

- Ensured that organizations such as political parties and trade unions, which may not be subject directly to obligations under the Convention, do not discriminate against women

Not applicable in the case of Iran, because there are no legal and genuine political parties or trade unions in the country.

- Collected and analyzed data on women's political participation, including in appointed and elected positions

According to the World Economic Forum's Global Gender Gap report 2020, Iran ranks 148 among 153 countries preceding only Congo, Syria, Pakistan, Iraq and Yemen.
The global gender gap index for Iran is 0.584, denoting a wide gender gap where men's benefits are twice as much of women's.
The hierarchy of decision-making and political power in Iran is completely male-dominated with no opportunity for women's participation.
The Supreme Leader is a man, the president is a man, the Guardians Council is comprised of 12 men and no women, the State Expediency Council is made up of 44 men, and all the 33 Cabinet ministers are men.
Women's presence in the cabinet has always been among the promises made in the presidential election campaigns, but Mahmoud Ahmadinejad was the only president who managed to

appoint a woman, Marzieh Vahid Dastjerdi, as Minister of Health (2009-2012), who was relieved of her duties after three years.

Presenlty, Laya Jonaidi, Shahindokht Molaverdi and Massoumeh Ebtekar are the only women who have non-minister roles in the 12th cabinet, as assistants and deputies to Hassan Rouhani, the mullahs' president, and do not enjoy executive powers.

Shahindokht Molaverdi, who served as head of the presidential directorate for women and family affairs, during Rouhani's first term, repeatedly complained about not having any executive powers to advance her directorate's projects.[718]

Massoumeh Ebtekar, Rouhani's deputy in Women and Family Affairs, once acknowledged that "women almost disappear in senior management positons."[719]

In eleven rounds of elections in Iran since the mullahs took power 40 years ago, only 12 women held positions of mayors.[720]

According to the Global Gender Gap Report 2020, the average women's political participation in the parliament stands at 0.298.[721]

In the current Iranian parliament, there are only 17 women among 290 members of parliament, making up a mere 5.8% participation for women.

There are 31 provincial governors (*Ostandar*) and no woman is among them.

There are 430 posts for governors of counties (*Farmandar*). Only five women were appointed as county governors.[722]

According to earlier reports from 2013 to 2015 by official sources, women held only 13 out of 2653 positions as provincial governors, governors, district governors, and mayors in the administration of Iranian cities and provinces. The breakdown is as the following:

The number of female provincial governors (*ostandar*): Zero from 31 [723]

The number of female governors (*farmandar*): 4 out of 440 governors (about 0.9%). However, with the death of the Governor of Turkeman, the number of women governors decreased to 0.7%. [724]

Two female mayors out of a total number of 1148 of mayors run small towns of Louleman in the Province of Gilan and Kalat in the Province of Sistan and Baluchestan. These small towns are not even registered in the list of cities.[725]

The number of female district governors (*bakhshdar*): 7 out of 1034 [726]

---

[718] In an interview which was published by the Tnews.ir, on August 24, 2015, Shahindokht Molaverdi revealed that "since we do not have an executive status, we have not yet found any desirable, effective relationship with other systems and provinces, and have faced serious obstacles from the beginning."
[719] The state-run ISNA news agency, October 31, 2017
[720] The state-run Jamejamonline.ir, August 22, 2017
[721] Global Gender Gap Report 2020, page 189
[722] The state-run Borna.news, May 23, 2017
[723] The state-run Raja News website – March 6, 2014
[724] The state-run Ham Ava website – April 19, 2015; the state-run Mashregh news website – October 6, 2015
[725] The state-run Mehr news agency – December 15, 2013
[726] The state-run Ham Ava website – April 19, 2015

A report published by the parliament on the city councils' elections, accounting only for the main cities, claims that women constitute some 12% of the city councils and concludes a 1% drop in women's participation.[727]

Another state-run news outlet studied the decrease in women's participation only in provincial centers estimating a 36.4% drop and setting the current number of women at 42.[728]

The NCRI Women's Committee compiled the latest elections outcome in more than 500 Iranian cities and towns from the statistics published in the state-run media in Iran and concluded that: In a total of 500 big and small cities, only 64 women were elected as members of City Councils compared to 3724 male members. That amounts to a meager 1.7% participation for women in the City Councils.[729]

A study on the outcome of the elections for the City Councils[730]
Women's participation compared in the fourth and fifth major City Councils

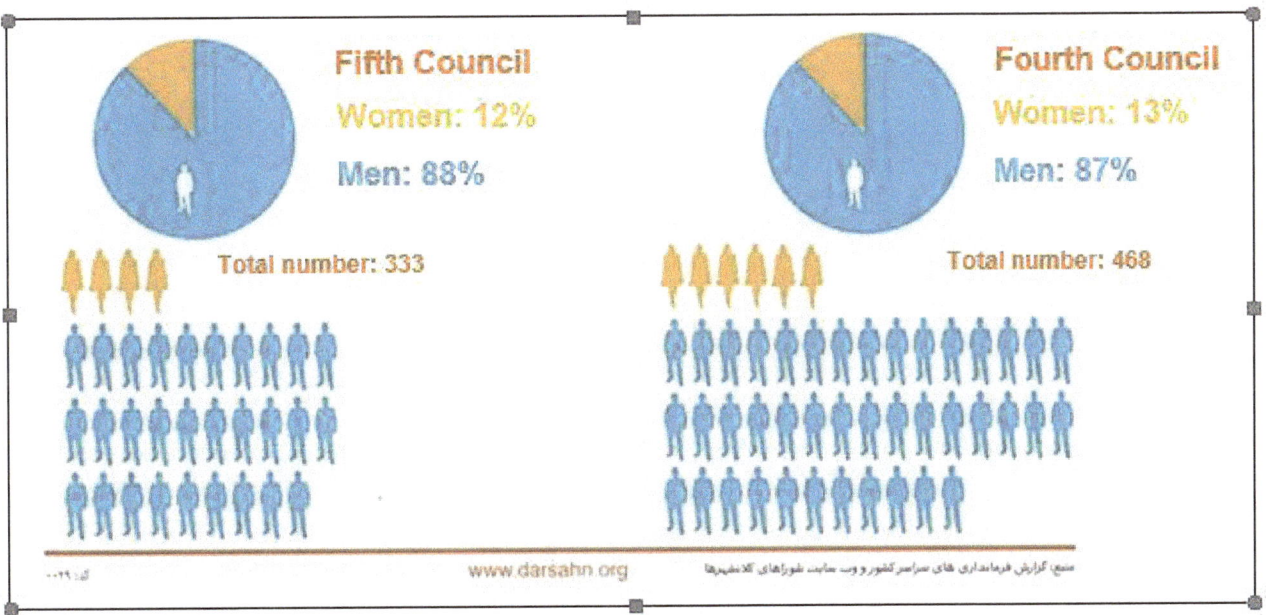

---

[727] The state-run Darsahn-e Majlis va Showraha, June 6, 2017 http://www.darsahn.org/1396/03/16/zanan-dar-kalanshahrha
[728] The state-run Iran newspaper, May 29, 2017
[729] A study of Iranian Women's Participation as governors, mayors, and members of city councils, NCRI Women's Committee website, June 2017
[730] Ibid.

- Other

Exclusion of women also applies to the realm of judgement

The guidelines for appointment of judges in the judiciary system states: "Judges should be elected from among men…"

As for female judges, after the Iranian Revolution in 1979, the instruction was to observe principles of *Sharia* in implementing Article 162 on the appointment of judges. Therefore, no woman was allowed to sit on the bench after the revolution when the mullahs seized power.

In 1983, a law was passed indicating the circumstances for becoming a judge. According to the new law, judges who issue verdicts must be chosen from among qualified MEN.

In 1984, the law was reformed, and it was stipulated that women can be appointed to some advisory posts.

19. What actions has your country taken in the last five years to increase women's access to expression and participation in decision-making in the media, including through information and communication technologies (ICT)?

This is not applicable to Iran as no freedom of expression exists for neither men nor women, and access to the internet is restricted.

20. Do you or the state track the proportion of the national budget that is invested in the promotion of gender equality and the empowerment of women (gender-responsive budgeting)?

No. As the Iranian regime spends the greater portion of the country's wealth on funding wars, terrorism and proxy groups, and its nuclear and missile programs, and a good portion of the country's funds and revenues is embezzled by the ruling hierarchy, including the supreme leader Ali Khamenei, and the Revolutionary Guard Corps (IRGC), little remains to pay the salaries of government employees, create jobs, and provide support to the vulnerable sectors.

Not only there is no chance for gender-responsive budgeting, but issues of women and girls do not have any priority in the Iranian regime's budgeting and planning.[731]

In addition, the regime does not espouse gender equality and empowerment of women.

For example, in the fiscal year 1398 (March 2019-March 2020), the Iranian regime allocated 62 trillion tomans to security and intelligence, 3,351 billion tomans to religious propaganda, but only 14.2 billion tomans to the Directorate of Women and Family Affairs, and 138 billion tomans to support women heads of household.[732]

As a result of such budget policy 88 percent of women heads of household who were eligible to receive subsidies from the Poverty Preventing Plan were excluded due to lack of funds.[733]

---

[731] Issues of women and children are overlooked, website of the NCRI Women's Committee, December 27, 2017
[732] Budget Bill of 1398, BBC Persian website, December 26, 2018
[733] Ahmad Maidari, Deputy Minister of Cooperatives, Labour and Social Welfare, the state-run IRNA News Agency – February 12, 2019

The Labor Ministry supports only 40 daycare centers for female employees who have young children, but the budget for this limited support was also cut from 15.6 to 10 billion Rials in the 1398 budget.

In the Persian fiscal year 1399, the situation is worse. Although the Directorate on Women and Family Affairs boasts of receiving a budget of 25 billion tomans which is 19% compared to the previous year,[734] but other budgets for women have been totally eliminated, including the budget for insurance of housewives, and the budget for insurance of women heads of household.[735] No budget was allocated for empowerment of women.[736]

All this, while the exchange rate for Iran's currency, Rial, has dropped even further bringing down the value of the allocated budget for the women's directorate from $2.17 million to $1.6 million.

22. Does your country have a valid national strategy or action plan for gender equality?

The Iranian regime's general planning and macro policies have been listed in a document called the "20-year Prospect Document" and "the Sixth Development Program."

Under the clerical regime, all issues concerning women are dealt with in the context of family. For example, the presidential Directorate on Women and Family Affairs, the parliamentary faction on family and women, etc.

Likewise, in the Sixth Development Program, the general policies concerning women are outlined in articles 101 and 102 promoting family as an institution.

Article 101 of the Sixth Development Program states that all executive agencies are obliged to implement the goals listed in the 20-year Prospect Document and the Sixth Development Program <u>to implement gender equity</u> in their agencies.

Article 102 of the same program instructs the government <u>to promote and strengthen a society centered around family, childbearing, and raising good children</u>. It further seeks to bring down the average age of marriage, increase the average number of children per family to 2.5, and turn marriage and childbearing into a value.

None of the 11 paragraphs of Article 102 focuses on gender equality.

23. Does your country have an action plan and timeline for implementation of the recommendations of the Committee on the Elimination of Discrimination against Women (if a State party), or of the recommendations of the Universal Periodic Review or other United Nations human rights mechanisms that address gender inequality/ discrimination against women?

No. The Iranian regime is not a state party of the Convention on the Elimination of all forms of Discrimination against Women.

---

[734] Zahra Javaherian, deputy for planning and coordination in the Presidential Directorate on Women and Family Affairs, the state-run ISNA news agency, December 11, 2019

[735] Zahra Javaherian, deputy for planning and coordination in the Presidential Directorate on Women and Family Affairs, the state-run ISNA news agency, December 11, 2019; Tayyebeh Saivoshi, member of the mullahs' parliament, the state-run javanonline.ir, January 2, 2020

[736] Farideh Olad Ghobad, member of the mullahs' parliament, the state-run ICANA.ir, December 17, 2019

Nor does it have any action plan or timeline for implementation of the recommendations of the Committee on the Elimination of Discrimination against Women, or the recommendations of the UPR or other UN human rights mechanisms.

In its submission for the UN Universal Periodic Review, 34th session of the UPR Working Group, November 2019, Amnesty International wrote:

Iran rejected 31 of the 56 recommendations it received regarding women's rights, including those calling for ratifying the Convention on the Elimination of All Forms of Discrimination Against Women, raising the minimum age of marriage to 18 years and eliminating the practice of forced and early marriage, criminalizing domestic violence, and reforming discriminatory laws. Iran has failed to make progress on the 25 recommendations it accepted, including to prevent and punish discrimination and violence against women, and enhance their participation in political decision-making processes.

Amnesty International's research shows that women face entrenched discrimination in family law and criminal law. Iran's legal system puts women in a subordinate status relative to men. Under the penal code, the testimony of a woman is accorded half the value of that of a man. The age of criminal responsibility is set at nine lunar years (eight years and eight months) for girls but at 15 lunar years (14 years and six months) for boys.

Women are also discriminated against under the Civil Code, notably in matters relating to marriage, divorce, child custody and inheritance.

Iran has failed to criminalize gender-based violence, including domestic violence and marital rape. A bill to protect women against violence has been stalled since 2012.

Under Iranian law, women and girls as young as 9 who are seen in public without a headscarf can be sentenced to prison, flogging or a cash fine. Millions of women and girls face daily harassment and abuse at the hands of state agents enforcing Iran's strict Islamic dress code for women and girls. Women peacefully protesting against degrading forced hijab (veiling) laws have been violently arrested and sentenced to imprisonment.

Child marriage continues to be permitted under the law. A proposed amendment to Article 1041 of the Civil Code that would have raised the age of marriage for girls from 13 to 16 was rejected by the parliament's judicial and legal committee in December 2018.

24. Is there a national human rights institution in your country?

No. Iran's clerical regime has claimed drafting a bill to establish a National Human Rights Institution, which is supposedly on its way to be reviewed and adopted. The bill contains no direct reference to the rights of women and fails to provide any concrete guarantees for the observance of human rights in Iran. Rather, it relies on the same agencies that are themselves, the prime violators of human rights in Iran.[737]

---

[737] Website of Abbas Akhoundi, former Minister of Roads and Transportation, April 10, 2019
https://www.abbasakhoundi.ir/archive/ID/1232

PEACEFUL AND INCLUSIVE SOCIETIES

28. What actions has your country taken in the last five years to eliminate discrimination against and violations of the rights of the girl child?

- **Taken measures to combat negative social norms and practices and increased awareness of the needs and potential of girl children**

Early marriages are considered the worst negative social practice with regards to the rights of the girl child. It is also violence against women and the worst form of oppression of Iranian girl children and future women of Iran.

- Institutionalized in the clerical regime's laws, the legal age of marriage for Iranian girl children is 13 years, and they can be given to marriage even younger if the father and a judge decide that they are mature enough.[738]
- In view of the bankrupt economic situation in Iran, rampant unemployment, and 80% of the population living under the poverty line, forced marriage of girl children has turned into the only way for a large number of families in Iran to reduce their expenses or earn some income.
- Forced early marriage is also the most significant contributor to school dropouts among girl children in Iran.
- In addition to creating various mental and physical problems for young girls, forced early marriages of girl children in Iran have paved the way for a plethora of social ills such as early divorces, child widows, domestic violence against women, and murder.[739]
- A proposed amendment to Article 1041 of the Civil Code that would have raised the age of marriage for girls from 13 to 16 was rejected by the parliament's judicial and legal committee in December 2018.[740]
- The Iranian census organization released new statistics on early marriages in Iran. According to the new data, 234,000 marriages of girl children under 15 years of age were officially registered by this organization from March 2017 to March 2018 (Persian year 1396). 194 of these were marriages of girl children under 10 years old.[741]
- Ali Kazemi, advisor to the legal deputy of the Judiciary Branch, announced in March 2019, that between 5 to 600,000 girl children get married every year (in Iran). This figure relates to officially registered marriages and does not include those which were not officially registered.[742]

---

[738] Amendment to Article 1041 of the Civil Code allows the father to wed his daughter even before 9 years of age after receiving endorsement of a judge.
[739] Early marriages of girl children in Iran have dire consequences, website of the NCRI Women's Committee, July 6, 2018; Child marriages and girl children who become widows, website of the NCRI Women's Committee, August 15, 2017
[740] Marriage age increase rejected by Iran parliament, website of NCRI Women's Committee, December 25, 2018
[741] The state-run IRNA news agency, January 6, 2019
[742] The state-run daily Entekhab, March 4, 2019

- The latest news is that after the Iranian regime facilitated granting marriage loans, the applicants for these loans increased 90 folds in the first five months of the year compared to the same period in previous year. [743]
- A government expert asserted that poor families are literally selling their daughters, and according to the Central Bank's figures, the number of early marriages of girls under 15 in six months increased four times the under-15 marriages throughout the previous year. [744]

- **Strengthened girls' access to quality education, skills development and training**

Access to quality education, skills development and training has not been strengthened in recent years but further weakened. This is mainly due to insufficient budget and budget cuts as well as the low quality of teaching.

- Each year the budget allocated to the Ministry of Education can only cover teachers' salaries and the day to day expenses of this ministry. Even this salary is still two-folds under the poverty line. [745]
- In the past few years, Rouhani has ordered shutdown of many schools in rural communities to cut down on budget.
- Such lack of budget has consequences for teachers, as well. Unfortunately, the living conditions for teachers, over 50% of them women, are far below acceptable standards. Going unpaid for months, instead of providing a good education, teachers in Iran are preoccupied by making their ends meet. [746]
- According to the Minister of Education, teachers have always had a second job to earn a living. If a teacher just wants to live on his/her salary, to be honest, he/she cannot even have a middle-class life. [747]
- 69% of the teachers are taxi drivers as a second job and 54% of them don't have enough income and no time left for themselves. [748]

---

[743] Tayyebeh Siavoshi, a member of the mullahs' parliament, the state-run Sarpoosh.com, December 29, 2019
[744] Mohammad Mehdi Tondguyan, deputy Minister of Sports and Youths, the state-run Sarpoosh.com, December 29, 2019
[745] Mojgan Bagheri, the state-run salamatnews.com, September 26, 2018
[746] Seyyed Mohammad Javad Abtahi, a member of the Parliamentary Education and Research Commission, the state-run Salamatnews.com - September 26, 2018
[747] Mohammad Bathaii, Minister of Education, the state-run Tasnim news agency - March 3, 2019
[748] Vahid Mahmoudi, an economist and a university professor, the state-run Tasnim news agency - March 3, 2019

- **Implemented policies and programmes to reduce and eradicate child, early and forced marriage**

The UN General Assembly resolution on December 18, 2019 urged the Iranian regime "to address the concerning incidence of child, early and forced marriage, as recommended by the Committee on the Rights of the Child."[749]

In February 2016, the UN Committee on the Rights of the Child addressing the Iranian regime said, "The committee is seriously concerned about the reports of increasing numbers of girls at the age of 10 years or younger who are subjected to child and forced marriages to much older men."[750]

Obviously, the Iranian regime has not tackled early marriages, and consequently the health outcomes due to early childbearing, in the period spanning from 2016 to 2019.

Additionally, a bill called the Law to Support Abandoned Children and Teenagers was passed by the Iranian Parliament on September 22, 2013 which in the addendum to Article 26, sanctions marriage of the guardian with the girl under his guardianship with approval of a court:

"Marriage, either during guardianship or after between the child and guardian is forbidden unless the court, after advisory opinion from the organization, determines that it is in the interest of the child." [751]

---

[749] UN General Assembly censures Tehran regime for rights abuses in Iran, website of the NCRI Women's Committee, December 19, 2019
[750] UN Committee Strongly Censures Abuse of Girl Children in Iran, website of the NCRI Women's Committee, February 7, 2016
[751] Under new law in Iran, Men Allowed to Marry their Adopted Children, a special report by the NCRI Women's Committee, October 2014

- According to an Iranian Justice Ministry lawyer, laws related to underage marriages are insufficient, and child marriages in Iran have been on the rise in recent years.[752]
- Another Judiciary official recently revealed that around 600,000 early marriages take place in Iran every year, without considering the large number of unofficial marriages that are not registered.[753]
- The Iranian census organization also released new statistics indicating that 234,000 marriages of girls under 15 years were officially registered from March 2017 to March 2018. 194 of these were marriages of girl children under 10 years old.[754]
- The legal age of marriage for girls in Iran is 13. The parliamentary judicial and legal committee rejected the plan to increase the minimum age of marriage for girls in December 2018.[755]
- Some families force girls as young as 9 or 10 years old to get married with old men just to earn some money to support the rest of the family's needs.[756]
- The general director of the Welfare Organization in Ardabil, announced that early marriages have become common practice in that province.[757] He pointed out, "Out of a total of 12,000 marriages over the past year in this province, 37 percent (i.e. 4,400) have been from among girls between 10 to 14 years of age."
- The number of girl children under 10 who have gotten married was 220 in 2011; 187 in 2012; 201 in 2013; 176 in 2014; and 179 in 2015. These figures are probably higher because of unregistered marriages.[758]
- The average marriage age for girl children in Zaweh village is 11.[759]
- The marriage age for girls in Zainub village is under 10.[760]

---

[752] The state-run IRNA News Agency, August 3, 2019
[753] Ali Kazemi, advisor to the legal deputy of the Judiciary Branch, the state-run daily Entekhab – March 4, 2019: "Between 5 to 600,000 children get married every year (in Iran) according to the officially-registered data. The main problem is that there are marriages taking place beyond those officially registered."
[754] The state-run Iran daily newspaper – October 30, 2019
[755] The state-run Fars news agency – December 23, 2018
[756] Massoumeh Agha-Alishahi, member of the mullahs' parliament, the state-run ROKNA news agency, May 28, 2018
[757] Behzad Sattari, the general director of the Welfare Organization in Ardabil, meeting with the Governor of Khalkhal, the state-run didarnews.ir, September 4, 2019
[758] Batool Salimi Manesh, a social researcher, the official IRNA news agency, August 5, 2018
[759] Ali Baghdar Delgosha, advisor in youths' affairs to the Governor of Razavi Khorasan Province, told a meeting at the School of Literature of Ferdowsi University of Mashhad on May 14, 2018. Zaweh is located in Razavi Khorasan Province in northeastern Iran.
[760] Amir Taghizadeh, cultural and youth affairs deputy in the General Department of Youths and Sports in East Azerbaijan Province, the state-run ISNA news agency, May 24, 2018

- Tackled disadvantages in health outcomes due to malnutrition, early childbearing (e.g. anemia) and exposure to HIV/AIDS and other sexually transmitted diseases

Malnutrition and early childbearing are among the most obvious problems Iranian girl children have to deal with. No accurate or even inaccurate statistics, however, have been reported on these problems.

Depression, suicide, divorce, school dropouts, and poverty are among the physical and psychological consequences of early marriage and childbearing in Iran.
- According to the regime's experts, 50 per cent of early pregnancies in Iran lead to the deaths of the mother or her baby. There is also 70 per cent higher chance of cancer in such mothers.[761]
- In 2017, it was announced that nearly 1,700 pregnant mothers less than 15 years of age were experiencing their first pregnancy.[762]
- More recently, the Director of Iran's Census Organization in Hamadan Province stated that 44 girls under the age of 15 were pregnant in Hamadan in 2018.[763]
- There have been no more admissions to early pregnancies. However, with the rising number of early marriages, one could assume that a large percentage of these underage brides get pregnant.

One of the horrible health outcomes of early marriages is suicide.
- A 16-year-old young woman by the name of Ziba set herself on fire to evade her family's insistence that she marries an old man.[764]
- There were reports in June 2019 that Souma Khedri, 19, from Baneh, and Sara Esmaili, 17, from Piranshahr, committed suicide to evade forcible marriage due to lack of legal protection for women under the law.[765]
- Within six months from March to August 2019, 11 women set themselves ablaze in the small town of Dishmuk, in Kohgiluyeh and Boyerahmad Province, southwestern Iran.[766]
- Early marriages, domestic violence against women and girls, and poverty are among the main reasons of self-immolations of women in Dishmuk. One of these women by the name of Sorayya had got married at age 11. Another was 17 when she set herself alight in August, and two others, 14 and 17 years old, set themselves ablaze in April.

---

[761] The state-run Shafaghna website - December 14, 2017
[762] The official IRNA news agency, July 30, 2017
[763] The state-run IRNA News Agency, August 3, 2019
[764] The state-run Khorasan daily, August 26, 2019
[765] Women burn themselves to evade oppressive marriage laws in Iran, website of the NCRI Women's Committee, August 28, 2019
[766] The state-run ILNA news agency- August 11, 2019; the state-run KABNA news website- May 16, 2019

Another issue is that some of these children are forced to marry men who are old. Sometimes, the age difference is up to 30 years and the girls are forced into such marriages.[767]
Unfortunately, the largest number of marriages take place in the southern part of Sistan and Baluchestan. Girls often are between 12 and 13 years old in these types of marriages. They are mostly wed to old men who have multiple spouses. The main reason for this type of marriages is poverty. Families receive houses, cars, and cash in return for their daughter's marriage. These young girls unfortunately undergo depression and other internal problems until the end of their lives, because their husbands turn 70 or 80 when they are not even 20.[768]
Another example is the case of Samira, 8, was given to marriage to a boy, 14 years old, to compensate for her father's debt to the boy's father. Samira's father worked at a brick kiln in Pakdasht, Tehran Province. He had borrowed 20 million tomans from his friend, but was not able to return his debt, so he decided to wed his daughter to his friend's son.[769]
According to the official statistics, there are some 24,000 widows under 18 years of age in Iran, and most of the early marriages end up in divorce.[770] Out of this number, an estimated 15,000 young widows are under 15 years of age in Iran.[771]

- **Implemented policies and programmes to eliminate violence against girls**

Child abuse and violence against children is the first social ill in Iran, but accurate data are unavailable.[772]
A government official admitted in 2017 that 12,000 cases of child abuse had been registered by the National Welfare Organization.[773]
One social expert reported of over 16,000 instances of violence against children being registered in just six months in 2018, without specifying the number of provinces.[774]

A Welfare Organization deputy announced that 13,000 cases of child abuse had been reported only to one emergency center in West Azerbaijan Province in the year 2017.[775] He did not say how many emergency centers exist in the province.

---

[767] The state-run Fararu news agency, August 14, 2017
[768] The state-run ILNA news agency – January 27, 2017
[769] The state-run ROKNA news agency – January 31, 2018
[770] Massoumeh Agha-Alishahi, member of the mullahs' parliament, the state-run ROKNA news agency, May 28, 2018
[771] Shahrbanou Imami, member of Tehran's City Council and former member of the mullahs' parliament, IWD gathering at Tehran's Melli University, the state-run ILNA news agency, March 8, 2018
[772] Kamel Delpasand, sociologist and a researcher in social sciences, interview with the official IRNA news agency, July 18, 2018
[773] The state-run ILNA news agency – March 4, 2017
[774] Reza Jafari, head of the Social Emergencies, interview with the state-run ILNA news agency, February 25, 2018
[775] Mehrdad Motallebi, Social Affairs deputy of the Welfare Organization of West Azerbaijan, the state-run Uromnews.com, August 7, 2018

As explained in answer to question 13, the Iranian regime has not yet adopted the bill to prevent violence against women. After obstructing the bill for 8 years and changing the contents and goals of the bill, it has remained in the hands of the government without any prospect to be adopted in the current parliament before the elections in February 2020.

Furthermore, the bill on the rights of children has been stalled in the parliament for 10 years. Civil and Penal codes do not clarify limits on physical punishment by parents. Fathers are not punished even for killing their children, because they are considered owner of their children's blood. The Iranian Law to Protect Children and Adolescents (2002) does not protest against physical abuse, no mention of sexual abuse.

Some case examples of violence against girl children follow:
- A 15-year-old student, Ma'edeh Shabani-Nejad, was arrested on January 25, 2018, by the IRGC's Department of Intelligence and detained under interrogation in Sepidar Prison of Ahvaz, for over three months in an undetermined state. She suffered GI bleeding while in prison.[776]

---

[776] Ma'edeh Shabani-Nejad remains in detention without legal warrant, website of the NCRI Women's Committee, May 31, 2018

- A 5-year-old girl in Mashhad suffered brain death. After a quarrel with the child's mother, the stepfather banged the girl on the floor several times which led to serious physical injuries and brain death.[777]
- In Damavand, Tehran Province, it was reported that a two-year-old girl was burned by her father and stepmother.[778]
- A three-year-old girl in a village in Marand, East Azerbaijan Province, went into coma after being brutalized by her addicted father.[779]
- A six-year-old girl by the name of Haddiseh died after eight days of brain death, on January 2, 2019, at Kamyab Hospital in Mashhad. There were scars of infected burns by cigarettes and hot wire on her body and genitalia.[780]
- Neighbors discovered three children in the backyard of a house in the town of Taleghan, in Mahshahr, southwestern Iran, in April 2018.[781]
Fatemeh, 12, Omolbanin, 8, and their five-year-old brother, Ali Akbar, had been kept out in the hot weather and tortured physically and psychologically by an ax, a hammer, hot iron rods, etc. Various parts of the children's bodies had been burnt. Their mouths had been closed by adhesive tape to prevent them from screaming.

- **Implemented policies to prevent and eliminate sexual violence and harmful practices**

No, the Iranian regime has not taken any specific steps to prevent and eliminate sexual violence and harmful practices.
An increasing number of rape accounts has been mushrooming in different parts of Iran, including the rape and murders of 6 and 7-year-old girl children.

- A seven-year-old girl, Atena Aslani, became victim of sexual violence and murder in Parsabad on June 19, 2017. Atena's father was a street peddler who sold clothes. The state media identified the suspect as Ismail, a local businessman selling paint.
- A 5-year-old girl in Mashhad suffered brain death due to harsh beating by her stepfather. Multiple scars of injury were evident on the girl's abdomen, head, and face upon admission to hospital. After clinical examinations, it became clear that in addition to broken legs and hip, she had also suffered brain damage.[782]
- The rapes of 41 women and girls in Iranshahr, in southeastern province of Sistan and Baluchestan, was one of the most horrific cases stirring controversy across the country in June 2018. The victims were between 18 and 30 years of age assaulted by a gang of four men, linked to the city's wealthy and influential families, the Bassij and IRGC.[783]

---

[777] The state-run IRNA news agency – May 3, 2017
[778] The state-run Tasnim news agency, September 1, 2019
[779] The state-run ISNA news agency, May 27, 2019
[780] The state-run Khorasan daily, January 2, 2019
[781] The state-run Asriran.com, April 24, 2018
[782] The state-run IRNA news agency, May 3, 2017
[783] Gang rapes of 41 young women and girls in Iranshahr, website of the NCRI Women's Committee, June 20, 2018

- Zahra Navidpour, 28, was raped and murdered in Malekan, a small city in East Azerbaijan Province. She had been raped by the parliamentary deputy of Malekan, Salman Khodadadi, and had filed a suit against him.[784]
- She was found dead at her mother's home on January 6, 2019. The coroner's office was supposed to perform autopsy to determine the reason for her death, but security forces stole and secretly buried her body in a village before the autopsy.
- A young woman, 20, divulged that she had been abused and raped by her father since she was eight, but had feared to talk about it.[785]
- In November 2017, following a research done on 400 child laborers, it was revealed by an official of Social Services in Tehran's Municipality that some 90% of child laborers are sexually abused. "We are going to prove that 90 per cent of child laborers get raped."[786]

- **Implemented policies and programmes to eradicate child labour and excessive levels of unpaid care and domestic work undertaken by girl children that prevents them from going to school and accessing health services**

Every year, at least a quarter of Iran's students are forced to drop out of school, with many of them becoming child laborers.[787] The Iranian regime does not have any policy of eradicating child labor and excessive levels of unpaid care and domestic work undertaken by girl children that prevents them from going to school and accessing health services. Instead, the government's wrong policies, mismanagement of the economy, and the corrupt kleptocratic rule further contribute to poverty and spread of child labor.

- In October 2015, the director-general of Tehran's Department of Education disclosed that 25,000 school-aged children in this city are working instead of attending school.[788]
- The girls in Tehran's Herandi district are unable to pursue their education or even leave home because of the detrimental atmosphere in this region, namely the large number of homeless and addicted people sleeping in the parks and the streets.[789]
- Generally, rural girls are converted to unpaid domestic workers at an early age. Nomad girls are forced to go to livestock breeding, sheep minding and hard labor with no opportunity to study.[790]

---

[784] Body of rape victim Zahra Navidpour secretly buried without autopsy, website of the NCRI Women's Committee, January 12, 2019
[785] The state-run Fararu website, June 2, 2019
[786] The executive director of the Organization of Social Services in Tehran's Municipality, the state-run Salamatnews.com – November 8, 2017
[787] Nahid Tajeddin, member of the board of directors of the Social Commission of the Majlis, the state-run salamatnews.com, September 27, 2017
[788] The state-run ANA news agency, December 6, 2015
[789] Ibid.
[790] The state-run mehrkhane.com, July 30, 2017

- A member of the mullahs' parliament, asserted, "Currently, there are some 15,000 scavengers in the capital, 5,000 of whom are children. 40% of them are 10 to 15 years old and their families' only breadwinners."[791]
- State-run media have written about the girl children sifting through garbage saying they are more vulnerable to diseases than boys. Their long hairs are full of lice and they have not enough water to wash their hair. The little water they use is contaminated.
- Sexual abuse is the greatest ailment among young child scavengers.[792]
- The state-run Salamatnews.com and Rokna.ir website published a report run by the official Iran newspaper which included some painful examples of sexual assault on deprived girl children and child laborers. The report narrated the stories of girl child laborers who are assaulted and raped since very young age due to poverty and addiction of their parents.[793]

- **Other**

Runaway girls

Due to the patriarchal culture promoted and advocated by the clerical regime, and lack of any form of support for abused children, recent years have seen a rise in the number of runaway girls in Iran as a major social issue. However, there are no accurate statistics available on it. Unfortunately, there have been reports that the limited number of shelters made for runaway girls have been used by authorities for human trafficking and prostitution.

Hossein Assadbeigi, head of the Social Emergency of the Welfare Organization, said the organization had been informed of a total of 5,000 runaway girls over the past year.[794]

---

[791] Hossein Maghsoudi, member of the mullahs' parliament, the state-run ICANA news agency - October 18, 2019
[792] Elham Fakhari, member of Tehran's City Council, the official Iran newspaper, November 8, 2017
[793] State media confess to rape of girl child laborers, the website of the NCRI Women's Committee, November 9, 2017; the state-run Salamatnews.com, November 8, 2017
[794] The state-run Tasnim news agency, January 10, 2018

Water shortages and drowning of girl children

Another issue worth examining, is the impact of water shortages on girl children.
In summer 2018, 48% of the country's population was under water stress.[795]
No budget was allocated for water from the National Development Fund in 2019.[796]
Two-thirds of the population of Sistan and Baluchestan province do not have access to sanitary drinking water.[797]
For example, women and girls in Chabahar have to walk almost 30 minutes, five or six times a day to provide drinking water to their families. They have to bring water with jerry cans.[798]

Monireh Khedmati, Maryam Khedmati and Sierra Delshab drowned while drinking water from *Hootag* on May 29, 2019

---

[795] The website of Tehran's Chamber of Commerce, Industry, Mines and Agriculture, www.tccim.ir/news/, January 6, 2019
[796] The website of Tehran's Chamber of Commerce, Industry, Mines and Agriculture, www.tccim.ir/news/, January 12, 2019
[797] www.bbc.com/persian, January 6, 2019
[798] The state-run Tasnim news agency, December 22, 2015

In the absence of pipelines and even tankers, people in this deprived region dig ditches to collect rainwater. These ditches are called *Hootag* and are considered as water reservoirs for village inhabitants. The water is used for both humans and animals and is extremely contaminated. There have been numerous reports of little girls and women drowning in these ditches.

- Monireh Khedmati, Maryam Khedmati and Sierra Delshab drowned while drinking water from *Hootag* on May 29, 2019. They were were studying in the second and third grade in the Kambazar village near Chabahr.[799]
- Two teenage Baluchi girls, Sara and Basmeh Kalamati, 14 and 16, were drowned in a water ditch or *Hootag* while doing their dishes and laundry.[800] The girls had gone to the *Hootag* outside of school hours to help their families, when they fell into the *Hootag* and lost their lives. Many students lose their lives while getting water from the *Hootag*.[801]
- Three girls and a woman drowned in a waterhole in the village of Zirdan, central Nik Shahr, located in south of Sistan and Baluchestan Province on August 28, 2018. The four victims included three girls, 8, 11 and 14 years old, and a 25-year-old woman who had gone to bring water.[802]

---

[799] The official IRNA news agency – May 29, 2019
[800] Jamshid Sarani, governor of Dashtyari County of Chabahar, the state-run Khabar Fori, October 10, 2019
[801] Anvar Badpa, director of the Education Department of Dashtyari, the state-run Khabar Fori, October 10, 2019
[802] Naseh, head of the pre-hospital emergency ward and accident management at the School of Medical Sciences of Iranshahr, the official IRNA news agency, August 28, 2018

ENVIRONMENTAL CONSERVATION, PROTECTION AND REHABILITATION

29. What actions has your country taken in the last five years to integrate gender perspectives and concerns into environmental policies?

The Iranian regime is not protecting the environment but destroying it. As a result, it could not integrate gender perspectives and concerns into its non-existent environmental policies. In fact, the destruction of environment in Iran has led to poverty and destitution of a large portion of the populace as explained in the following paragraphs.

- Drying up of Lake Urmia in the northwestern province of West Azerbaijan,[803] drying of Zayandeh Rood in Isfahan in central Iran and other rivers, dust storms and haze in southwestern Khuzestan Province, scarcity of water all across the country, as well as alarming air pollution levels in Tehran and other metropolises, are some of the major environmental disasters in recent years.
- Iran is now among the countries with the highest rate of soil erosion, exploitation of water resources, desertification, and so forth. Today, there's not a single living wetland or lake in the country.[804]
- While part of the problem can be attributed to the global climate change, the regime must be blamed for adopting wrong policies which have aggravated the conditions.
- The Iranian regime does not have any policy to conserve and protect the environment. In fact, it has done the opposite throughout its rule, destroying the country's natural resources and its infrastructures.
- The Islamic Revolutionary Guard Corps (IRGC), which dominates the country's Armed Forces and economy, has had an extremely destructive role in this regard. The IRGC has changed the path of rivers and built numerous dams in wrong locations to serve the regime's nuclear and military projects. The drying of Lake Urmia, Zayandeh Rood river and other major rivers in Khuzestan and Kohgilouyeh and Boyer Ahmad provinces are attributed to the IRGC projects.
- The regime has issued permission to raze large parts of Iran's jungles and forests to smuggle wood out of the country, to construct hotels and buildings in the natural course of rivers to earn more money. They export the country's water for economic and political profits;[805] they have sold out the Caspian Sea and allowed Chinese companies to use industrial fishing methods causing irreversible damages to the Persian Gulf environment. By doing so, they have virtually eliminated the source of income for local people and vastly contributed to the destructions caused by

---

[803] [Lake Urmia drying danger of disease for 14 million people](http://www.ncr-iran.org), www.ncr-iran.org, July 26, 2017

[804] Isa Kalantari, the head of the Environment Protection Agency, the state-run ISNA news agency, October 15, 2017

[805] A report aired on an Iraqi TV channel, Iran's Foreign Affairs Minister, Javad Zarif had negotiations with Iraq last year on exporting Khuzestan's water to Basra. The event was not carried by Iranian news agencies and Iranians were unaware of it until the al-Baladi TV station covered it. A number of amateur videos were also published online showing large pipes carrying fresh water to Iraq.

natural disasters such as the case in the flash floods which washed away large parts of the country in spring 2019 and afterwards.
- As a result of such destructive policies, whoever attempts to take any step to voluntarily conserve the environment and natural resources, comes automatically into collision with the state interests and is accused of jeopardizing the country's national security.
- Employees of the Environmental Protection Organization held a protest on October 26, 2015, where they protested mismanagement of the country's environment, overlooking experts' views. The organization's response, however, was to order protesters to leave if they were discontented.[806]

Drying up of Lake Urmia
- The rapid drying up of Lake Urmia has been the worst disaster taking place under the rule of the clerical regime in Iran. The drying of the lake endangers the lives of residents of East and West Azerbaijan Province, and has affected the lives of neighboring provinces, over time.
- The salty shores surrounding the lake are gradually expanding, and the salinity of aquifers has been increasing. With the drying of Lake Urmia, a vast salty desert will replace it and change the face of life of local people.
- Experts say the clerical regime's disorderly construction of big dams as well as the construction of a road with military purposes which passed through the middle of this lake upset its ecological balance and accelerated the speed of its dehydration.[807]

Drinking water
- People living in Khuzestan, located on the banks of Iran's largest river, and cities bordering bodies of sea, are struggling with shortage of drinking water. According to official statistics, around 334 cities from the 1,157 cities in Iran are struggling with water shortages.[808]
- According to the Ministry of Energy, 165 cities with a population of 5.10 million people are in the yellow zone, 62 cities with a population of 8.6 million are in the orange zone while 107 cities with 2.17 million people are in the red zone in terms of water shortages. In total, 334 cities are struggling with a water shortage.[809]
- A water official said 88 dams built for providing potable water are in bad conditions, and 56 dams in critical conditions.[810] 15% of the rural population do not have access to quality potable water. 107 cities suffering from water shortages are

---

[806] The state-run Fars news agency, TNews.ir, October 26, 2015
[807] The state-run Mashreqnews.ir, June 26, 2018
[808] Reza Ardakanian, Minister of Power, the official IRNA news agency, April 24, 2018
[809] Ibid.
[810] Hamidreza Janbaz, Head of the Water and Sewage Company, the state-run ISNA news agency, August 8, August 8, 2018

mostly overpopulated and currently 17 million people are subject to water shortage.[811]
- The head of Meteorological Organization's National Center for Drought and Crisis Management acknowledges that nearly 95 percent of the country is suffering from drought.[812]

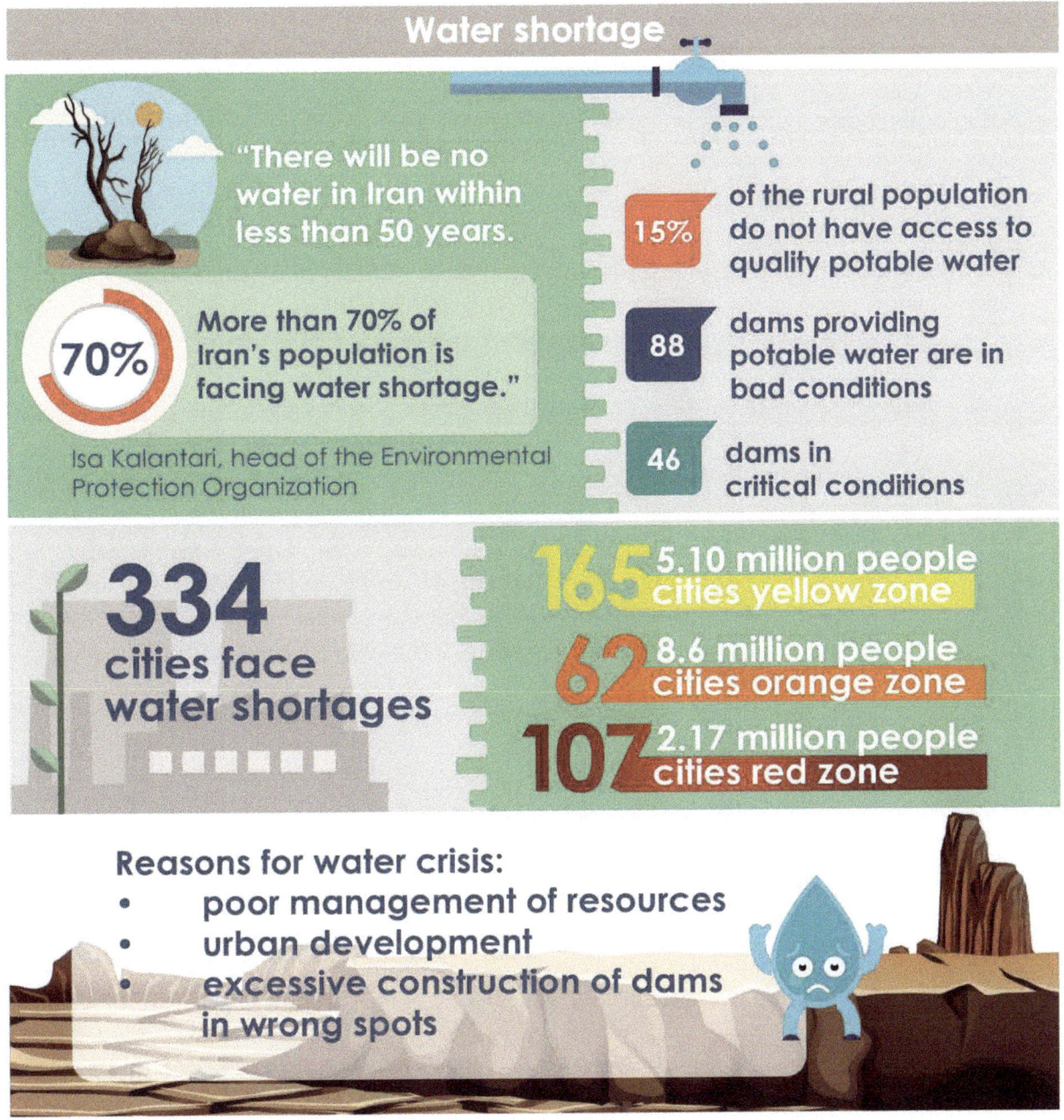

---

[811] Ibid.
[812] The state-run ISNA news agency, August 9, 2017

- Isa Kalantari, head of the Environmental Protection Organization, warned there will be no water in Iran within less than 50 years.[813] He also asserted that more than 70% of Iran's population is facing water shortage.[814]
- According to other experts, Iran's central plateau will be facing water crisis within half a century.[815] They blame the aggravating water crisis on poor management of resources, urban development, and excessive construction of dams in wrong spots.
- No budget has been allocated for water from the National Development Fund in 2019.[816] Officials predict that due to shortage of water for agriculture, Iran's eastern and southern areas will be completely deserted in less than 25 years, and 50 million people will have to emigrate.[817]
- Groundwater resources in Isfahan, used for drinking water in the province, are depleting. Currently, only 160 million cubic meters of drinking water remain behind the dam, while the annual consumption of drinking water in Isfahan is about 420 million cubic meters.[818]
- From the 570 springs in Kohgiluyeh and Boyer Ahmad province, 360 springs and water sources for drinking water have completely dried out in the tribal regions.[819] The drought in the province has also led to early migrations by nomadic tribes.
- The southern province of Kerman which produces one of the country's main exports, pistachios, suffers from a "Drought Tsunami" and 800 villages are supplied by water tanks.[820]
- Also, in Mazandaran Province in northern Iran, 2,471 acres of agricultural soil have turned into arid lands and 617 acres of paddy fields have dried up.[821]
- In the plains and plateaus of Iran and areas such as Semnan and Fars, about 70% of the plains have been declared as "forbidden water plains" due to the reduction of groundwater.[822] The condition of aquifers of the southern province of Fars, once one of the top producers of wheat in Iran, has become irreversible.[823]

---

[813] The state-run ILNA news agency, August 8, 2018
[814] Ibid.
[815] Parviz Kardovani, prominent professor of geology and director of the Desert Studies Center,
[816] The website of Tehran's Chamber of Commerce, Industry, Mines and Agriculture, January 12, 2019
[817] Isa Kalantari, head of the Environmental Protection Organization, the state-run ILNA news agency, October 11, 2016
[818] The state-run ISNA news agency – Mar. 12, 2018
[819] Majid Alipour, Director General of Kohgiluyeh and Boyer Ahmad Tribal Affairs, the official IRNA news agency, April 23, 2018
[820] The state-run Qods Online - October 14, 2017
[821] The state-run Tasnim news agency, August 6, 2018
[822] Ahmad Reza Lahijanzadeh, deputy for Marine Environment and Wetlands in the Environmental Protection Agency, the state-run Mehr news agency, November 2, 2019
[823] Ibid.

Forests

Most of Iran's forests are in the north of Iran which borders the Caspian Sea where the inhabitants of the provinces of Gilan, Mazandaran, and Golestan enjoy a subtropical climate. The northern provinces of Iran used to be known for their lush greenery and forests. Over the past 40 years, however, deforestation has destroyed half of Iran's northern forests.

- According to the data collected by the Natural Resources and Forestry Organization, the area of the northern forests has gone from 3,600,000 to 1,800,000 hectares during the past 40 years.[824] Some 100,000 hectares of forests are destroyed in Iran every year.[825]
- The Caspian Hyrcanian mixed forests in Alborz have been vastly devastated.[826] Hyrcanian forests are 55,000 square kilometers and extend from the Republic of Azerbaijan to Iran and the greater part of this millions-year-old jungle is located in Iran. It is one of the oldest jungles on earth. Some parts of these forests have turned into a garbage land.
- Rain has decreased by 20 percent in the past 50 years while floods have increased by 50 percent, according to environment officials.[827] Rain is considered a disaster in northern Iran these days because trees have been cut down under the excuse of development, building industrial plants, roads and villas. Deforestation means that flood water is directed better. When half of the forests are gone, the rain is no longer a blessing and turns into floods.[828]
- Deforestation is taking place extensively and at a high speed, so much that it could be physically detected. Experts say it is soon going to lead to a huge catastrophe in Iran's semi-arid climate.[829] Not much time is left before all the forests in the north are destroyed, warned a study.[830] It has already led to the erosion of soil, pollution, reduction of biodiversity and extinction of various animal and plant species.[831] Another study says that in 10 years' time, there would be no trace left from the forests in western Iran and in Golestan Province in the north.

Wetlands

Most of the wetlands in Iran are drying up.

- Low water levels of Karun River caused by irresponsible official measures, have led to the drying of Hoor-ol Azim wetland, contributing to the remarkable warming of weather in Khuzestan Province.

---

[824] The state-run Hamshahrionline.ir, March 12, 2014
[825] Ibid.
[826] Ahmad Reza Lahijanzadeh, deputy for Marine Environment and Wetlands in the Environmental Protection Agency, the state-run Mehr news agency, November 2, 2019
[827] Violating the sanctity of forests, main cause of floods, the official IRNA news agency, April 9, 2019
[828] Massoud Molana, a member of the Iran Environment and Natural Resources Network Coordination Council, the state-run ISNA news agency, October 24, 2018
[829] The state-run Mehr news agency, March 2, 2016
[830] The state-run donya-e-eqtesad.com, October 9, 2017
[831] The state-run Mehr news agency, March 2, 2016

- The oil-rich Khuzestan Province in southwestern Iran is an embodiment of unstable development in the country. Despite abundant water, fertile soil, and oil and gas resources that could nourish all of Iran's populace, lagoons and rivers in this province have dried up. Consequently, dust storms have crippled Khuzestan, for years.[832]
- Low water levels and increasing salt concentration of Karun river, have resulted in rising fish fatalities at the Khorramshahr Fish Farming Complex.[833]
- Salt mountains overlooking Iran's biggest earth-fill dam called the Gotvand Dam have caused high salinity of billions of cubic meters of water collected behind this dam, transferring the salt into Karun River and destroying all the farmlands across the river's path. Gotvand Dam was built by the IRGC.[834]
- Anzali Wetland, one of the most famous in Iran, has been drying up since more than 30 years ago. But the regime has taken no practical measures to save the wetland. Then in 2015, the wetland caught fire. Authorities of the Environmental Protection authorities of Gilan Province later said the fire was an arson.[835]
- In the deprived province of Sistan and Baluchestan, Hamun Lake has dried up, creating a serious environmental crisis in this province.[836]
- The famous Gavkhouni wetland and Bakhtegan Lake in Fars Province, southern Iran, are also drying up.[837]

Marine environment

The Caspian Sea's coastline has been gradually and steadily disappearing in both Mazandaran and Gilan provinces in northern Iran.[838]

- The destruction of marine environment of the Caspian Sea, and the gradual and steady coastal erosion is evident in both Mazandaran and Gilan provinces to the extent that one cannot even find 100 meters of shore area.
- The IRGC-linked Fisheries Organization has "rented out" Iran's southern waters to Chinese fisheries allowing them to fish in Iran's southern waters, causing major problems for Iranian fisherman.[839]
- The Chinese bottom trawling methods and the industrial fishing practices of thousands of Chinese boats leave nothing for native fishermen. Even fish eggs, and

---

[832] Ahmad Reza Lahijanzadeh, deputy for Marine Environment and Wetlands in the Environmental Protection Agency, the state-run Mehr news agency, November 2, 2019

[833] The state-run Mehr news agency, August 6, 2018: This complex started its activities as a conglomerate of 55 cooperatives in 1998 and expanded to include 88 cooperatives in 2016. The farm grows a variety of fish, and it has more than 1,000 employees.

[834] tribunezamaneh.com, June 7, 2018

[835] The state-run Tabnak website, October 16, 2015

[836] tribunezamaneh.com, June 7, 2018

[837] tribunezamaneh.com, June 7, 2018

[838] Ahmad Reza Lahijanzadeh, deputy for Marine Environment and Wetlands in the Environmental Protection Agency, the state-run Mehr news agency, November 2, 2019

[839] The state-run Tabnak website, August 20, 2018

shellfish get stuck in the Chinese trawling nets. The overfishing in the Gulf waters has led to serious and irreversible damage to the environment.
- Environmental experts say the Persian Gulf has turned into the world's most contaminated body of water on earth.[840]

Impact of petrochemical industry on the environment

- The development of the petrochemical industry in Mahshahr, in southwestern Iran, has reduced the city's fishing capacity down to about 900 tons. Officials admit they have sacrificed long term interests for a short term one.[841]
- The southern industrial city of Asaluyeh is "the most polluted city" in Iran and has reached the point of no return. The area is witnessing widespread slaughter of aquatic species and reduced environmental diversity.[842]
- Asaluyeh, located in Bushehr Province is believed to house one of the largest oil, gas and petrochemical projects in Iran. The power and petrochemical plants were built without observing the minimum environmental standards and their detrimental effects on the people of the surrounding areas. The concentration of heavy industrial activities on the shores of Bushehr Province and the absence of wastewater treatment facilities is a major threat to the Persian Gulf environment.
- A report by the Parliamentary Research Center, entitled the Comparative Environmental Economics Review from a Legislative and Regulatory Perspective, indicates that pollution and environmental degradation have undermined health of Iranian citizens.
- Ghaed Bassir Petrochemical Plant[843] owned by Ali Khamenei, the mullahs' Supreme Leader,[844] located in Golpayegan, Isfahan Province, has had a devastating impact on the life of the surrounding villages since its construction in 1997.

---

[840] Hambastegimelli.com, October 17, 2015
[841] Ahmad Reza Lahijanzadeh, deputy for Marine Environment and Wetlands in the Environmental Protection Agency, the state-run Mehr news agency, November 2, 2019
[842] Ibid.
[843] The Ghaed Bassir Company is owned by the Tadbir Energy Development Group, overseen by Tadbir Economic Development Group, which is controlled by the Execution of Imam Khomeini's Order (EIKO) or "*Setad*" which in turn is overseen by Iran's Supreme Leader himself.
[844] According to a report by Reuters, November 11, 2013, "Khamenei controls massive financial empire built on property seizures. (The *Setad* has become) one of the most powerful organizations in Iran, and has morphed into a business juggernaut that now holds stakes in nearly every sector of Iranian industry, including finance, oil, telecommunications, the production of birth-control pills and even ostrich farming."
"The organization's total worth is difficult to pinpoint because of the secrecy of its accounts. But Setad's holdings of real estate, corporate stakes and other assets total about $95 billion, Reuters has calculated".

- The plant has dug more than 200 deep water wells sucking out all the water in the area. As a consequence, the villages once known for their natural springs and sparkling water, are now barren. The people have lost their agriculture and the lands are no longer productive.[845] According to the villagers interviewed by the official IRNA news agency, their water is contaminated and the smoke from the plant has robbed them of clean air. The factory's sewage system is right next to the village's drinking water source. Toxins have found their way into the water which has resulted in the many cases of cancer among the villagers. The report shows that the government of Iran is responsible for yet another environmental crisis which has led to many cancer-related deaths and hardships for people in Golpayegan, Isfahan.

Air pollution

Toxic industrial emissions cause heavy air pollution in all major Iranian capitals and especially Tehran. Coupled with dust and sandstorms, air pollution leads to the deaths of thousands of people every year.[846]

---

[845] The state-run ISNA news agency, July 30, 2019
[846] tribunezamaneh.com, June 7, 2018

30. What actions has your country taken in the last five years to integrate gender perspectives into policies and programmes for disaster risk reduction, climate resilience and mitigation?

Not only there are no governmental mechanisms in Iran to deal with natural disasters such as earthquakes and floods, but due to widespread corruption in the ruling hierarchy even popular and international aid cannot get to the victims. In such situation, women bear the brunt and pay the heaviest price.

Earthquakes

- In the 2003 earthquake which shook the city of Bam in Kerman Province in southern Iran, two thirds of the city's residents died and in some regions all of the houses were destroyed.
- The official plan was to finish reconstruction of this city by summer 2005. To this date, however, the residents of Bam continue to lack the most basic needs of a simple life and hundreds of people live in the outskirts of the city in trailers.[847]
- Example: A woman by the name of Azam lives in a shanty town with her three children. Two of her daughters go to school and she also has a little boy. Her husband is a daily worker who is an opium addict and practically does not work at all. For the past 11 years, Azam has been working in a date farm to pay for her daughters' school expenses. She and her family live in two small trailers with no bathrooms. There is no electricity and every now and her water supply is cut off.[848]
- There is a similar situation in Kermanshah Province, western Iran, which was struck with a 7.3 Richter earthquake in November 2017. Some 450 people died, 7,100 people were wounded, and 70,000 people became homeless.
- By a conservative estimate, at least 100 women lost their husbands and turned into their family's bread winners.
- After the earthquake, the region ran out of water and electricity for a long time and hospitals could not deal with such a large volume of disaster. The government was not even capable of supplying food to the victims. The earthquake in Kermanshah caused great pain and suffering to many women who lost their properties and entire wealth and belongings.
- The health situation is dreadful, particularly for pregnant women many whom suffered miscarriages. Pregnant women were promised to receive trailers, but this did not happen. Many women gave birth in the tents and due to poor sanitary conditions, caught infections. Dozens of children died in the freezing cold of winter.[849]
- Toilets and bathrooms are scarce and in poor conditions. Lack of cleaning material, including soaps and shampoos, wet towels, diapers and sanitary napkins for women, underwear for children and women, and lack of bath towels are among other problems of the population of villages hit by the earthquake.

---

[847] The state-run qudsonline.ir, December 26, 2016
[848] The state-run ISNA news agency, December 26, 2017
[849] The state-run salamatnews.com, March 15, 2018

- Families with nine and even more live in one trailer.
- Lack of powdered milk, food and medicine have caused malnutrition and various kinds of diseases. Due to lack of regular bath for children, women and the elderly, many people have developed skin diseases such as acne, painful skin rash, skin fungus, lice and baldness.[850]

Floods

The heavy rainfalls in spring 2019 ravaged thousands of Iranian villages and towns and devastated people's lives. The scale of destruction caused by the devastating floods attested to the destruction of Iran's natural resources.

- Citing the European Commission, the United Nations estimated that at least 12 million citizens across Iran were affected by the devastating floods.
- The European Civil Protection Mechanism (EUCPM) said the incident was the worst natural disaster happening in Iran in 15 years, affecting 2,000 cities and towns in 31 provinces. ReliefWeb,[851] the specialized digital service of United Nations Office for the Coordination of Humanitarian Affairs (OCHA) said two million people were in need of humanitarian aid and over half a million people had been displaced from their places of residence.[852]
- In the past 40 years, the clerical regime's fraudulent agencies, particularly the Revolutionary Guard Corps (IRGC), have reaped huge profits through destruction of the environment and nature including by construction of hundreds of dams and tunnels in wrong spots, diversion of the natural paths of rivers, confiscation and sale of lands on river banks, illegal blocking and construction in the natural paths of flood, deforestation to sell the woods and lands, etc.
- They have done so without observing the basic rules essential to any construction. Consequently, they have left the people of Iran defenseless in the face of natural disasters. If the natural environment of Iranian cities and villages had not been so vastly damaged, the heavy rainfalls could have been reigned in and the deprived people of Iran would not have suffered such extensive losses of lives and properties.

---

[850] A year after the earthquake, deplorable plight of women and children, website of the NCRI Women's Committee, November 15, 2018
[851] Relief Web, OCHA services
[852] Iran floods: Two million people in need of humanitarian aid, Relief Web, April 15, 2019

The situation of women and children

Women and children suffered most in the devastating floods that swept through the country. Women are often left alone in taking care of their families. They have to endure tremendous pressure in circumstances where they have little or no access to food, water, health care and medical treatment.

- Women often suffer psychological harms while they lack any form of support, despite loss of their family members, homes and other properties. Such disruption of their routine life imposes an adverse impact on their mental health.
- According to the information collected from published news and reports, at least 20 women and girl children died in the devastating floods throughout Iran.[853] No exact figures were ever announced by the regime officials. But real evidence, including the number of submerged villages and the cities destroyed by floods, indicates that the actual figures must be much greater.
- In none of the disasters in recent years, including the earthquake in Kermanshah and the nationwide flood disaster the overwhelmed the entire country, the mullahs' regime has given any support to the people.

In remarks made on April 14, 2019, Pezeshkian, deputy speaker of the mullahs' parliament, revealed that the Iranian regime is neither capable nor it wants to compensate for the damages the people of Iran suffered as a result of the devastating floods. He said, **"It is impossible for the government to respond to these problems just by-passing legislations... When it gets to action, the government has no money to do it. It cannot dredge or repair the dams."**

Other

The clerical regime's approach to conservationists

- The State Security forces prevented women and girls from participating in the "Pure Tuesday" bicycle marathon on July 27, 2016. The event was held to promote a day without vehicles in support of a healthy environment.
- A number of environmental activists were arrested during a gathering on April 1, 2016, at Tehran's Laleh Park in defense of animals' rights and environment.
- At least three women, environmental activists, were arrested by security forces in Marivan, Iranian Kurdistan. These women had staged a protest gathering against burying the city's waste in a tourist area called, Samaghan Valley.[854]
- Twenty female environmental activists were arrested by security forces in Marivan on March 18, 2017.[855]

---

[853] Devastating floods in Iran: problems of women in the absence of aid, website of the NCRI Women's Committee, April 19, 2019
[854] Three female environmental activists are arrested, website of the NCRI Women's Committee, April 7, 2017
[855] Ibid.

- Sahar Kazemi, a civil rights and environmental activist and an athletics coach, was arrested in Sanandaj, capital of Iranian Kurdistan, on August 9, 2018.[856]
- Some 75 members of a group of environmental activists were arrested in February 2018 on the charge of espionage.[857]
- Tehran's Revolutionary Court sentenced two female conservationists, Niloufar Bayani to 10 years in prison and Sepideh Kashani to six years' imprisonment on the charge of "espionage."
- Niloufar Bayani and Sepideh Kashani went on hunger strike in Evin Prison in July 2019 to protest their continued detention without determining their case. They were illegally held in Ward 2A of Evin under distressful conditions.
- In February 2020, Niloufar Bayani announced in an open letter that she had been beaten and brutalized, threatened and tortured on numerous occasions by the Revolutionary Guards agents during her year-long detention, and was forced to make false confessions against herself.[858]

---

[856] Sahar Kazemi and Zahra Modarres-Zadeh arrested in Sanandaj, Karaj, website of the NCRI Women's Committee, April 12, 2018
[857] Ibid.
[858] Environmental activists interrogated for 1200 hours under severe torture, website of the NCRI Women's Committee, February 20, 2020

NATIONAL INSTITUTIONS AND PROCESSES

31. What is your country's current national machinery for gender equality and the empowerment of women? Please name it and describe its location within Government.

- What is the line of accountability for the national machinery for gender equality? Does it report annually to the Cabinet and Parliament? Are those reports accessible to the public?

To begin with, the Iranian regime openly opposes gender equality and uses the term gender EQUITY rather than equality, even in international women's forums and in their reports. Consequently, the ruling regime in Iran does NOT seek to promote gender equality and the empowerment of women. It does NOT have an institutional process for SDG implementation. In fact, they have so far opposed every attempt for SDG implementation, specifically the implementation of the Education Document 2030.[859]

Furthermore, the Iranian regime is not a signatory of CEDAW and does not seek to implement the Beijing Declaration and Platform for Action as they contradict the principles and foundations of the clerical regime which is based on gender discrimination. Article 1 of CEDAW, alone, contradicts the articles of the Constitution, the Civil Code, the Islamic Penal Code and etc. in 90 instances.[860]

However, under the pressure of domestic and international public opinion, the regime took a cosmetic measure of establishing an entity called, directorate for women and family affairs (NOT FOR GENDER EQUALITY) in the presidential office. This is the exact and accurate translation from Farsi title of *"Mo'avenat-e Zanan va Omour-e Khanevadeh dar daftar-e Ra'is Jomhour."*

In their propaganda and gestures for western public opinion, the clerical regime insists that this is a Vice Presidency.[861]

In reality, however, this directorate does not enjoy any executive powers and its duties are limited to "planning, policy-making and monitoring." The directorate on women and family affairs has to work with other ministries' advisors or counsels on women's affairs to advance or implement their proposed plans and policies only after they are adopted, and "if these counsels do not participate in the decision-making processes in their departments, they would not be able to implement the devised policies."[862]

---

[859] Education 2030 Framework for Action (SDG 4) and Iranian officials' hysteric reactions to it, a special report by the NCRI Women's Committee, June 2017

[860] Why the Iranian regime does not join the CEDAW? A study by the NCRI Women's Committee – March 2016

[861] The regime translates the same title as "Vice Presidency for Women and Family Affairs" and claims that it is "a member of the government cabinet and with the level of ministry."

[862] Interview with ISNA news agency, May 10, 2015: Sussan Bastani, director for strategic studies at the presidential Directorate for Family and Women's Affairs: "The duty of the women's directorate is planning, policy-making and monitoring and it does not engage in implementation. Therefore, the directorate finds direct relations with the advisors on women's affairs in other departments. If these advisors do not partake in their respective department's decision-making, it is going to create problems in implementing the programs planned in the women's arena."

Shahindokht Molaverdi who headed this directorate from 2013 to 2017 once acknowledged: "Since we do not have an executive status, we have not yet found any desirable, effective relationship with other systems and provinces, and have faced serious obstacles from the beginning."[863]

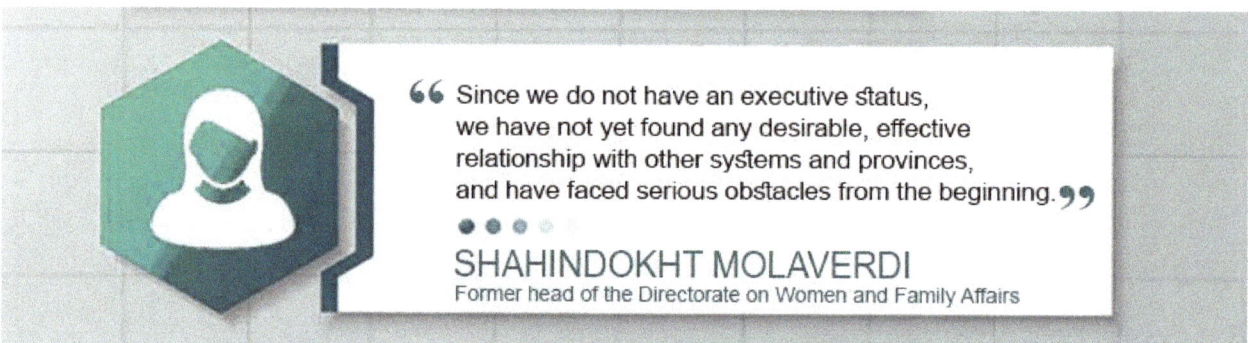

In its biannual "Report on the Conduct of Directorate of Women and Family Affairs (2014-2015)"[864] released on August 30, 2015, the directorate had listed 90 items in an "executive summary" table of measures and plans it has undertaken in two years under Rouhani to advance Iranian women's conditions.

Of the 90 listed items, hardly 28 of them were practical, concrete measures which were only carried out through other agencies and ministries. They included measures such as providing multi-vitamins to 11,000 pregnant and lactating women, educating pregnant women about the benefits of natural childbirth, giving consultations to 2410 women and girls on the verge of marriage or divorce, setting up a women's website and at best, teaching skills to women recovering from addiction.

The other 62 items included making proposals (12 items); following up on various issues from treatment of acid attack victims, membership in a certain council, to adoption of the bill on insurance of housewives, etc. (12 items); holding or taking part in meetings and paying visits to various institutions (9 items); writing the drafts of various bills (5 items);[865] preparing various forms of reports (4 items); signing agreements with other ministries and countries (4 items); cooperation with other agencies and supporting specific projects (2 items); conducting interviews with the 229 national and international media (1 items); and items that are not specifically related to women (13 items).[866]

---

[863] TNews.IR, August 24, 2015: "She continued by pointing to the cooperation of the Directorate on Women and Family Affairs with other systems and provinces and said, "Since we do not have executive status, we have not yet found any desirable, effective relationship with other systems and provinces and have faced serious obstacles from the beginning."

[864] *Gozaresh-e Amalkard-e Mo'avenat-e Omour-e Zanan va Khanevadeh dar Dowlat-e Tadbir-o Omid, 1392-1394*, pp. 7-14

[865] Some of the items in the table, including some of the drafts, have been marked with zero per cent achievement meaning that they have not been done at all or have been rejected altogether, but are still listed as actions undertaken by the directorate.

[866] *Gozaresh-e Amalkard-e Mo'avenat-e Omour-e Zanan va Khanevadeh dar Dowlat-e Tadbir-o Omid, 1392-1394*, pp. 7-14

The same is true for the National Report on Women's Status in the Islamic Republic of Iran (Beijing + 25) published by the office of international affairs, of the Vice Presidency for Women and Family Affairs in 2019.

The 200-page report has been filled with general statements without listing any practical, on-the-ground measures taken in favor of women. At the same time, they have refrained from answering many crucial questions posed by the UN Women and UN Committee on the Status of Women (CSW).

For example, in the section dealing with social protection and eradication of poverty (Question 9, page 54 of the National Report on Women's Status in the Islamic Republic of Iran (Beijing+25)), the Iranian regime's Women and Family Affairs directorate has listed a number of so-called measures which are devoid of substance.

They have not taken any measures to help the poor or eradicate poverty through social protection, unemployment benefits, public works programs, or social assistance. Their hollow claims are instead based on the idea of entrepreneurship, mini-finance funds, training workshops and exhibitions, all of which have been attempts to use the people's own resources for the government's theatrical measures. The government has not even taken any steps to support the female entrepreneurs with the initial capital,[867] but has extracted and collected the minimum resources people have to form the mini-finance funds to give loans to those seeking to start a small business in a village. And even the outcome of this is not clear in their report and whether it produced result.

Most of their activities are holding workshops where the government agents spend 60 hours but they multiply it by the number of people who attended the workshop to claim having done 820020 hours of work. In this way, they have exaggerated the little they have done in cosmetic measures.

One of the most absurd items included in the list of measures undertaken to provide social protection to women is at the bottom of page 54: "Adjust expectations and attitudes of graduate girls in terms of work and economic activities in accordance with labor market environment." This means that they convince girls with higher education to stay home and do not participate in the male-dominated job market in Iran.[868]

> Parvaneh Mafi, a former government official and active in women's affairs, evaluated the conduct of the presidential directorate on women and family affairs as the following:
> **"This directorate has addressed mostly ultra-structural and superficial works, gatherings and meetings, etc.** These are not bad, but they must comprise only a small part of their conduct. (The directorate) must undertake infrastructural works that could cause fundamental change in women's affairs or at least initiate basic and infrastructural work with regards to women."[869]

---

[867] Fatemeh Zolqadr, member of the Labor Committee of the parliament, said, "Many women who wish to start a business, do not have the initial capital despite their capability to run one. When we speak of supporting employment and occupation for women, the first thing is to provide the initial capital, and accordingly, women who wish to start a business must be able to be granted loans... Getting loans is more difficult for women compared to men. Thinking that women would have more problems in paying back their loans compared to men, banks refuse to grant them loans." The state-run ILNA news agency, October 9, 2019
[868] The official IRNA news agency, January 17, 2019
[869] The state-run Iran-e Zanan Network website, September 3, 2015.

> In a country with so many college-educated women and a large work force of 15 to 49 year old women, women's economic and political participation is
> **NON-EXISTENT**
> they have no presence in the administrative councils and their 3% role in the parliament has not solved any of the existing problems.

The women's directorate does not account to any authority, does not report to the parliament

As for accountability of this directorate, Zohreh Tabibzadeh, member of parliament, said, "The Directorate on Women and Family Affairs presently does not account to any authority... No report has been provided by the Directorate on Women and Family Affairs to the parliament so that we know what they have done...We cannot examine an unprofessional report containing only generalities on the conduct of the directorate. Only exact figures and accurate explanations on the conduct of an entity can explain the quality of its work, not the number of memoranda and contracts signed with other centers. They must report on the number of coops they have set up, the number of books they have published, the amount of support they have provided to elite women, etc. Statement of generalities and highlighting just a few agreements as the report of conduct is totally unacceptable. Instead, they must provide exact details of their conduct."[870]

The Directorate for Women and Family Affairs has also been criticized for being "ineffective." The former director of this agency was accused of making hollow promises. "She is good at rhetoric and making promises in line with women's demands, but in practice, she has not taken any steps that could be evaluated... Her work has been mostly for propaganda, protocol and showcase... She has not undertaken any infrastructural steps to advance the cause of women even one step further." [871]

The current director, Massoumeh Ebtekar has done even less as she is often preoccupied with justifying the regime's misogynistic conducts, notably in the international media since she is fluent in English. A former hostage taker involved in the takeover of the American Embassy in Iran in 1979, Ebtekar was removed in 2017 as head of the Environmental Protection Agency and replaced Shahindokht Molaverdi, as head of the presidential directorate on women and family affairs.

Regrettably, in a country with so many college-educated women[872] and with a large work force of 15-49 year old women,[873] "women's economic and political participation is non-existent" [874]

---

[870] The state-run Iran-e Zanan Network website, September 3, 2015

[871] The state-run Iran-e Zanan Network website, August 17, 2015, interview with a civil activist on women's affairs, Touran Vali-Morad on the record of the Directorate on Women and Family Affairs.

[872] Sussan Bastani, deputy for strategic studies in Rohani's presidential directorate for Women and Family Affairs, the state-run ISNA news agency, February 13, 2016: "Two million girls have graduated from universities in the past 20 years. However, unemployment rate among women has increased. Women's economic participation has also dropped from 39.5 to 27 per cent."

[873] The state-run Asr-e Banovan website, August 5, 2015: The former minister of science, Jafar Tofighi Darian, admitted that "more than 77 per cent of Iranian women who are between 15 and 49 years of age, enjoy a great potential for activity in social, economic and political arenas" but they have not been recruited as much as they

and women have no presence in the administrative councils[875] and their 3% role in the parliament[876] has not solved any of the existing problems.[877]

32. Is the head of the national machinery a member of the institutional process for SDG implementation (e.g. inter-ministerial coordinating office, commission or committees)? YES/NO If YES, what is their role in decision-making in the national machinery?

There is no national process for SDG implementation in Iran. Massoumeh Ebtekar, head of the Directorate on Women and Family Affairs, is officially entitled as a deputy to Hassan Rouhani. The directorate does not have any executive powers and or any impact on decision-making processes in the country.[878]

33. Are there formal mechanisms in place for different stakeholders to participate in the implementation and monitoring of the Beijing Declaration and Platform for Action, CEDAW and the 2030 Agenda for Sustainable Development?

No, there is no formal mechanism in place for the implementation and monitoring of the Beijing Declaration and Platform for Action, CEDAW and the 2030 Agenda for Sustainable Development

34. Is gender equality and the empowerment of all women and girls included as a key priority in the national plan/strategy for SDG implementation?

No, there is no national plan/strategy for SDG implementation to have any priority on gender equality and the empowerment of all women and girls.

---

should have. "The rate of employment for women is very small compared to world averages, indicating that educated women have not been employed as much as they deserved."
[874] Massoumeh Ebtekar, Rouhani's deputy in Women and Family Affairs, asserted that "women almost disappear in senior management positons." The state-run ISNA news agency, October 31, 2017
[875] The state-run ILNA news agency, August 25, 2015: On women's appointment to managerial positions, Shahindokht Molaverdi, presidential deputy on Women and Family Affairs, said, "Initially, there were some good moves in terms of appointment of female governors, which were halted after a while for reasons that I would not get into right now." She added, "Unfortunately, we do not see women's presence in the administrative councils of provinces."
[876] The state-run Mizan website, September 8, 2015: "Women's presence in the parliament is about 3 per cent and, in the most optimistic estimations, only one per cent in other decision-making and power structures, a situation that is embarrassing for the government," said Shahindokht Molaverdi, presidential deputy on Women and Family Affairs.
[877] The state-run Zanan-e Iran Network website, August 5, 2015: Tooran Vali-Morad, secretary of the Women's Islamic Coalition: "In the past 36 years and especially the past 26 years, our country has moved in the wrong direction in tackling women's issues... Unfortunately, all that has been done for women is summarized in gatherings and meetings. Women's mandatory presence both in the parliament and government have not solved any of the existing problems."
[878] Women demoted in new Rouhani Cabinet, website of the NCRI Women's Committee, August 17, 2017

DATA AND STATISTICS

35. Out of the following, which are your priorities for strengthening national gender statistics over the next five years?

- Promoted new laws, regulations, or statistical programme/strategy to develop gender statistics
- Establishment of an inter-agency coordination mechanism on gender statistics (e.g., technical working group, inter-agency committee)
- Use more gender-sensitive data in the formulation of policy and implementation of programmes and projects
- Conduct new surveys to produce national baseline information on specialized topics (e.g., time use, gender-based violence, asset ownership, poverty, disability)
- Greater utilization and/or improvement of administrative-based or alternative data sources to address gender data gaps
- Production of knowledge products on gender statistics (e.g., user-friendly reports, policy briefs, research papers)
- Development of a centralized web-based database and/or dashboard on gender statistics
- Institutionalization of users-producers' dialogues mechanisms
- Statistical capacity building of users to increase statistical appreciation on and use of gender statistics (e.g., trainings, statistical appreciation seminars)
- Other
- Please explain your plan (2 pages max.)

Since misogyny and anti-feminine attitudes and approaches are institutionalized in the Constitution and other laws of the clerical regime in Iran, it is most important to eliminate the existing laws against women and replace them with gender sensitive laws.
This, however, would not be possible with a tyrannical regime in power that guns down peaceful protesters in the streets as the world witnessed in December 2017-January 2018, November 2019 and January 2020.

Presently, bills and proposals for minimum changes are being rejected or totally overhauled by the parliament for contradicting the Constitution and *Shari'a* laws.
The bill to increase the age of marriage for girl children was rejected in December 2018.[879]
The bill to eliminate violence against women got stuck in the parliament and Judiciary for eight years before being thoroughly re-written in 2019 by the Judiciary. The bill has been kept in depot since September 2019 when it was passed to the government.[880] Officials say that it would not be adopted before the parliamentary election in February 2020.[881]

---

[879] Marriage age increase rejected by Iran parliament, website of NCRI Women's Committee, December 25, 2018
[880] Provision of Security for Women bill finalized by Judiciary after 8 years, website of the NCRI Women's Committee, September 19, 2019
[881] Fatemeh Zolqadr, member of the Cultural Committee of the mullahs' parliament: "The bill has been sent from the judiciary and returned to the government, but we do not know why it has remained silent in the government...

And the bill on the rights of children has been stalled in the parliament for 10 years.
Instead, a bill called the Law to Support Disadvantaged, Defenseless and Abandoned Children was passed by the Iranian Parliament on September 22, 2013, which sanctions marriage between the child and her guardian (stepfather), with the approval of a court.[882]
Actually, women and children do not enjoy any priority in the clerical regime's agenda.[883]

37. Has data collection and compilation on SDG 5 indicators and on gender-specific indicators under other SDGs begun?
If NO, explain the main challenges for collecting and compiling data on these indicators

For those following up on the statistics in Iran, it is very difficult to come up with figures accurately reflecting the reality.
While there are no effective systems for collecting the statistics, government officials often speak of percentages and not actual numbers. But when and if they do, they present varying figures on the same issue.
Another problem is lack of transparency, since officials try to conceal the gravity of the situation to avoid adding fuel to the flames of widespread social discontent.
In the meantime, the percentages and figures provided are intended to downplay the severity of the situation or to conceal the reality.
There are no gender-specific indicators for collection of data.
This issue has been thoroughly examined in the answer provided to **Question 1-e, Does the government have gaps in data? If so, what are these?**

38. Which of the following disaggregation17 is routinely provided by major surveys in your country?
- Geographic location
- Income
- Sex
- Gender
- Age
- Education
- Marital status
- Race/ethnicity
- Migratory status
- Disability
- Other characteristics relevant in national contexts

A month ago, at a meeting with Massoumeh Ebtekar, the issue was raised that the bill was being considered by the Government Committee to make the final amendments, but so far nothing has been reported and it is unlikely it will reach the parliament this year." The state-run ROKNA news agency, December 27, 2019

[882] Under new law in Iran, Men Allowed to Marry their Adopted Children, a special report by the NCRI Women's Committee, October 2014
[883] Issues of women and children are overlooked, website of the NCRI Women's Committee, December 27, 2017

None of the above is routinely provided by major surveys.

There are occasional reports on education and marital status (marriage and divorce and child marriages), however, it is never clear if the statistics provided by officials are from a recent survey or from the old one.

Officials usually speak in terms of percentages without providing exact figures.

If they do so, they are for only one province or two, and they never provide a complete picture in terms of real numbers.

This issue has been thoroughly examined in the answer provided to **Question 1-e, Does the government have gaps in data? If so, what are these?**

www.ingramcontent.com/pod-product-compliance
Ingram Content Group UK Ltd.
Pitfield, Milton Keynes, MK11 3LW, UK
UKHW060214240426

12048UKWH00031BB/1728